The Sugar Mill Caribbean Cookbook

THE SUGAR MILL

CARIBBEAN COOKBOOK

Casual and Elegant Recipes Inspired by the Islands

JINX AND JEFFERSON MORGAN

Illustrations by Dorothy Reinhardt

THE HARVARD COMMON PRESS
BOSTON, MASSACHUSETTS

THE HARVARD COMMON PRESS
535 Albany Street
Boston, Massachusetts 02118

Printed in the United States of America

Library of Congress Cataloging-in-Publication Data

Morgan, Jinx.
The Sugar Mill Caribbean cookbook : casual and elegant recipes
inspired by the Islands / Jinx and Jefferson Morgan.
p. cm.
Includes index.
ISBN 1-55832-120-9.—ISBN 1-55832-121-7 (pbk.)
1. Cookery, Caribbean. 2. Sugar Mill Hotel (Road Town, V.I.)
I. Morgan, Jefferson. II. Title.
TX716.A1M6697 1996
641.59′1729—dc20   96-9929

Cover and text design by Kathleen Herlihy-Paoli, Inkstone Design
Cover photographs by Roberto Santos/Southern Stock (border) and
Peter Johansky/Envision (center)
Illustrations by Dorothy Reinhardt

Special bulk-order discounts are available on this and other Harvard Common Press books.
Companies and organizations may purchase books for premiums or for resale,
or may arrange a custom edition, by contacting the Marketing Director at the address above.

10 9 8 7 6 5 4 3 2 1

This book is dedicated
to the people of the British Virgin Islands,
who welcomed two strangers from far away
and made us feel right at home.

CONTENTS

ACKNOWLEDGMENTS

In the fifteen years we've lived in the British Virgin Islands dozens of people have befriended us, offered us wise advice, shared their picnics, fed our cats, helped us clean up after storms, sailed us to their secret harbors, taught us how to clean a conch, and generously passed along their knowledge of Caribbean ingredients and cooking techniques. In the process they also set a standard for friendship that would be hard to duplicate. They all know who they are and we give them our deepest thanks.

Our thanks also to a great lineup of chefs, including Rick Buttafuso, Ivor Peters, Jeff Oakley, Chris Griffiths, and Mona Donovan, who, over the years, helped make the Sugar Mill a special place to dine and contributed much to this book.

We're grateful to Cheryl and Bill Jamison, who gave us a push in the right direction, and to Belle and Barney Rhodes, who were there at the beginning to support us in a most tangible way.

We salute our editors at *Bon Appétit*, especially Bill Garry and Barbara Fairchild, for sticking with us for all these years and sending us to all corners of the Caribbean on delicious voyages of discovery.

A good editor is to writers what a sturdy net is to high-wire performers. Linda Ziedrich is one of the best, combining sensitivity and precision in just the right balance. Dan Rosenberg's enthusiasm and hard work guided the project from the beginning, and Dorothy Reinhardt's illustrations add charm and style to the book.

We thank Carl Brandt, as always, both agent and friend. Carl also has fallen prey to the wacky lure of paradise, and now, during our favorite part of the year, he and his wife Clare are fellow residents of Tortola.

The staff of the Sugar Mill has shouldered a bigger load than usual to give us the time to complete this book, and we are most appreciative of that. A special thanks is owed to our General Manager, Patrick Conway, who leads the team, and Assistant Manager Joanna Samuels-Watson, who keeps us all sane.

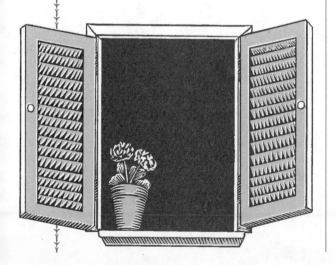

A Caribbean Cooking Adventure

Like romantics everywhere, we are always at the mercy of our fantasies. At no time was this more evident than one starry night more than a dozen years ago when we walked into a hotel and restaurant in a beautiful old stone building on the Caribbean island of Tortola and fell head over heels into the craziest period of our lives.

The place was for sale.

And so began our Caribbean saga, an adventure that took us from our home in California to a new life as owners of a small hotel and restaurant in the British Virgin Islands. From the first it was a madcap scheme, since we were neither seasoned hoteliers nor restaurateurs. As writers specializing in food and wine, we had traveled the world and stayed at a variety of hotels, but that experience qualified us for owning a hotel in much the same way that being frequent flyers would qualify us to handle the controls of a DC-10.

It didn't take us long to realize that it would take hard work and an abiding sense of humor to fulfill our dream of creating a special small resort with a certain style and a *soupçon* of elegance; in other words, the sort of hotel we liked to stay in when we traveled.

Fortunately, the Sugar Mill itself gave us a head start toward our dream. The hotel is built on the site of the old Appleby Plantation, from which Tortola's Apple Bay gets its name. Only a small, crumbling wall remains of the Great House, which we suspect was great more in name than in elegance. But the beautiful old stone boiling house, where rum was made, still stands, and it now houses our main restaurant.

The old Sugar Mill has been witness to more than three centuries of Caribbean history. Sometimes on a starlit night, when a breeze blows softly through the candlelit dining room, we think we can almost hear the whispers of those plantation days long ago.

Clearly, however, it would take more than such romantic notions to make the Sugar Mill a success. When we came to Tortola we were long on theory and woefully short on hotel and restaurant experience. We listened, learned, and eventually began to get the hang of things. But, as always in the islands, each day brought a new challenge.

The problem of getting supplies is a complaint that runs up and down the islands, and we were no exception. The ferry that brought us most of our provisions was a leaky lifeline to suppliers, who appeared to see the Sugar Mill as a place where that last crate of antediluvian lettuce might find a home.

Electricity, too, can be a sometimes thing in the West Indies, and equipment such as blenders and food processors have a way of expiring just as the first diners are being seated. The romantic dining room is suddenly plunged into darkness (to say nothing of the chaos that ensues in the kitchen) and guests begin feeling their way through the crowd, often making lifelong friendships along the way. This event is usually followed by the discovery that the propane bottle feeding the ranges has run out of gas, and that the lantern batteries appear to be so old and corroded that they might have been salvaged from Truk Lagoon.

It is inevitable that, on an evening when all of the foregoing has taken place, when the cisterns have run dry, and when a group of surfers is in the bar delighting the cocktail crowd with unsavory college drinking songs, the food critic from the *New York Times* strolls in.

Faced with such new challenges, we did what so many others in the islands have done. We improvised. With more optimism than good sense, we planted a vegetable garden and watched our neighbors shake their heads at our folly in trying to grow herbs and lettuce and mysterious vegetables in the dry and rocky soil we called our own. Eventually, though, the vegetable garden thrived, and tided us over until boats and planes began bringing a wider variety of fresh produce and a couple of new ferries linked us more reliably with overseas suppliers.

However, it was the native ingredients that really intrigued us. What cook could resist the temptation of trees weighted with mangoes, papayas, soursop, sugar apples, guava, coconuts, plantains, bananas, and avocados? We learned to work with local vegetables that we found at Tortola's colorful open-air market, including pumpkins of all shapes and varieties, breadfruit, christophene, a type of spinach that grows on a vine, and "provisions"—

knobby and strange-looking root crops, including dasheen and taro, that are essential to many local recipes. At the market, too, we found friendly farmers who told us about guavaberry wine and sold us bundles of homegrown parsley, rosemary, thyme, and green onion, tied together and called "seasonings," and explained the incendiary properties of the various peppers they displayed.

Hot peppers have always played a vital role in the Caribbean kitchen. To many people there is no discernible difference among chile peppers except for the degree to which they incinerate the palate. To islanders, however, each pepper has a personality of its own, and each dish dictates the pepper of choice. In Jamaica, otherwise gentle folk have argued for years over the relative merits of the country pepper versus the Scotch bonnet. Other islands have their own special favorites. In our recipes we've tried to keep the BTUs within the guidelines of the Geneva Convention.

The fruitful sea surrounding our islands is another inspiration to any cook. The local lobster is a succulent creature (really a large crawfish) that makes up for what it lacks in claws with the tasty meat in its tail. Conch (pronounced "conk") is a wondrous sea critter, as temperamental as California's famed abalone. When properly handled it presents a gentle, appealing flavor of the sea. Ground and seasoned into spicy little morsels wrapped in a fragile batter, it becomes conch fritters, a perfect accompaniment to cocktails. In salads or delicious chowders, conch is queen on many island menus. Whelks are another gift from the sea. Living on rocks just at the tide line, whelks are the islands' answer to escargots and often are prepared in a similar manner—steamed in sea water and served with garlic-laden butter.

The happy combination of rice and beans (or "peas," as beans are known on some islands) is popular all over the Caribbean. In Jamaica the beans are red, and the mixture is flavored with coconut cream. In Cuba black beans are served on top of rice, and the combination is known fondly as Moors and Christians. Topped with a fried egg and sautéed plantains, it's a satisfying meal. On some islands the local bean-and-rice variation might be seasoned with sweet peppers and tomatoes, bacon, beef bones, or hot peppers. In Haiti, *djon djon* is rice and a form of lima beans cooked in broth from the earthy, dark mushrooms grown in the Haitian highlands. In the British Virgin Islands, rice snuggles up with pigeon peas, yellow pea-like seeds that originally came from Africa and in some other places are called *gungo, gunga, goonga,* or *Congo peas.*

In all the islands, outdoor cooking has been a popular social event since Caribs and Arawaks were the hosts. Given our star-splashed nights, warm tropical beaches, a casual lifestyle, and a party-loving population, it's not surprising that the barbecue grill has little chance to cool off in these islands. What makes BVI barbecues so special is the locally made charcoal. Whereas others may sing the praises of food grilled over mesquite or grape vines, anyone who has been to a fish fry here, with fresh seafood grilled over local charcoal, has experienced a very special treat.

Any discussion of Caribbean tastes is incomplete without a mention of the island libation: rum. Mixed with colorful fruit juices and garnished in sometimes improbable ways, rum is for many visitors one of the most memorable tastes of the tropics.

When we arrived in the British Virgin Islands, about as many people came to the Caribbean for fine dining as went to Paris for the beaches. Like many natural beauties, the islands had gotten along on their looks for years. Dining

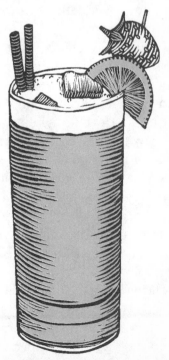

took a dim second place to the sugary beaches, gin-clear water, and winters full of sunshine that lured the snow-weary visitor. In recent years, though, things have changed, and we've seen restaurants in the Caribbean transformed with a swiftness that in these slow-paced islands is truly remarkable.

Perhaps it began when others took up the banner of Caribbean cuisine and began serving jerked pork, *accras*, and goat stew in such unlikely venues as New York and Los Angeles. Sometimes food has to travel before it gains honor in its own land. Old Caribbean kitchen hands, who'd once imported everything to dazzle their patrons with truffles and flourishes, now began to find inspiration in tropical fruits, fish so fresh it swims into the pan, and seasonings that dance in the mouth with a reggae beat.

Then new young chefs came along who studied ingredients native to their islands and looked for new ways to use them. With intelligence and creativity they began developing elegant new dishes with island pedigrees: duck breast with mango coulis, breadfruit vichyssoise, grilled grouper with tropical fruit salsa, pasta with conch sauce, curried banana soup, soursop gelato, and other intriguing delights. We like to think the Sugar Mill played a role in these changes.

The menu in the Sugar Mill dining room has evolved over the years to take advantage of Caribbean ingredients, and to use them in unexpected ways that reflect our love of fresh and bold flavor combinations. Many years of living in and around the food-loving city of San Francisco led us to create a menu that over the years reviewers have dubbed "California-Caribbean cuisine."

Once the main restaurant began to flourish, we decided the hotel was ready for a second eating spot, and Islands was born. A casual beachside restaurant where lunch is served daily and dinner is available during the winter season, Islands features an all-Caribbean menu. Over the years our travels through the West Indies have led us to discover that each of the lovely dots of land anchored in the Caribbean Sea has its own style of cooking and favorite ingredients. We've recreated much of what we've tasted for the menu at Islands.

In the Caribbean, an eclectic blend of influences from Africa, Asia, Europe, and America has spawned a cuisine featuring vivid seasonings, luscious fruits, spanking fresh seafood, and dramatically prepared meats and poultry that is as colorful and exotic as the islands themselves. Like all exciting cuisines, that of our islands and our restaurants evolves constantly. Each newcomer has brought fresh ideas and new recipes to add to our delicious simmering pot. We hope you'll enjoy the result.

And now, as we say in the Caribbean at carnival time—

"Alay, alay—go eat and have fun."

—JINX AND JEFFERSON MORGAN
Tortola, British Virgin Islands

SUNRISE SPECIALS

SUNRISE SPECIALS

TROPICAL TREAT
MANGOES
PRE COOLED

BEACH BREAKFAST

This spicy combination of Caribbean black beans and eggs gives any morning a zingy lift-off.

. . . .

BEANS:
    6 slices bacon, diced
    ⅓ cup chopped onion
    ⅓ cup minced red or green bell pepper
    1½ cups (1 15-ounce can) cooked black beans, drained, liquid reserved
    Salt and pepper to taste
    Sazón seasoning to taste (optional; see "Sazón")

. . . .

FRIED PLANTAINS:
    3 ripe plantains or green bananas, peeled and sliced diagonally
    Vegetable oil

. . . .

CREOLE SAUCE:
    1 jalapeño pepper, seeded and minced
    ½ yellow onion, minced
    3 to 4 ripe fresh tomatoes or 7 to 8 ounces canned plum tomatoes, chopped
    2 tablespoons tomato sauce
    2 to 3 sprigs cilantro or parsley
    Salt and pepper to taste
    Lime juice to taste

. . . .

    6 to 12 eggs, poached or fried
    Grated parmesan cheese
    6 lime slices

. . . .

To prepare the beans, cook the bacon until the fat is rendered. Add the chopped onion and pepper, and cook until they are limp. Add the black beans, and mash some of them with the back of a spoon. Cook the beans over low heat, moistening the mixture with the reserved bean juice as needed. Season the beans with salt, pepper, and, if you like, Sazón seasoning. Keep the beans hot.

To prepare the plantains, heat ½ inch oil in a skillet, and fry the plantain slices on both sides until they are golden brown. Drain them on paper towels.

For the sauce, stir together all the sauce ingredients. Season with salt, pepper, and lime juice.

To assemble each serving, spoon a portion of beans onto a plate. Place one or two freshly poached or fried eggs on top. Arrange plantain slices on the side, and spoon a small amount of sauce beside the egg. Sprinkle with parmesan cheese, and garnish with lime slices.

Serve at once.

Makes 6 servings

SAZÓN

. . . .

Sazón, a seasoning mixture containing ground annatto seeds, cilantro, and other Caribbean seasonings, is available in many Latin American markets and from Goya Foods, Inc., Secaucus, New Jersey 07094.

SURF SIDER EGGS

Surfers and sailors like to start the day at the Sugar Mill with this heavy-duty breakfast of poached eggs on a beef-and-spinach bed topped with a smooth cheese sauce.

....

CHEESE SAUCE:
  ½ cup flour
  ¼ cup butter
  1¼ cups milk
  ⅔ cup grated cheddar cheese
  Salt and pepper to taste
  1 pinch nutmeg
  A few drops hot pepper sauce

....

  1 tablespoon vegetable oil
  1½ pounds ground beef
  1 medium onion, chopped
  1 large garlic clove, minced
  1 teaspoon salt
  1 tablespoon minced fresh oregano,
    or ½ teaspoon dried oregano
  1 teaspoon ground nutmeg
  ¼ teaspoon ground black pepper
  1 package (10 to 12 ounces) frozen
    chopped spinach, thawed, drained,
    and squeezed to remove excess
    liquid
  ½ cup grated parmesan cheese
  6 to 12 poached eggs

....

To make the cheese sauce, combine the flour and butter in a saucepan, and cook the mixture about five min-

POACHED EGGS

....

The elegant oval of a skillfully poached egg is a whole lot easier to attain if the egg is very fresh. Most of us, however, have only store-bought eggs of uncertain vintage on hand and so must use a few tricks to make the eggs behave.

We find that a little vinegar in the cooking water (about 2½ tablespoons vinegar for every quart of water) helps coagulate the surface of the white. Stirring the water into a small whirlpool and slipping the egg from a dish into the vortex also helps the egg form a neat shape.

If you're nervous about preparing poached eggs while your guests are waiting, simply cook the eggs at your leisure a day or two ahead, submerge them in a container of cold water, cover the container, and refrigerate it. When you're ready to serve breakfast, slip the eggs into simmering water, heat them for 2 minutes, and remove them with a slotted spoon.

utes over low heat. Stir in the milk, and whisk vigorously as the sauce thickens. When the sauce is thick, add the cheese and seasonings. Keep the sauce warm. (It may be reheated over hot water or in a microwave.)

Heat the oil in a heavy skillet. Add the beef, and cook it until it is brown and crumbly. Stir in the onion and garlic, and cook, stirring, until the onion is limp, about 5 minutes. Add the salt, oregano, nutmeg, and pepper. Add the spinach, and continue cooking and stirring until the liquid has evaporated. Add the cheese. Spoon the mixture into six ramekins. Top each serving with one or two freshly poached eggs, and spoon on the hot cheese sauce. Serve immediately.

Makes 6 servings

LOBSTER OR CRAB EGGS BENEDICT

Start the day the elegant Caribbean way with lobster swathed in lime hollandaise in an island version of classic eggs Benedict.

....

1 tablespoon butter
½ cup sliced green onions
1 pound cooked lobster or crab meat, drained
4 English muffins, split and toasted

....

LIME HOLLANDAISE SAUCE:
4 large eggs
½ teaspoon salt
½ teaspoon grated lime zest
2 tablespoons lime juice
½ cup butter, melted

....

Loose-leaf lettuce
8 poached eggs
Paprika
1 cup chopped fresh tomatoes

....

Melt the butter in a large skillet over medium heat, and add the green onions. Sauté them, stirring constantly, for 1 minute. Add the lobster or crab meat, and cook until it is thoroughly heated. Keep the mixture warm.

To make the lime hollandaise sauce, whirl the eggs, salt, lime zest, and lime juice together in a blender. While the machine is running, slowly add the hot melted butter. Whirl until the sauce is thick and smooth. You can keep it hot in the top of a double boiler over simmering water.

Arrange the English muffin halves on individual plates lined with lettuce. Spoon the lobster or crab mixture evenly over the muffin halves. Top with poached eggs, and spoon on the lime hollandaise sauce. Sprinkle each serving with paprika, and garnish with chopped tomato.

Makes 4 to 8 servings

SALT FISH SCRAMBLE

"Salt fish and ackee" is a favorite breakfast in Jamaica, but ackee is a tricky fruit. Until it bursts open and "smiles," revealing its yellow meat and characteristic black seeds, it's poisonous. When cooked, ackee is very similar in taste and appearance to scrambled eggs. So we prefer to live a

ANNATTO

These rusty-red seeds, also known as achiote, are used by Caribbean cooks to color cooking oil a bright yellow-orange. A great inexpensive substitute for saffron, annatto also imparts its own delicate flavor. In the United States, butter and cheddar cheeses owe their sunny appearance to the pigmentation provided by annatto seeds. Annatto seeds are available in Caribbean and Latin American markets.

To make annatto oil, heat 1 cup vegetable oil in a saucepan, and add ½ cup annatto seeds. Heat the oil gently, stirring occasionally, for about 5 minutes, or just until the oil turns a rich red-orange. Strain out the seeds. The oil will keep indefinitely in a sealed glass jar in the refrigerator.

little less dangerously by making a similar dish using the less exotic egg.

You can make your own annatto oil for this recipe (see "Annatto"), or substitute plain oil with a pinch of saffron or turmeric added.

....

⅓ pound dried, salted codfish
4 cups water
2 tablespoons vegetable oil
3 onions, minced
⅓ cup tomato sauce
3 tablespoons annatto-seasoned oil
  (see "Annatto")

12 eggs, beaten
Salt and pepper to taste

....

Cover the salt cod with cold water, and let the fish soak for 4 to 12 hours.

Drain the fish, and place it in a saucepan with the 4 cups water. Boil the fish 15 minutes.

Drain the cod, and rinse it in fresh water. With your fingers, shred the fish, discarding the skin and bones.

Heat the 2 tablespoons oil in a skillet. Add the onions, and cook them slowly until they are golden and tender. Stir in the codfish. Add the tomato sauce and annatto oil. Pour in the eggs, and cook the mixture over low heat, stirring with a wooden spoon from time to time to scramble the eggs. Season with salt and pepper, and serve immediately.

Makes 6 servings

ISLAND STYLE: JAMAICA

Salt fish and ackee. Jerked pork and rock lobster. Blue Mountain coffee and curried goat. Rum and Red Stripe beer. Jamaica's cuisine is as diverse as the people who populate this cosmopolitan island, where a bounty of tropical foods is seasoned with the flavors of Spain, Africa, India, and China as well as the Caribbean. Jamaica's traditional dishes are a happy fusion of many ethnic influences.

Jamaica's cooks must also be both poets and wags, for how can we otherwise explain the names of some of their dishes? Where else can you eat duckunoo (a pudding made from cornmeal, coconut, sugar, and spices steamed in a banana leaf)? And if you don't like that name you can call it by another. The dark blue color imparted by the banana leaf and the shape of the fold leads some to call this dessert blue drawers.

Matrimony is a fruit salad made with star apples and oranges with cream. Mannish water is a highly seasoned soup believed to be a, well, let's say, a tonic, and as such is often served at weddings. Run-down is salted cod-fish (salt fish) simmered in coconut milk that's been thickened to custard consistency. Stamp and go is Jamaica's name for the Caribbean's popular salt-fish fritters.

Some dishes, though available on other is-lands, are intrinsically Jamaican. Salt fish and ackee is the Jamaican national dish, available all over the island at all hours of the day. When the fishing wasn't good in the old days, Jamaicans depended on salt cod, and liked to pair it with ackee, a fruit that, when cooked, tastes remarkably like scrambled eggs.

Rice and peas with coconut is often called the Jamaican coat of arms, and home-sick Jamaicans living in the United States dream of their native island when they smell the fragrance of spices, onions, and coconut simmering on the stove. Some Jamaican culi-nary inventions were inspired by recipes brought by colonizers. Britain's Cornish pasty, a meat- and potato-filled pastry, became to-day's Jamaican beef patty—minus the potato and plus enough West Indian seasonings to fry most Anglo-Saxon tonsils.

One of our favorite dishes is Jamaican jerk, which is almost as popular on the island as rum and reggae. Created by the Arawaks and perfected by the Maroons, jerk pork is the ultimate island barbecue. Jerked food is hot, but it's flavors are also complex and exciting. They dance like a spicy festival in your mouth. Scallions, onions, thyme, Jamaican pimento (allspice), cinnamon, nutmeg, and fiery Scotch bonnet or bird peppers combine in a pungent medley that is rubbed on the meat before it is slowly cooked over a smoky open fire.

SULTRY CHILE SOUFFLÉ ROLL

This easygoing soufflé, sizzling with hot peppers, can be served warm or at room temperature.

....

2 tablespoons vegetable oil
2 onions, chopped
1 garlic clove, minced
2 tablespoons oil
1 Scotch bonnet (or habanero)
  pepper, finely minced; or 2 minced
  fresh green jalapeño peppers;
  or 7 ounces canned diced green
  jalapeño peppers
½ cup flour
2 cups milk
¼ teaspoon ground cumin
Salt and pepper to taste
4 eggs, separated
½ cup shredded Monterey Jack cheese

....

SAUCE:
1 avocado, mashed
2 tablespoons lime juice
2 green onions, all of the white parts
  and some of the green, chopped
1 garlic clove, minced
½ cup sour cream
¼ teaspoon ground cumin
Salt and pepper to taste

....

GARNISH:
Cilantro sprigs
Black olives

....

In a skillet, heat the oil. Sauté the onions and garlic until the onions are limp. Stir in the peppers, and set the pan aside.

Line a 10-by-15-inch jelly-roll pan with parchment paper or foil. Butter the lining generously, and dust it with flour, shaking off the excess. Place a sheet of waxed paper on a baking sheet the same size or larger. Preheat the oven to 325°.

Put the flour in a saucepan, and gradually pour in the milk, whisking until the mixture is smooth. Stir in the cumin, salt, and pepper. Place the pan over medium heat, and cook the mixture, stirring, until it is thickened.

In a bowl, lightly beat the egg yolks, then beat in several spoonfuls of the heated flour-milk mixture. Stir the egg-yolk mixture into the flour-milk mixture in the saucepan, add the cheese, and cook, stirring, for 1 minute. Set the pan aside.

In a clean bowl, beat the egg whites until they are foamy, then continue beating until moist, stiff peaks form. Stir some of the beaten whites into the yolk mixture to lighten it. Fold the remaining whites into the yolk mixture just until they are blended. Pour the mixture into the prepared jelly-roll pan, spreading it evenly. Bake for 40 to 50 minutes, until the soufflé is golden brown and puffy.

To make the sauce, stir together the avocado, lime juice, green onion, garlic, sour cream, cumin, and salt and pepper.

Turn the soufflé onto the waxed paper-lined baking sheet, and carefully peel off the parchment or foil. Spread the onion-pepper mixture evenly over the soufflé. Using the waxed paper as a support, roll the soufflé from one long side into a cylinder.

To serve, cut the roll into thick slices, spoon on some avocado sauce, and garnish with cilantro sprigs and black olives.

Makes 6 servings

RUM FRENCH TOAST

It's amazing how a tot of rum can transform ordinary French toast into something special enough for guests.

....

4 eggs
1 cup milk, half-and-half, or heavy cream
3 tablespoons dark rum
2 tablespoons sugar
¼ teaspoon ground nutmeg
1 pinch salt
6 thick slices home-style white or whole-wheat bread
4 tablespoons butter
2 tablespoons vegetable oil

....

GARNISH:
Berries, pineapple, bananas, oranges, or whatever fruit is fresh and colorful, sliced or cubed as appropriate

....

Stir together the eggs, milk (or half-and-half or cream), rum, sugar, nutmeg, and salt in a shallow bowl. Dip both sides of each bread slice in the batter, and place the slices on a piece of waxed paper.

Heat 2 tablespoons butter and 1 tablespoon oil in a skillet large enough to hold three slices at a time. Fry the bread over medium heat, turning once, until it is lightly browned. Keep the cooked slices warm while you fry the remaining three in the rest of the oil and butter.

To serve, cut each slice of bread in half, and arrange the pieces on plates. Garnish the plates with fruit, and serve with butter and warm maple syrup.

Makes 6 servings

VANILLA RUM

On some Caribbean islands, vanilla flavoring was once a rare treat. When a lucky cook got hold of a vanilla bean, it was put right into a bottle of rum, to preserve the bean and to flavor the rum. You can make this special West Indian flavoring, too.

Split a vanilla bean, put it into a handsome decanter, and fill the decanter with your favorite rum. Close the decanter, and let the rum stand for at least two days. Use the rum for baking or for flavoring special coffee drinks. Vanilla rum will keep indefinitely.

BANANA-STUFFED FRENCH TOAST

The surprise is tucked inside of each slice of this delicious French toast.

....

6 to 12 1-inch-thick slices French or
    Italian bread
3 bananas, sliced crosswise
3 eggs
¾ cup milk
½ teaspoon vanilla extract
Vegetable oil, for deep frying
⅔ cup sugar
1½ teaspoons ground cinnamon

....

Cut a 2-inch crosswise pocket in each slice of bread. Stuff the banana slices into the bread pockets. In a bowl, whisk together the eggs, milk, and vanilla. Pour the mixture into a square glass baking pan. In another bowl, mix together the sugar and cinnamon.

In a deep skillet, heat about 2 inches of oil to 350°. While the oil heats, lay the stuffed bread in the egg-and-milk mixture. Let the bread soak up the liquid for a few minutes.

Fry the bread, turning it once, until it is lightly browned, about 3 minutes. Drain the slices on paper towels. Sprinkle them with the sugar-and-cinnamon mixture, and serve them at once.

Makes 6 servings

PIÑA COLADA PANCAKES

You can enjoy the flavors of the islands' favorite creamy cocktail in these delicious pancakes.

....

2 eggs
5 tablespoons melted butter
¾ cup milk
¼ cup sweetened cream of coconut,
    such as Coco Lopez
2 tablespoons rum
1¼ cups flour
1 tablespoon sugar
4 teaspoons baking powder
¾ teaspoon salt

....

In a mixing bowl, beat the eggs. In another bowl, combine the melted butter and milk, and stir this mixture into the eggs. Stir together the flour, sugar, baking powder, and salt in a third bowl. Pour the egg mixture into the flour mixture, and stir just until the dry ingredients are uniformly moist.

Heat a griddle or skillet until a few drops of water will dance on it, then lightly brush it with oil, and ladle on the batter. Cook the pancakes, turning them once, until they are golden brown on both sides.

The pancakes are especially good served with a warmed mixture of equal parts sweetened cream of coconut and maple syrup.

Makes 6 servings

GINGERBREAD PANCAKES

This warm and comforting breakfast dish is subtly spiced with one of the Caribbean's favorite flavors.

....

1½ cups flour
¼ cup sugar
1½ tablespoons baking powder
½ teaspoon salt
1½ teaspoons unsweetened cocoa
½ teaspoon ground ginger
½ teaspoon ground cloves
½ teaspoon ground cinnamon
2½ tablespoons minced pecans
3 egg whites, lightly beaten
1¼ cups milk
2½ tablespoons molasses
1 tablespoon vegetable oil

....

Combine all the dry ingredients in a bowl. Make a well in the center of the mixture.

In another bowl, whisk together the egg whites, milk, molasses, and oil. Add these to the dry ingredients, and stir to mix thoroughly. Heat a griddle or skillet until a few drops of water will dance on it, then lightly brush it with oil, and ladle on the batter. Cook the pancakes, turning them once, until they are golden brown on both sides. Serve them with warm maple syrup or honey.

Makes 6 servings

TROPICAL FRUIT WAFFLES WITH PECANS AND TOASTED COCONUT

Top your waffles with an array of luscious tropical fruits, and you'll start the day dreaming of swaying palms and aquamarine waters.

....

2 cups flour
2½ teaspoons baking powder
¾ teaspoon baking soda
½ teaspoon salt
2 tablespoons sugar
4 eggs, separated
1 cup vanilla-flavored yogurt
1½ cups milk
½ cup melted butter
¾ cup toasted pecans
½ cup toasted coconut (see page 69)

....

TOPPINGS (CHOOSE ONE OR MORE):
Chopped banana
Chopped mango
Chopped papaya
Pineapple chunks
Toasted coconut (see page 69)
Maple syrup

....

Sift together the flour, baking powder, baking soda, salt, and sugar. In a separate bowl, beat together the egg yolks, yogurt, milk, and melted butter. Stir this mixture into the dry ingredients.

In another bowl, beat the egg

whites until they are stiff but not dry, and fold them into the batter along with the nuts and coconut. Spoon the batter into a hot waffle iron, and bake until the waffles are golden brown. Serve the waffles with your choice of tropical toppings.

Makes about 8 waffles

SWEET-POTATO WAFFLES WITH ORANGE BUTTER

Caribbean sweet potatoes grow on a trailing vine and have orange skins and flesh that varies in hue from pale white to reddish orange. In the French islands sweet potatoes are called *patates douces*, and in the Spanish islands *patatas dulces*.

....

ORANGE BUTTER:
> ½ cup butter, softened
> 2 tablespoons curaçao liqueur
> 1 tablespoon grated orange zest

....

SWEET-POTATO WAFFLES:
> 2 cups flour
> 1 tablespoon baking powder
> ½ teaspoon salt
> 3 eggs, separated
> 1½ cups cooked and puréed sweet
>   potatoes
> 1¼ cups milk

> ¼ cup brown sugar, firmly packed
> ¼ cup melted butter
> 2 tablespoons grated orange zest

....

GARNISH:
> Fresh orange slices

....

In a small bowl, whip together the butter, curaçao, and orange zest until the mixture is light and fluffy.

Sift the first four ingredients into a large bowl, and set the bowl aside. In another bowl, combine the egg yolks, sweet potatoes, milk, sugar, and butter. Stir this mixture into the flour mixture. Beat the egg whites until stiff but moist peaks form, and fold the whites into the batter. Spoon the batter into a hot waffle iron, and bake until the waffles are golden brown and no steam appears.

Garnish the waffles with fresh orange slices, and serve with the orange butter and warm maple syrup.

Makes about eight 8-inch waffles

Brunch on the Patio

....

GINGER-POACHED SPICE ISLANDS PEARS

◆

LOBSTER EGGS BENEDICT

◆

CARIBBEAN SPICY SAUSAGE WITH CREOLE SAUCE

◆

COCONUT BREAD

COCONUT BREAD

This delicious breakfast bread is also a wonderful accompaniment to lunchtime fruit salads.

....

2 cups flour
1½ teaspoons baking powder
1 teaspoon salt
⅓ cup butter
⅔ cup sugar
2 eggs
¼ cup milk
1 cup shredded coconut

....

Preheat the oven to 350°. Sift together into a bowl the flour, baking powder, and salt. In another bowl, cream the butter with the sugar. Add the eggs, milk, and coconut to the butter and sugar mixture, and beat. Add the flour mixture, and stir (but don't overbeat). Add a little more milk if the batter seems too dry. Pour the batter into an oiled loaf pan. Bake for 50 to 60 minutes, or until a wooden pick inserted in the center comes out clean. Let the bread cool in the pan for 10 minutes, and then remove it to a rack to finish cooling.

Slice the bread while it's still warm, or let it cool, then slice it and toast it in the oven (because it's fairly fragile, it can fall apart in a toaster).

Makes 1 loaf

A JAMAICAN BREAKFAST

....

"*Such eating and drinking I never saw [as in Jamaica]! I observed some of our party today eat at breakfast as if they had never eaten before. A dish of tea, another of coffee, a bumper of claret, another large one of hock; then Madeira, sangaree, hot and cold meats, stews and pies, hot and cold fish pickled and plain, peppers, ginger-sweetmeats, acid fruit, sweet jellies. . . .*"

—LADY NUGENT'S DIARY, 1801

PINEAPPLE BRAN MUFFINS

Hearty and healthy, these toothsome muffins are chock-full of things that are good for you.

....

2½ cups bran
1⅓ cups whole-wheat flour
¼ cup brown sugar, firmly packed
½ teaspoon salt
2½ teaspoons baking soda
1 cup raisins
2 eggs, lightly beaten
½ cup milk
½ cup plain yogurt
½ cup vegetable oil
⅓ cup molasses

⅓ *cup honey*
½ *cup drained canned crushed*
   pineapple

....

Preheat the oven to 425°. Grease muffin pans.

Stir together the bran, flour, sugar, salt, baking soda, and raisins in a large mixing bowl. In another bowl, stir together the eggs, milk, yogurt, oil, molasses, honey, and pineapple. Combine the two mixtures, and stir just until all ingredients are blended (the batter will be quite moist).

Spoon the batter into prepared muffin pans (an ice cream scoop makes this job easy), filling each cup about two-thirds full. Bake the muffins for about 15 minutes, or until a toothpick inserted in the center of one comes out clean. Remove the muffins from the oven, and let them cool on a rack.

Makes about 12 muffins

TROPICAL FRUIT PLATTER WITH MANGO SILK SAUCE

We like to arrange our fruit on dark green hibiscus leaves, but you could use any nontoxic leaves as a background for this beautiful fruit display.

....

MANGO SILK SAUCE:
   Flesh of 1 mango
   ¼ *cup frozen orange juice concentrate*
   2 tablespoons lime juice

....

1 pineapple, halved, cored, peeled,
   and cut crosswise into ½-inch slices
1 papaya, peeled and sliced
1 melon, peeled and sliced
Mint or watercress sprigs

....

To make the sauce, purée the mango in a blender. Add the orange juice concentrate and lime juice, and whirl until the sauce is smooth. Pour the sauce into a small bowl, and refrigerate the sauce until you're ready to serve, as long as overnight.

Place the pineapple slices in a row down the center of a large platter, overlapping them, and arrange the papaya and melon slices on either side. Spoon the sauce over the fruit,

garnish with mint or watercress, and
serve.

GINGERED FRUIT COMPOTE

Fresh tropical fruit is so delicious that we often serve it au naturel. When papayas and mangoes are out of season, though, and the pineapples aren't quite ripe, we sometimes fall back on imported fruits, which we enhance with the island flavors of coconut and ginger.

....

2 pink grapefruits, peeled and
    sectioned, membranes removed
2 ripe pears, diced
½ pound red seedless grapes
1 cup dried figs, cut in half lengthwise
⅓ cup fresh lime juice
¼ cup honey
2 to 3 teaspoons peeled and minced
    gingerroot
½ cup freshly grated coconut

....

Put all the fruit into a bowl. Mix together the lime juice, honey, and ginger, and toss the dressing with the fruit. Sprinkle the coconut on top. Allow the fruit to marinate in the refrigerator for about an hour before serving.

Makes 6 servings

PINEAPPLE IN RUM CREAM

Pineapple and rum form a perfect flavor alliance in this dish, which is wonderful for breakfast, and makes an equally pleasing dessert.

....

2 pineapples, peeled, cored, and cut
    into 1-inch cubes
¾ cup sugar
¾ cup rum
8 egg yolks
2 cups warm milk
1 teaspoon vanilla extract
1 cup heavy cream, whipped

....

Put the pineapple cubes into a bowl, and sprinkle them with ¼ cup sugar and ¼ cup rum. Chill the pineapple until serving time.

Combine ½ cup sugar and the egg yolks in the top of a double boiler, and beat until the mixture is pale yellow and smooth. Add the warm milk, and place the pan over simmering water. Cook the custard, stirring constantly until it thickens and heavily coats a spoon.

Pour the custard into a bowl, and stir in ½ cup rum and the vanilla extract. Chill the custard for 2 to 3 hours.

Fold the cream into the custard. Spoon a few tablespoons of the accu-

PINEAPPLE POINTERS

Pineapples weren't designed for easy access. Some people favor a gizmo called a pineapple parer, whereas others attack the problem with only a sharp knife. We've tried all sorts of pineapple corers and trimmers, but we usually find they waste too much of the good fruit.

So, with a heavy, sharp chef's knife, we cut off the top and bottom of the pineapple. Then, if it is to be used as an ingredient, we skin the pineapple and cube, slice, or chop the fruit. Sometimes we leave the skin on, cut the pineapple into wedges, cut out the core, and serve the wedges for breakfast or dessert.

Pineapple is a great mixer. It has a special affinity for other fruits that grow in the tropics; avocado, papaya, and banana are always excellent companions. Poultry and fish combine with pineapple to make super salads, and, of course, pineapple is a prime ingredient in many desserts. A simple and delicious way to finish a meal is by removing some fresh pineapple from the shell, chopping it, and combining with vanilla ice cream or fruit sherbet. Spoon the mixture into a quarter pineapple shell, and sauce it with a liqueur.

mulated juices from the pineapple into the rum cream to thin it. Spoon the sauce over the pineapple cubes, and serve immediately.

Makes 8 servings

SUNRISE SMOOTHIE

This healthful, delicious breakfast-in-a-glass is the perfect way to start the day lightly. It combines piña colada yogurt, orange juice, and a fresh banana. We like to serve it with warm, whole-grain Pineapple Bran Muffins.

....

1 8-ounce carton piña colada–
   flavored yogurt (we use Yoplait)
⅓ cup orange juice
1 banana
4 ice cubes

....

Combine the first three ingredients in a blender. With the blender on high speed, add the ice cubes one at a time, and whirl until the mixture is smooth. Serve immediately.

Makes 1 serving

KIWI YOGURT COOLER

Kiwifruit came recently to the Caribbean, via cargo boats, and was an instant hit. In an area where strange-looking fruits and vegetables are not unknown, this fuzzy little charmer won everyone's heart.

Sweetened cream of coconut is

available in liquor stores and departments. Coco Lopez is a popular brand.

....

1 kiwifruit, peeled and sliced
1 tablespoon sweetened cream of
*   coconut, such as Coco Lopez*
½ cup plain yogurt
Juice of 1 lime

....

Combine all the ingredients except one slice of kiwifruit in a blender, and blend until the mixture is smooth. Pour it into a tall glass, garnish with the remaining slice of kiwifruit, and serve immediately.

PAPAYA YOGURT SMOOTHIE

Papayas come in many shapes and sizes. In our garden we grow a variety that is the size of an overstuffed football and has deep red flesh with a delightful flavor. In the tropics papayas grow easily and quickly from seed into tall fruit-laden trees.

....

½ cup plain yogurt
1 cup peeled and diced papaya
3 tablespoons frozen orange juice
*   concentrate*
1 tablespoon honey
1 cup low-fat milk

....

Put all the ingredients into a blender, and blend until the mixture is smooth. Serve immediately.

Makes 2 servings

Snacks, Nibbles, and Island Appetizers

SNACKS, NIBBLES, AND ISLAND APPETIZERS

CONCH FRITTERS

Every cook in the islands has a recipe for this island snack. Now one of the most popular of our gifts from the sea, conch was also much appreciated by Columbus and his crew. In the journal of his second voyage on the *Niña*, in 1494, Columbus records seeing conches "as large as a calf's head" on the ocean floor off the south coast of Cuba.

In its natural state conch can be tough and chewy. Some conch is sold already tenderized, but if yours isn't you can beat it into submission by placing it between two pieces of waxed paper on a flat surface and pounding it with a mallet, the flat side of a cleaver, or a rolling pin.

For these fritters, mince the conch and carrots in the food processor, run them through a meat grinder, or mince them by hand.

....

1 pound conch, cleaned, peeled, and
    tenderized
1 carrot, minced very fine
4 green onions, minced
2 garlic cloves, minced
¼ cup melted butter
2 tablespoons minced basil
½ teaspoon ground ginger
Salt and pepper to taste
Hot pepper sauce to taste
1½ cups flour

1½ teaspoons baking powder
Milk
Vegetable oil, for deep frying

....

In a bowl, combine the conch, carrots, onions, garlic, and butter. In another bowl, combine the flour and baking powder. Begin heating the oil. When the oil has reached 375°, stir the flour mixture into the conch mixture. Season with the basil, ginger, salt, pepper, and hot pepper sauce, and stir in just enough milk to give the batter a good consistency.

Drop the batter by the heaping tablespoonful into the hot oil, and cook the fritters until they are golden brown on all sides. Serve them with your favorite hot sauce.

Makes 6 servings

CARIBBEAN COCONUT CHICKEN BITES

These tropical tidbits are blissfully simple to prepare. You can make them early in the day, then later reheat them or serve them at room temperature.

You can use unsweetened coconut cream instead of the sweetened kind, but we like the contrast of the nippy mustard and sweet cream of coconut.

....

3 pounds boned and skinned chicken
    breasts, cut into 1-inch pieces
¼ cup Dijon mustard
1½ cups sweetened cream of coconut,
    such as Coco Lopez
1½ cups fine, soft bread crumbs,
    tossed with ½ teaspoon salt, ¼
    teaspoon pepper, and ½ teaspoon
    paprika
¼ cup melted butter

....

Spread each piece of chicken with
Dijon mustard. Dip the pieces into the
cream of coconut and then into the seasoned bread crumbs. Place the chicken
pieces on buttered baking sheets, and
drizzle the chicken with melted butter. Preheat the oven to 400°.

Bake the chicken pieces for 10 to 12
minutes, turning them once. Serve
them hot or at room temperature.

VEGETABLE FRITTERS

You can use whatever vegetables
you like for these tasty fritters. In
the Caribbean we might use pumpkin, sweet banana peppers, sweet potato, or okra.

....

1 cup flour
2 teaspoons dry mustard
1 teaspoon grated nutmeg
½ teaspoon salt
4 eggs, separated
2 teaspoons Dijon mustard

1 cup beer
½ cup minced fresh basil, or 2
    tablespoons dried basil plus 6
    tablespoons chopped fresh parsley
Vegetable oil, for deep frying
Salt to taste
3 pounds vegetables, trimmed and
    cut (asparagus stalks; whole
    mushrooms or green beans;
    cauliflower or broccoli flowerets;
    zucchini, eggplant or pumpkin
    cubes; whole sweet banana
    peppers; sweet-potato slices; whole
    okra; etc.)

....

Combine the flour, dry mustard,
nutmeg, and salt in a bowl. In another
bowl, whisk together the egg yolks,
Dijon mustard, and beer. Add this mixture to the flour mixture, and whisk until the batter is smooth. Cover the bowl,
and refrigerate the batter for 2 hours.

Stir the chopped basil (or basil
and parsley) into the batter. Beat the egg
whites until they are stiff but not dry.
Fold the whites into the batter. Heat the
oil to 375°.

Dip your choice of vegetables into
the batter, allowing the excess to run
off. Fry the vegetables, a few at a time,
until they are golden, about 4 to 5 minutes. Drain the vegetables on paper
towels. Sprinkle them with salt, and
keep them warm in the oven while you
fry the remainder.

Serve the fritters with Fire Coral
Hot Sauce (recipe follows) for dipping.

Makes 6 to 8 servings

FIRE CORAL HOT SAUCE

Fire coral is the seductive scourge of divers and snorkelers near tropical reefs. A scrape from fire coral stings like crazy, but a little lime juice cools the pain. The peppers in this sauce have a sting of their own, so use care (and rubber gloves).

....

2 cups tomato purée
½ cup strained lime juice
2 cups minced onions
2 tablespoons minced celery
2 to 4 teaspoons minced Scotch
    bonnet, habanero, or bird peppers
    (or minced milder peppers, such
    as jalapeño, to taste)
Salt and pepper to taste
¼ cup minced pimiento-stuffed green
    olives

....

Combine the tomato purée, lime juice, onions, celery, hot peppers, and salt and pepper in a bowl, and stir until the ingredients are thoroughly blended. Stir in the minced olives. Serve the sauce immediately, or store it in the refrigerator. It will keep for about 5 to 7 days.

Makes about 4¾ cups

MUSSELS WITH CREAMED DILL SAUCE

We often make this dish with local whelks, but the simple but sumptuous sauce is equally good with mussels.

....

2 cups heavy cream
1 tablespoon chopped fresh dillweed
    or 1 teaspoon dried dillweed
Salt and white pepper to taste
Kosher salt
2½ dozen mussels, cleaned

....

GARNISH:
Lettuce, sea grape, or hibiscus leaves
Dill sprigs
Orange slices, cut partly in half and
    twisted

....

In a saucepan, simmer the cream until it is thickened. Season it with dill,

MUSSEL BEACH

....

Once considered the poor man's shellfish, mussels are now chic. To clean mussels, put them in salted water with a sprinkling of oatmeal or flour for an hour or two, so they will rid themselves of grit. Then scrape the shells clean with the back of a knife, and rinse the mussels in cold water. Pull out the stringy beard, and cut it off. Rinse the mussels again in clean water. Discard any that float to the surface or have damaged or open shells.

salt, and white pepper. Preheat the oven to 300°.

Spread a layer of kosher salt on a baking sheet, and arrange the mussels on top (the salt will hold them in place). Spoon the sauce under and over the mussels in their shells. Bake the mussels for 6 to 8 minutes.

Serve the mussels on leaves, garnished with dill and orange slices.

Makes 6 servings

PAPAYA AND TAMARIND–GLAZED BABY RIBS

Papaya, garlic, tamarind, and hot chiles combine in this piquant barbecue sauce to showcase a medley of island flavors.

. . . .

BARBECUE SAUCE:
    1 medium onion, chopped
    2 tablespoons minced garlic
    1 large tomato, diced
    1 cup diced fresh papaya
    ½ to 1 Scotch bonnet (or habanero)
        pepper or other hot pepper of your
        choice
    2 tablespoons minced fresh
        gingerroot
    ¾ cup red wine vinegar
    ¼ cup soy sauce
    2 tablespoons tamarind drink
        concentrate (see page 169) or 2
        tablespoons Worcestershire sauce

Sailing Lunch

. . . .

BREADFRUIT VICHYSSOISE

◆

PAPAYA AND TAMARIND–GLAZED
BABY RIBS

◆

RED BEAN AND RICE SALAD

◆

CARROT SALAD VINAIGRETTE

◆

PEANUT BUTTER–FUDGE TART

    ¼ cup brown sugar
    Salt and pepper to taste

. . . .

    2½ pounds baby back ribs, cut into
        individual portions

. . . .

Put all of the barbecue sauce ingredients into a large saucepan, and simmer them over medium heat for 15 to 20 minutes, stirring occasionally. Remove the pan from the heat, and let the sauce cool.

Remove and discard the hot pepper (unless you are not afraid of internal combustion). Purée the sauce in a food processor or blender.

When you are ready to cook the ribs, preheat the oven to 300°, and line a baking sheet with foil (the dishwasher will be very grateful). Arrange the ribs in a single layer, and spoon some of the barbecue sauce on each rib. Bake the ribs for 30 minutes.

Turn the ribs over, and spoon the

remainder of the sauce on the other side of the meat. Continue baking for another 30 minutes.

Serve the ribs at once.

Makes 10 to 12 servings

FLYING FISH WITH LIME AND CAPER AÏOLI

If you have a young fishing enthusiast in your family, this is a great way to serve the catch of the day, since any small firm-fleshed fish can stand in for the fliers.

....

FLYING FISH

These sleek, silver-blue fish make their home off the coast of Barbados. With fins that look like the wings of dragonflies, flying fish are the delight of sailors, who marvel at the aerodynamic lift the sight of a predator can inspire in them. By vibrating their tail fins in the water, they gather enough force to propel themselves into the air at nearly 30 miles per hour.

Flying fish are so important to the economy of Barbados that their image is part of the national emblem. When leaving the airport there, you can pick up a carton of these delicacies to bring home with you.

LIME AND CAPER AÏOLI:

6 egg yolks

1 tablespoon roasted garlic purée (see page 27)

Grated zest and juice of 1 lime

½ teaspoon white pepper

1 teaspoon salt

2 tablespoons balsamic vinegar

1 dash hot pepper sauce

2½ cups olive oil

3 tablespoons herbs

½ cup drained capers

....

Vegetable oil, for deep frying (optional)

¾ cup flour

¾ cup cornmeal

Salt and pepper to taste

6 to 12 flying fish or other small whole fish, cleaned and patted dry

2 eggs, beaten with 2 tablespoons water

....

In a bowl, whisk the egg yolks well. Add the garlic purée, lime juice and zest, pepper, salt, and vinegar. Whisk again. Slowly add the olive oil, a drop at a time, while whisking constantly. Continue until all the oil is incorporated and the sauce is thick. Fold in the herbs and capers. Refrigerate the sauce until you're ready to use it.

Prepare a fire for grilling, or heat about 2 inches of vegetable oil to 375° in a heavy pot.

In a bowl, stir together the flour and cornmeal. Season the mixture with salt and pepper. Dip the fish in the egg wash, then coat them on both sides

ROASTED GARLIC PURÉE

Trim the tops off one or two heads of garlic. Place the garlic on a square of foil, sprinkle it with 2 teaspoons olive oil, and close the foil around the garlic. Bake the garlic at 425° for about 45 to 60 minutes, until the garlic is soft when pierced with a knife. Remove the garlic from the oven, and let it cool.

Using your fingers, squeeze the soft garlic pulp into a small jar. Cover the jar, and refrigerate the purée until you're ready to use it.

with the cornmeal mixture. Grill the fish over the hot coals for about 5 minutes, turning them once; or fry them in the hot oil for about the same amount of time, turning them once or twice, until they are golden on both sides.

Top each serving with a dollop of the aïoli.

Makes 6 to 12 servings

PLANTAINS WITH CAVIAR

The slightly sweet plantains and salty caviar make a great combination in this elegant cross-cultural first course. Ripe plantains are dark yellow with

black spots. To peel them, cut off their ends and score the skin lengthwise in several places.

....

½ cup dried black beans
1 small onion
1 garlic clove, peeled
1 teaspoon salt
3 cups cold water
3 ripe plantains, peeled and cut into
   ½-inch diagonal slices
2 cups peanut or other vegetable oil
1 cup sour cream
6 ounces red caviar
6 ounces black caviar
1 red onion, peeled and sliced into
   thin rings

....

Put the beans into a saucepan with the onion, garlic, salt, and water. Cover the pan, and bring the beans to a boil. Reduce the heat, and simmer the beans, covered for about 2½ hours, or until they are tender but not mushy. Remove the onion and garlic, and drain the beans well. Mash them with a fork.

Soak the plantain slices in salted water for 30 minutes. Drain the slices, and pat them dry with paper towels.

Heat the oil in a deep skillet. When the oil has reached 375°, add the slices of plantain. Fry them until they are golden, then drain them on paper towels. Press them with the back of a spoon until they are ¼ inch thick. Fry them again for 30 seconds, and drain them well on paper towels.

Place a row of hot plantain slices

down the center of a plate, and lay stripes of the beans, sour cream, and two caviars on either side of them. Arrange red onion rings over the top, and serve.

Makes 6 servings

LOBSTER CORNUCOPIA WITH BANANA CHUTNEY

This vivid first course was created by one of our former chefs, Jeff Oakley, who used a variety of island ingredients to create a sizzling symphony of flavors.

The spiny lobsters found in the Caribbean have no claws, but the tail meat is lean, white, and firm-textured. For this recipe, frozen spiny-lobster tails, which are readily available in most supermarkets, work very well. Be sure to select solidly frozen packages that are stacked well below the freezer's frost line.

If you are using a live lobster, sever the spine by inserting a sharp pointed blade at the joint where the body and tail section join. Split the shell lengthwise from the head to the tail. Remove and discard the black intestinal vein and sac located near the back of the head.

BANANA CHUTNEY:
1 red bell pepper, diced small
1 yellow bell pepper, diced small
1 medium onion, diced
1 tablespoon chopped garlic
2 apples, diced
¾ cup apple cider vinegar
1 teaspoon salt
1½ cups light brown sugar
½ teaspoon ground cloves
½ teaspoon ground ginger
½ teaspoon ground cinnamon
Chopped parsley, basil, or cilantro to taste
4 ripe bananas, diced

....

RED PEPPER–MANGO SAUCE:
2 red bell peppers or 3 pimientos
3 tablespoons minced onions
1 cup dry white wine
½ cup water
2 cups heavy cream
1 large mango, peeled and cubed
1 tablespoon lemon juice
Salt and pepper to taste

....

6 flour tortillas
1½ cups uncooked shelled lobster
Caribbean seasoning (see page 29) to taste
2 tablespoons fresh lime juice
2 tablespoons dry white wine
2 tablespoons cold butter, cut into bits

To make the banana chutney, sauté the peppers, onion, and garlic in a skillet. Add all of the remaining ingredients except the herbs and bananas. Cook the mixture over low heat until it thickens, approximately 45 minutes. Remove the pan from the heat, and fold in the herbs and diced bananas. Let the chutney cool to room temperature.

Make the red pepper–mango sauce. If you are using fresh peppers, turn them over a low flame, using a long fork, until their skins are charred black. Put the peppers into a plastic bag, seal the bag, and let the peppers steam for about an hour.

Peel the skins from the peppers, and slice them. Remove the seeds.

If you're using pimientos, slice them.

In a heavy pan, boil together the red peppers, onions, white wine, and water until the liquid is reduced to about 3 tablespoons. Add the cream, and simmer until the mixture is thickened. Put the mixture into a blender or food processor, and whirl until the mixture is smooth. Add the mango cubes, and blend until the mango is completely incorporated. Season with the lemon juice and salt and pepper, and set the sauce aside.

Wrap the flour tortillas in foil. Heat them in the oven until they are warm. This will soften them and make them easier to roll.

Meanwhile, dust the lobster pieces lightly with Caribbean seasoning. Put the lobster into a hot pan with the lime juice and white wine. Cook the lobster until it is firm, about 5 minutes.

While the lobster cooks, gently reheat the red pepper–mango sauce. Stir the cold butter into the hot sauce until the butter is melted and thoroughly incorporated.

Cut the warm tortillas in half, and put approximately ¼ cup hot lobster meat on each half. Roll the tortilla half into a cone shape. Serve the cornucopias surrounded with banana chutney, chopped parsley, and red pepper–mango sauce.

Makes 6 servings

CARIBBEAN SEASONING

2 teaspoons cayenne
2 teaspoons salt
1 teaspoon ground white pepper
1 teaspoon black pepper
1 teaspoon dried basil
½ teaspoon dried thyme
2 teaspoons paprika

Mix together all the ingredients, and store the mixture in a tightly covered container in a cool, dark place.

STAMP AND GO

These Jamaican salt-fish fritters are popular throughout the Caribbean, where salt fish is a staple. Although salt fish will never win any fragrance awards—some compare its odor to that of a thirteen-year-old boy's gym locker—it tastes delicious.

....

½ pound dried, salted codfish

....

KEY LIME SAUCE:

    1 cup mayonnaise
    1 cup sour cream
    2 tablespoons Gulden's mustard
    2 tablespoons lime juice
    Grated zest of 1 lime

....

    2 green onions, all of the white part
        and some of the green, minced
    2 jalapeño peppers, minced
    1 small tomato, peeled, seeded, and
        minced
    2 cups flour
    2 teaspoons baking powder
    About ¼ cup cold water
    Vegetable oil, for deep frying

....

Cover the salt fish with cold water, and let the fish soak 4 to 12 hours.

Drain the fish, then place it in a saucepan, and cover it with fresh cold water. Bring the water to a boil, and simmer the fish 15 minutes or until tender. Let it cool in the cooking water.

Combine the ingredients for the key lime sauce, and chill the sauce until you're ready to serve it.

Skin and flake the fish. Mix the flaked fish, green onions, peppers, and tomatoes in a bowl. Stir in the flour and baking powder, and add enough water to make a soft, sticky batter. Heat the oil to between 350° and 375°. Drop the batter by the teaspoonful into the oil. Fry the fritters, a few at a time, until they are golden brown. Drain them on paper towels, and serve them immediately with the key lime sauce for dipping.

Makes 6 servings

SALT FISH

....

From street stalls along the highways of Puerto Rico to beach shacks in the French islands, salt fish is one of the threads that run through the cuisine of the Caribbean. First brought to the area as food for plantation slaves and servants, salt fish is now a well-loved dish throughout the islands.

Known as morue in the French-speaking islands and bacalao where Spanish is the mother tongue, salt fish is found in most Caribbean markets, where local cooks will look for pieces with firm white flesh (a yellow tinge indicates age). Of all the dried, salted fish available, most cooks think cod has the best flavor.

CURRY IN THE CARIBBEAN

When East Indian workers migrated to Caribbean islands such as Martinique, Guadeloupe, and Trinidad, they brought with them the ingredients for curry powder, thereby introducing a whole new taste to the islands. A rainbow of spices is fried or toasted to release the flavors, then combined with pork, chicken, goat, seafood, lamb, or vegetables.

In the Caribbean, curries take on the national flavors of the islands on which they are encountered. Some cooks flavor curry with tamarind pulp, while others smooth the mixture with coconut milk. On the French islands white wine is often included, while on other islands rum might spike the dish.

CURRIED VEGETABLE AND CASHEW-NUT PATTIES

These spicy turnovers are inspired by Jamaican patties, plump pastries with a peppery beef filling.

CURRIED PATTY PASTRY:
2 cups flour
2 teaspoons curry powder
½ teaspoon salt
½ cup vegetable shortening
¼ to ½ cup ice water

VEGETABLE AND CASHEW FILLING:
2 eggplants, about 1 to 1¼ pounds each
1 tablespoon salt
2 garlic cloves, chopped
¼ teaspoon cayenne
2 teaspoons ground coriander
1 teaspoon ground cumin
1 teaspoon ground turmeric
1¾-inch piece gingerroot, sliced
1 small cauliflower, broken into flowerets
4 medium tomatoes, peeled and diced
2 potatoes, peeled and diced
1 jalapeño or other fresh hot pepper, minced
½ cup water
½ cup minced parsley
4 ounces raw cashew nuts, toasted in a 350° oven for 3 to 4 minutes

To make the pastry, sift together the flour, curry powder, and salt, then cut in the shortening until the mixture resembles coarse sand. Sprinkle in enough ice water, tossing with a fork, to hold the dough together. Wrap the dough, and refrigerate it for several hours.

To make the filling, peel and dice the eggplants. Sprinkle them with salt, and allow them to drain in a colander for about 30 minutes. In a large, heavy pan, heat the oil, and add the garlic and spices. Cook the mixture 1 to 2 minutes to bring out the flavors. Add the eggplant, cauliflower, tomatoes, potatoes, and hot pepper. Add the ½ cup water, cover the pan, and cook the mixture over medium heat 20 minutes. Add the parsley and cashews, and let the mixture cool.

Remove the dough from the refrigerator 15 minutes before you're ready to use it.

Roll the dough out ¼ inch thick on a lightly floured board. Using a saucer as a guide, cut the dough into 4-inch circles. Sprinkle a little flour on each circle, stack the circles, and cover them with a damp cloth.

Preheat the oven to 400°. Place one-twelfth of the filling on half of the first circle. Fold the other half over, and seal the edges by pressing down with a fork. Repeat with the remaining filling and pastry circles. Place the patties on baking sheets, and bake them for 30 minutes or until they are golden brown. Serve them hot.

Makes about 12 patties

CURRIED LOBSTER PATTIES

Another take on the patty, this time using Caribbean lobster. You can substitute crab or firm fresh fish.

....

Curried patty pastry (see page 31)
¼ cup vegetable oil
1 large tomato, chopped
1 onion, chopped
2 green onions, chopped

2 tablespoons curry powder
1 cup water
2 pounds uncooked shelled lobster, chopped (from 3 to 4 2-pound lobsters)
Salt and pepper to taste
2 tablespoons butter

....

Prepare the pastry as directed for Curried Vegetable and Cashew-nut Patties.

For the filling, heat the oil in a large, heavy skillet. Add the tomato, onions, and curry powder, and sauté for 5 minutes. Slowly pour in the water, and stir.

CARIBBEAN LOBSTER

....

The movie *Annie Hall* made the great lobster chase a comic standard. Occasionally we've played out our own version of that memorable pursuit when we've tried to remove a gang of particularly lively critters from their crates.

The Caribbean's spiny lobster is a tasty relative of the northern variety. Although the spiny lobster lacks meaty claws, its tail meat is especially delicious.

In many areas of the Caribbean, lobster is growing scarce because of overfishing. Thankfully, steps are being taken to limit the numbers taken and to enforce lobster seasons. So if you don't find lobster on island menus during your visit, it's only because we're trying to protect this delectable crustacean.

When the liquid starts to bubble, add the lobster meat. Cover the pan, reduce the heat, and simmer the mixture gently for 15 minutes.

Add salt and pepper. Stir in the butter, and immediately remove the skillet from the heat. Let the mixture cool.

Roll out the pastry, and fill and bake the patties as described for Curried Vegetable and Cashew-nut Patties. Serve the patties hot.

Makes about 12 patties

Prosciutto and Mango with Pepper-Mango Coulis

The luscious perfumed fruit of the mango makes a dazzling partnership with tissue-thin slices of delicately salty prosciutto.

....

¼ medium onion, sliced thin
1 tablespoon butter
1 large mango, peeled and diced
½ cup dry white wine
About 1 tablespoon hot pepper sauce
16 very thin prosciutto slices
2 large ripe mangoes, peeled and
    sliced into 8 strips each

....

Sauté the onion in the butter until the onion is limp. Add the diced mango and white wine. Simmer the sauce for 5 minutes over moderate heat, then purée it in a blender or food processor. Add hot pepper sauce to taste. Let the pepper-mango sauce cool, then chill it.

Wrap the prosciutto around the mango slices. Spoon the sauce onto plates, and place the prosciutto-wrapped mango slices on top, or serve the sauce separately.

Makes 4 servings

Oysters Caribe

If we lived near the Caroni Swamp in Trinidad, we'd be able to take a boat into the swamp and find tree oysters amid the tropical vegetation. On other islands the mangrove oyster is still available, though it is growing scarcer as the mangroves disappear under the pressure of development. Whatever fresh oysters are available to you will be delicious in this dish.

To clarify butter, melt it slowly in a pan over very low heat. Remove the pan from the heat, and let the butter stand for a few minutes. Carefully skim off the foam of butterfat on the top, and gently pour off the clear yellow liquid, leaving behind the milk solids at the bottom.

....

4 ounces sliced bacon, diced
1 garlic clove, minced
½ cup chopped onion
l large red bell pepper, peeled,
*   seeded, and diced small*
1 mango, peeled and diced small
2 cups fine dry bread crumbs
1 cup crushed buttery crackers (such
*   as Ritz)*
Salt and pepper to taste
2 tablespoons lime juice
Hot pepper sauce and Worcestershire
*   sauce to taste*
12 large fresh oysters, scrubbed
¼ cup clarified butter

....

In a skillet, fry the bacon until it is brown. Remove all but about 1 tablespoon of the fat from the pan. Add the garlic, and cook briefly over medium heat. Add the chopped onion, and cook until it begins to turn a light caramel color. Add the roasted pepper and mango. Stir to combine the ingredients.

Put the bread crumbs and cracker crumbs into a bowl, add the mango mixture, and stir. Season with salt, pepper, lime juice, hot sauce, and Worcestershire sauce. Preheat the oven to 500°.

Open the oyster shells, reserving as much liquid as you can. Discard each top shell, and loosen each oyster from the bottom shell. Place some of the stuffing on each oyster. Brush the oysters with clarified butter, and bake them for 8 to 10 minutes, until the stuffing is golden brown.

Serve the oysters with lemon wedges and chopped parsley or cilantro.

Makes 4 servings

ALLISON'S MARINATED CONCH

Allison Piotrowski, a fabulous caterer on Tortola, gave us this recipe. Her conch is wonderful to munch with drinks, or you can lay it on a bed of lettuce with some stuffed eggs, olives, and quartered tomatoes for a great salad. If you can't get conch, you can substitute lightly cooked scallops or cubes of cooked firm fish.

....

2 pounds cleaned and peeled conch,
*   cooked for 30 minutes in a*
*   pressure cooker*
1 onion, sliced thin
2 garlic cloves, mashed
1 teaspoon salt
½ teaspoon freshly ground black
*   pepper*
1 teaspoon sugar
¾ cup vegetable oil
3 to 4 tablespoons white wine
*   vinegar*
1 tablespoon hot pepper sauce

....

Cut the conch into small pieces, and let it cool. Mix together the remaining ingredients, and add the conch. Chill the mixture at least 8 hours before serving. The conch will keep for several weeks in the refrigerator.

CRAB CAKES WITH SHRIMP SAUCE

Our small crabs are not sea dwellers; they prefer the landlubber's life. You can often see them darting across dark roads on moonlit nights. Once caught, they are fed on bread and spices until the time comes for them to find their way into some delectable dish like these crab cakes. Whatever local crab meat is available to you will work just fine in this recipe.

....

SHRIMP SAUCE:
- *2 garlic cloves, chopped*
- *2 shallots, chopped*
- *4 ounces raw shrimp, shells removed and reserved*
- *1 tablespoon vegetable oil*
- *1 teaspoon paprika*
- *¼ cup dry sherry*
- *¼ cup heavy cream*
- *Salt and pepper to taste*

....

CRAB CAKES:
- *1 cup green, red, or yellow bell peppers, or a combination, diced*
- *4 tablespoons butter*
- *3 eggs, separated*
- *2 cups soft bread crumbs*
- *8 to 10 ounces cooked crab meat*
- *1 tablespoon Caribbean seasoning (see page 29)*
- *Flour, for dusting*
- *Worcestershire sauce, Tabasco sauce, and salt and pepper to taste*

....

In a small saucepan, sauté the garlic, shallots, and shrimp shells in the oil until the shells turn red. Add the paprika and sherry, and cook over medium heat until the sherry is reduced by half.

Strain the sherry, and return it to the pan. Dice the shrimp, and add it with the heavy cream to the saucepan. Reduce the sauce until it coats the back of a spoon. Season it to taste with salt and pepper, and keep the sauce warm.

In a small skillet, sauté the peppers in 2 tablespoons butter until they are soft.

Beat the egg whites until soft peaks form. Put the bread crumbs and crab meat into a bowl. Fold in the egg whites. Add the yolks and the seasonings. Form the mixture into 3-inch cakes, dust them in the flour, and fry them in the remaining 2 tablespoons butter, turning them once, until they are golden brown.

Serve the hot cakes with the warm shrimp sauce.

Makes 8 servings

GARDEN VEGETABLE STRUDEL

When sliced, the brightly colored vegetables rolled in flaky, crisp phyllo make a mosaic pattern as bright as carnival costume.

....

3 medium carrots
1 small zucchini, cut lengthwise into
    spears
1 small christophene (chayote), cut
    lengthwise into spears
6 asparagus spears
1 1- to 1½-pound eggplant, peeled
    and cut into ½-inch cubes
½ red bell pepper, cut into strips
½ yellow bell pepper, cut into strips
2 tablespoons dry bread crumbs,
    mixed with 2 tablespoons ground
    toasted pecans
1 medium onion, halved and sliced
½ cup melted butter
½ cup dry bread crumbs
8 sheets phyllo dough
1 egg, beaten with 1 tablespoon
    water
Sesame seeds

....

Preheat the oven to 350°. Blanch all of the vegetables except the peppers and onion. Drain the vegetables, and put them into a bowl with the peppers and the bread crumb–pecan mixture. In a small skillet, sauté the onion in 2 tablespoons of the butter, and add the onion to the other vegetables. Stir the mixture together.

On a cloth towel, place two sheets of phyllo, one on top of the other. Brush them with some of the melted butter, and sprinkle them with bread crumbs. Lay two more sheets of phyllo on top, and brush with butter and sprinkle with crumbs as before. Repeat the process until the phyllo sheets are used up.

Spoon the vegetable mixture down the middle of the phyllo stack, parallel to the long edges, arranging the vegetables in an attractive pattern. Fold one long edge of the phyllo over the vegetables, and roll the strudel, tucking in the short edges. Brush the top of the roll with the egg wash, and sprinkle with sesame seeds. Bake the strudel for 45 minutes or until the top is golden brown.

Allow the strudel to cool for a few minutes before you slice it.

Makes 8 servings

SWEETBREADS SOFRITO IN PUFF PASTRY

When the Spanish settled in the Caribbean, they brought with them many of their native dishes. This flavorful sauce is the basis for many dishes in Spanish-speaking islands.

....

½ pound salt pork, diced

2 red bell peppers, diced

1 medium onion, diced

4 garlic cloves, minced

2 teaspoons annatto oil (see page 7),
or 2 teaspoons vegetable oil and a
pinch of saffron or turmeric

1 cup chopped peeled tomatoes

1 cup chicken broth

1 tablespoon minced cilantro

Salt and pepper to taste

¾ pound veal sweetbreads, cleaned
and poached (see "Sweetbreads
and the Yuck Factor") and cut into
bite-size pieces

6 commercial puff pastry shells,
baked according to package
directions

....

Sauté the salt pork in a skillet until it is golden. Remove the pieces of pork with a slotted spoon, and drain them on paper towels. Pour off most of the fat from the skillet, and add the peppers, onion, garlic, and oil. Sauté until the onions are soft and translucent. Add the tomatoes, chicken broth, cilantro, and salt pork, and simmer for 30 minutes, stirring occasionally.

Remove the pan from the heat, and season the mixture with salt and pepper. When you are ready to serve, add the poached sweetbreads and heat them in the sauce. Spoon the sweetbreads and sauce into the puff pastry shells, and serve.

Makes 6 servings

SWEETBREADS AND THE YUCK FACTOR

....

For years we hesitated to put sweetbreads on the menu, knowing they are one of those dishes that brings out a passionate response—either adoration or ughs. This recipe changed our minds.

The yuck factor arises when people learn that sweetbreads are thymus glands, an item in that unappealing gastronomic category called "variety meats." Never mind. This dish is so tasty that after trying it even the most finicky diner becomes a sweetbreads fan. Many of our guests have asked us how to make it at home.

The only tricky part about preparing sweetbreads is the precooking. Since sweetbreads are very perishable, precook them as soon as you get them home. Wash the sweetbreads, and then simmer them for 20 minutes in 1 quart water, to which 1 teaspoon salt, 1 tablespoon lemon juice or vinegar, and any other seasonings of your choice have been added. The acid will help to keep the sweetbreads white and firm. Drain them and let them cool. Remove the membrane that covers the outside of the sweetbreads, and refrigerate them at once.

Cooked sweetbreads can be cubed and added to salads or scrambled with eggs. Dipped into an egg wash and bread crumbs and sautéed, they are a crisp delight. They are also splendid stirred into a cream sauce seasoned with herbs and sautéed mushrooms and served in puff pastry shells.

ESCARGOTS CALYPSO

Garlic butter is the classic sauce in which escargots swim. This rum-enhanced preparation introduces a different and equally appealing approach. Whelks are also delicious in this dish.

....

6 slices firm white bread, cut into
    3-inch crustless rounds
6 tablespoons butter, melted with
    1 tablespoon minced garlic
6 medium mushrooms, chopped
2 tablespoons butter
2 tablespoons rum
2 medium tomatoes, peeled, seeded,
    and diced
30 to 36 canned escargots, drained
    and rinsed
1 tablespoon minced parsley

....

Preheat the oven to 350°. Place the bread rounds on a baking sheet, and brush them with 4 tablespoons of the garlic butter. Toast them in the oven for about 10 to 12 minutes, or until they are crisp and golden brown.

While the bread toasts, sauté the mushrooms in the remaining 2 tablespoons butter in a large skillet. Cook them until their moisture is released and evaporated. Add the rum, tomatoes, and escargots, and sauté until the escargots are heated through. Stir in the remaining garlic butter and parsley.

Spoon the mixture onto the toast rounds, and serve.

Makes 6 servings

SPINACH CREPES WITH SUNSET CREAM AND CARIBBEAN BLACK BEANS

A warm-weather plant with leaves very much like spinach grows as a vine in the tropics. Often our garden fence is covered with a profusion of "spinach" leaves, and these crepes are one way we like to use the crop.

....

CREPES:
    1 10-ounce package frozen chopped
        spinach, thawed and squeezed
        dry
    1 cup cold water
    1 cup cold milk
    4 eggs
    ½ teaspoon salt
    2 cups flour
    ¼ cup melted butter

....

    Vegetable oil

....

FILLING:
    8 ounces cream cheese
    Milk or cream

2 packages Sazón seasoning (see
    page 4)
2 cups (1 15-ounce can) cooked
    black beans, drained and rinsed

....

Put all the crepe ingredients into a blender or food processor, and whirl until they are well combined. Refrigerate the batter for at least 2 hours.

Brush a 6- to 7-inch crepe pan with oil, and place the pan over high heat. Pour ¼ cup of the crepe batter into the pan, and tilt the pan to spread the batter evenly over it. Cook the crepe for about 1 minute, until you can shake it loose from the bottom of the pan. Turn the crepe over, and cook it for about half a minute on the other side. Slide it onto a rack to cool. If you won't be filling the crepes right away, stack them between layers of waxed paper. (You can freeze the crepes, if you like. To reheat them, remove the waxed paper and wrap the crepes in foil. Warm them in a 300° oven.)

To make the filling, put the cream cheese and seasoning mix into a blender or food processor. Whirl to combine them, adding just enough milk or cream to make the mixture easy to spread. Spread some of the cheese mixture over each crepe. Spoon black beans down the center. Roll the crepes, and wrap them snugly in plastic wrap. Refrigerate them for at least 2 hours.

When you are ready to serve, un-wrap the crepes, slice them diagonally into bite-size pieces, and serve.

Makes about 14 crepes or about 84 bite-size pieces

CARIBBEAN SPICY SAUSAGE WITH CREOLE SAUCE

Rick Buttafuso, Sugar Mill chef, invented these piquant sausages, which he enhances with Caribbean spices and serves with a colorful Creole sauce.

....

3 pounds pork butt or loin
1 pound pork fat trimmings, diced

....

CARIBBEAN SPICE MIX:
    2 tablespoons salt
    1 tablespoon ground black pepper
    1 tablespoon cayenne
    1 tablespoon paprika
    2 teaspoons dried oregano
    2 teaspoons dried basil
    2 teaspoons dried thyme
    1 tablespoon dried hot red pepper
       flakes

....

2 tablespoons brown sugar
1 tablespoon ground cloves
½ cup red wine

....

CREOLE SAUCE:
    2 tablespoons vegetable oil
    1 cup chopped yellow onion
    1 tablespoon minced garlic
    ½ cup chopped green bell pepper
    ½ cup chopped red bell pepper
    *1 cup peeled and chopped
        tomatoes*
    2 cups chicken broth
    1 cup tomato sauce

    . . . .

    Vegetable oil, for frying
    *1 pound spinach fettuccine, cooked
        and drained*

    . . . .

Spread the pork meat and fat on a baking sheet. Combine the ingredients for the Caribbean spice mix. Sprinkle the pork with 2 to 4 tablespoons of the spice mix, with the brown sugar, and with the cloves, and toss the pork with the seasonings.

Run the spiced pork through the medium plate of a meat grinder. Put the ground meat into a bowl. Add the red wine, and mix well. Form the mixture into 2½-inch patties.

To make the Creole sauce, heat the oil in a saucepan. Add the onions and garlic, and sauté them until they are translucent. Add the peppers, and continue to sauté for about 5 minutes. Season the sauce to taste with the Caribbean spice mix, and keep the sauce warm.

Heat ¼ inch oil in a large skillet, and fry the patties, turning them once.

Serve the patties and the Creole sauce over the hot fettuccine.

*Makes 8-10 first-course servings or
6 main-course servings*

SMOKED SCALLOPS WITH SALSA AND DIJON CREAM

This is another of Rick Buttafuso's inventions. He likes the apple-wood chips for the delicate flavor they impart to the scallops. Be sure to have plenty of ventilation when smoking the seafood.

. . . .

SCALLOP BRINE:
    1 quart water
    ¼ cup kosher salt
    3 tablespoons mixed pickling spices
    ⅓ cup sugar
    3 tablespoons lemon juice
    30 scallops (preferably sea scallops)
    2 cups apple-wood chips

    . . . .

SALSA:
    ½ medium red onion, minced
    ½ medium red bell pepper, minced
    *1 medium tomato, peeled and
        chopped*
    *2 tablespoons chopped chives or
        green onions*
    2 tablespoons sugar
    3 tablespoons olive oil

Salt and pepper to taste

....

DIJON CREAM:
6 tablespoons sour cream
1 tablespoon Dijon mustard

....

CROUTONS:
¼ cup butter
½ teaspoon garlic powder
½ teaspoon paprika
1 teaspoon minced parsley
6 basil, mint, or parsley leaves
2 tablespoons minced chives
*6 slices firm white bread, cut into 3-
    inch crustless rounds*

....

GARNISH:
Minced parsley and chives

....

Combine the brine ingredients in a pot. Bring them to a boil, and let them cool.

Soak the scallops in the cooled brine for 20 minutes. Place them on a rack, and allow them to dry.

Put the wood chips between two bricks in the bottom of a roasting pan. Heat the pan over high heat until the wood chips begin to smoke. Preheat the oven to 300°.

Place a rack wrapped with aluminum foil on top of the bricks. Place the scallops on the rack, and cover the pan with a lid or tightly sealed foil. Put the pan in the oven until the scallops are a pale golden brown, about 30 to 40 minutes.

While the scallops are smoking, combine all the salsa ingredients in a bowl. Combine the sour cream and mustard in a small bowl, and thin the mixture, if necessary, with a little water. Put the Dijon cream into a pastry bag with a small tip.

Remove the scallops from the oven, and keep them warm. Raise the oven temperature to 400°.

To make the croutons, melt the butter, and combine it with the seasonings. Brush the bread rounds with the seasoned melted butter, and toast them in the oven until they are crisp and golden.

Place a warm crouton in the center of each plate, and spread some of the salsa across the crouton. Lay some of the scallops on top, and pipe some Dijon cream over the scallops. Sprinkle with minced parsley and chives, and serve immediately.

Makes 6 servings

RUM-GLAZED CHICKEN WINGS

Chicken wings are a favorite snack with sundown cocktails in the islands. We like the glossy mahogany glaze that the soy-and-rum marinade gives the wings.

½ cup soy sauce

¼ cup rum

⅓ cup chopped onion

1 tablespoon finely grated gingerroot

1 garlic clove, minced or mashed

5 pounds chicken wings, cut apart at
the joints, tips discarded

¼ cup melted butter

3 tablespoons catsup

1 teaspoon sugar

1 teaspoon red wine vinegar

⅛ teaspoon freshly ground black
pepper

In a large bowl, stir together the soy sauce, rum, onion, ginger, and garlic. Add the chicken pieces, turn them to coat them well, and cover the bowl. Chill the chicken for 6 hours, turning the pieces occasionally.

Preheat the oven to 325°. Butter a shallow pan. Drain the chicken, and arrange the pieces in a single layer in the pan. In a small bowl, stir together the remaining ingredients, and brush the mixture over the chicken. Bake the wings, turning them once, for 45 to 60 minutes, until they are tender. Serve them hot.

Makes 15 to 20 appetizer servings

SMOKED SALMON–WRAPPED SALMON MOUSSELINE

Even though we are surrounded by a sea teeming with fish, occasionally we get a taste for something that doesn't swim through the Caribbean. When smoked salmon is available from one of our purveyors, we jump at the chance to serve our guests this special dish.

1 pound smoked salmon

¼ cup cold water

1 tablespoon unflavored gelatin

2 cups heavy cream

1 tablespoon lime juice

2 teaspoons minced dillweed

GARNISH:

Green Herb Sauce (recipe follows)

Cucumber slices

Red or black caviar

Line each of six metal timbale molds with smoked salmon, using about half the fish.

Put the water into the top of a double boiler. Sprinkle the gelatin over the water, then set the pan over boiling water. When the gelatin has dissolved, remove the top of the double boiler from the heat, and let the mixture cool a bit.

Beat 1½ cups of the cream until soft peaks form, and refrigerate the whipped cream. Purée the remaining smoked salmon in a food processor with the lime juice and dill for about 10 seconds. Add the remaining ½ cup cream, and purée for 10 seconds longer. Add the dissolved warm gelatin, and whirl for 5 seconds. Remove the purée to a mixing bowl. Fold in the whipped cream. Fill the molds ¾ full with salmon mousseline, and refrigerate them for at least 1 hour.

When you are ready to serve, unmold the mousselines onto serving plates. Garnish them with Green Herb Sauce, cucumber slices, and caviar.

Makes 6 servings

GREEN HERB SAUCE

This is an extremely versatile sauce. It's great with almost any fish, and we often use it as a dip for crudités. Spread it on sandwiches to pep them up, or toss it with vegetables and cooked pasta for a great salad.

....

1 cup watercress leaves, firmly
    packed
1 cup parsley sprigs, firmly packed
1 shallot or 2 green onions, chopped
1½ teaspoons minced fresh tarragon,
    or ½ teaspoon dried tarragon
1½ teaspoons fresh thyme leaves, or
    ½ teaspoon dried thyme
½ teaspoon salt
¾ teaspoon dry mustard
2 tablespoons white wine vinegar
1 egg
1 cup vegetable oil

....

Purée all of the ingredients except the oil in a blender or food processor. With the motor running, add the oil. Pour it in a slow, thin stream until the mixture has thickened, then faster until all the oil is incorporated.

Makes about 2 cups

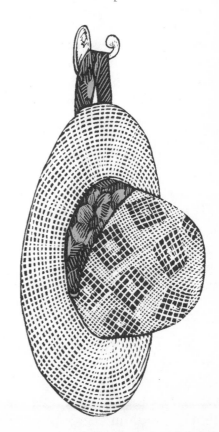

Conch Ceviche

The Hawaiians have their *lomi lomi*, the Tahitians their *poisson cru*, and the Mexicans their *ceviche*. We have borrowed the idea of "cooking" seafood in lime juice from our Caribbean neighbors in Cancun to create this dish using our local conch. Tenderize the conch by pounding it with a mallet until its tissue has broken down.

....

2 pounds fresh conch or thawed
    frozen conch, cleaned, peeled,
    trimmed and tenderized (or
    skinned and boned fresh halibut,
    tuna, or other firm fish)
2 cups strained fresh lime juice
½ cup chopped onion
2 teaspoons salt
3 tomatoes, peeled and chopped
½ cup minced green onions
¼ cup chopped green bell peppers
¼ cup chopped red bell peppers
1 cup fresh coconut cream, chilled
    (see "Coconut Milk or Cream")
Chopped fresh watercress or
    parsley

....

Chill the conch or fish briefly in the freezer to firm it.

Cut the conch or fish into bite-size pieces. Mix together the lime juice, onion, and salt in a large bowl. Add

Coconut Milk or Cream

To make coconut milk, pour 2 cups boiling water over 4 cups grated fresh coconut meat, and allow the mixture to stand for 30 minutes. Then strain it through a double layer of cheesecloth that has been rinsed and wrung dry, squeezing to remove all the milk.

To make coconut cream, allow the coconut milk to sit until it separates, and spoon the thickened cream off the top.

You can also make coconut milk with unsweetened dried shredded coconut, substituting dairy milk for the water.

the conch or fish, and turn it to cover it with the lime mixture. Cover the bowl with plastic wrap, and marinate the conch or fish at room temperature for about 2 hours, or in the refrigerator for 3 to 4 hours, stirring occasionally.

When ready, the conch or fish will be opaque and firm. Taste it to judge its texture. If it seems too soft, marinate it for an hour or so longer.

Drain the conch or fish, squeezing it slightly to remove excess moisture. Put it in a serving bowl, and add the tomatoes, green onions, peppers, and coconut cream. Toss the mixture together, and garnish with watercress or parsley. Serve the ceviche at once.

Makes 6 servings

ISLAND STYLE: THE ABC ISLANDS

They are called the ABC Islands not only because of the initials of their names—Aruba, Bonaire, and Curaçao—but because they are moored closely together in the Caribbean Sea. Dutch is the official language of these islands, and English is commonly spoken, but the prevalent idiom is Papiamento, an exotic linguistic blend of Dutch, Portuguese, Spanish, English, French, and African dialects.

Aruba's windswept, rocky terrain rises in the middle to a mere 617 feet. What little vegetation exists is mostly divi-divi trees, twisted and bent to the will of the trade winds.

Predictably, much of the food on Aruba comes from the sea, but the bounty of South America is also close by. On this arid island, ironically, more fresh fruits and vegetables are available than on other, lusher Caribbean islands that boast commercial farming.

With the ingredients at hand, cooks on the island developed a cuisine that marries Dutch and African influences. Specialties include kari kari, flaked fish cooked with local seasonings, which is most often served with cornmeal-and-flour pan bati. Sopito is a fish chowder made with coconut milk. Isoba di bestia chiquitis, a hearty stew of young goat and vegetables, and funchi, a fried version of Caribbean cornmeal mush, are also popular. One of Aruba's most unusual dishes is keshi yena, for which a whole Edam cheese is skinned, hollowed out, filled with spiced chicken or seafood, then baked.

Bonaire, the farthest east of the little archipelago, is also the least populated and most languid. Bonaire is a mecca for divers: The entire coastline is an underwater park, protecting 84 species of coral and 272 kinds of fish.

Unprotected varieties often find their way onto plates on this island, where the freshness of seafood is measured in minutes.

Curaçao is the bustling capital of the Netherlands Antilles. Although the Spanish discovered the island in the fifteenth century, they abandoned it as useless because it had no gold or arable land. When Dutch explorers arrived in 1634, however, they recognized the value of Curaçao's harbor, the seventh-largest natural deep-water anchorage in the world.

The cosmopolitan mix of cultures brought together by the Dutch created a rich culinary amalgam of West Indian, Indonesian, Spanish, African, and European ancestry. Indonesian rijsttafel banquets are common, as are sates, spicy grilled bits of meat and poultry on skewers served with peanut sauce. More challenging dishes to the timid diner include pickled pigs' ears and iguana soup.

On the quayside along Punda, Willemstad's historic downtown shopping district, schooners tie up to display their wares from Venezuela and nearby islands. Decks of these boats are bright with piles of tomatoes, carrots, leeks, okra, and strange hairy tubers that have made their way across the sea.

The Spanish planted orange trees during their brief tenure on Curaçao, but the sparse rainfall produced small, sour, inedible fruit. Much later, though, somebody discovered that the orange rinds yielded an aromatic oil ideal for flavoring drinks, and the liqueur named after the island was born. Still made from the descendants of the Spanish orange trees, today's Curaçao liqueur is produced at Chobola, one of the island's surviving Dutch colonial landhuis farmhouses.

CARIBBEAN GUACAMOLE

Everyone loves this glorious green dip, but we've added a tropical touch by including papaya and seasoning the combination with Caribbean peppers and local hot sauce.

. . . .

2 avocados, peeled and cut into
  chunks
1 papaya, peeled and cut into
  chunks
1 tomato, cored and cut into chunks
1 red onion, peeled and quartered
2 green onions, diced
2 to 3 garlic cloves, minced
¼ to ½ Scotch bonnet (or habanero)
  pepper, or 2 to 3 jalapeño peppers,
  seeded and minced
3 tablespoons minced fresh cilantro
¼ cup lime juice
1 tablespoon ground cumin
1 teaspoon hot pepper sauce
Salt and pepper to taste

. . . .

In a food processor, whirl all of the ingredients, scraping the side often and stopping before the mixture is completely smooth. Serve the guacamole at once with your favorite chips. We especially like it with chips made from West Indian vegetables, such as tannia and plantain.

Makes about 3 cups

Tailgate Party
. . . .
CARIBBEAN GUACAMOLE
◆
TANNIA OR PLANTAIN CHIPS
◆
TAMARIND AND ORANGE BRAISED
BRISKET ON CRUSTY ROLLS
◆
CURRIED TOMATO SALAD
◆
LEMON SHORTBREAD TART

TANNIA CHIPS

Tannia—also known as dasheen, taro, or yautia—is available in many supermarkets as well as in Asian and West Indian markets.

. . . .

Vegetable oil, for deep frying
1 pound tannia
Cayenne, salt, and pepper to taste

. . . .

In a large pot, heat 1½ inches oil to 375°. Peel the tannia, and slice it as thin as possible. Drop the slices into the oil a few at a time, and fry them until they are light brown. Remove the chips with a slotted spoon, and drain them on paper towels. Sprinkle the chips with seasonings.

Makes about 1 pound chips

KNOW YOUR ROOTS

Tropical tubers are an ungainly lot; they are knobby and gnarled, with odd shapes and obscure potential. Moreover, their confused nomenclature discourages many people from trying to sort out one from another. But it's worth becoming familiar with these interesting roots that are vital to the Caribbean diet.

The long, club-shaped tuber with shaggy, patchy skin that we call tannia on Tortola is known as malanga in Cuba and yautia in Puerto Rico. Fried tannia chips are fabulous with almost any dip, and tannia also makes a smooth thickener for soups. Choose tannias that are relatively light-colored, hard, and unblemished.

Scrub them under running water, trim and peel them, drop them into cold water, and refrigerate them in their soaking water for 24 hours.

Dasheen, or taro, is also tangled in a web of differing local names that make identifying it confusing. To add to the muddle, there are two distinct forms of dasheen. One is about the size of a turnip, with brown, shaggy skin and flesh that is white, cream, or lilac-gray. The other form is pale brown and elongated. It is delicious fried or roasted with garlic and butter, puréed, or added to soups and stews.

Yams are one of the world's largest crops and most important staples. In the United States, yams and sweet potatoes are often confused, although the true yam is no relation to the sweet potato. In the Caribbean, yams are scruffy, hairy brown tubers the size of footballs. They make super chips and, when boiled, provide a nice, starchy counterpoint to salt fish.

Cassava, also known as yuca and manioc, is the basis for tapioca. The roots are long and narrow and have a bark-like covering. The solid flesh is hard and white and as versatile as the potato. Bread made from the flour of this root is one of the treats of the Caribbean.

Sweet potatoes, also known as boniato and camote, grow on a trailing perennial plant and usually have orange-tinged skin and flesh that ranges from pale white to a deep red-orange. When cooked, they are dry, pale, and delicately flavored. Choose hard tubers with no moldy spots, peel them, and keep them in cold water in the refrigerator for 24 hours before cooking them. Then you can steam, roast, boil, fry, or bake them.

PLANTAIN CHIPS

Most greengrocers now carry plantains, which resemble bananas but are longer, thicker, and starchier. They are always cooked before eating, and never more delicious than when served as the island equivalent of potato chips.

If you can't get plantains, you can substitute green bananas in this recipe.

....

8 ripe plantains, peeled and cut into
  1-inch crosswise slices
Vegetable oil, for deep frying
6 cups cold water
Salt to taste

....

In a large pot, heat 1½ inches of oil to 375°. Add the plantain slices a few at a time, and fry them until they are golden, about 3 minutes. Remove them from the oil with a slotted spoon, and drain them on paper towels.

When the plantain slices are cool, use a mallet or a rolling pin to gently pound each slice to a thickness of ⅛ inch. Put the pounded chips into a large bowl of cold water, without crowding them. Allow them to stand until their edges have absorbed enough water to look puffy, about 2 to 3 minutes. Drain the slices on paper towels.

Heat the oil to 375° again, and cook the chips until they are brown and crisp, about 3 minutes. Drain them on paper towels. Sprinkle them with salt, and serve them hot. (Or allow them to cool, cover them, and refrigerate them for up to 2 days. To reheat the chips, spread them in a single layer on baking sheets, and bake them in a 450° oven until they are hot and crisp, 5 to 7 minutes.)

Makes about ½ pound chips

STONE CRAB CLAWS WITH KEY LIME MAYONNAISE

Stone crabs are very cooperative shellfish—their delicious claws can be removed without causing them too much dismay, and they will quickly grow new ones. When stone crab claws are not available, cooked, chilled shrimp, or cubes of poached firm fish served on toothpicks garnished with lime slices, are just as delicious with Key lime mayonnaise.

....

2 cups mayonnaise
¼ cup Dijon mustard
¼ cup Key lime juice (or Persian or
  Tahitian lime juice)
1 teaspoon grated lime zest
Hot pepper sauce or Tabasco sauce
  to taste
2 tablespoons Worcestershire sauce
¼ teaspoon cayenne
Salt and pepper to taste
30 to 36 (about 9 pounds) cooked
  stone crab claws
Lemon wedges

....

In a bowl, combine all of the ingredients except the crab claws and lemon. Cover the bowl, and refrigerate the mayonnaise for 2 to 4 days to develop its full flavor.

BRINGING THE CARIBBEAN HOME

Even if your view may run more to urban air wells, suburban lawns, desert, or mountains than reefs and breaking surf, you can still create a party atmosphere that soothes and beguiles with fanciful rum drinks, exotic food, and imaginary trade winds wafting through the festivities.

The key to dressing the set for such an event is a profusion of greenery and flowers. Potted plants and tropical blooms—orchids, hibiscuses, gardenias, or birds-of-paradise—form the magic carpet that will whisk your party from reality to some star-spangled Caribbean island.

A length of batik, pareu fabric, tapa cloth, or just a vivid flower-print fabric can cover any table with a touch of the tropics. We present finger-foods in a flotilla of leaf-lined baskets. Oversized clam or conch shells find new life displaying snacks or flowers.

Drinks should be tricked out in true island style with garnishes of fresh fruit, such as slices of pineapple, oranges, limes, or carambola (star fruit). If you're very ambitious, you can cut a coconut into perfect halves with a hacksaw, remove the meat, and fill the shell halves with a favorite rum concoction or dips for fruit, vegetables, or shellfish.

Make fresh fruit a centerpiece for your party. Cut a watermelon in half and scoop out the flesh (if you want to scallop or sawtooth the edges, so much the better). Thread pieces of fruit on wooden picks. Stick the picks into the green skin of the watermelon, creating a porcupine-like effect. You can concoct a delicious dip for the fruit from sour cream laced with curry powder, lime juice, and a little honey. Use the watermelon as a natural punchbowl for your drinks, or fill it with water and float more flowers on it.

So make up your guest list, shake out your sarong, and make plans for one of the best parties of the season. But don't forget that you still should come to the Caribbean for a real island fling.

Pile the stone crab claws on a platter, and place a small bowl of the sauce and several lemon wedges by each diner's place. Provide lobster crackers or small wooden mallets, and don't spare the napkins. If you value your dining room table, cover it with newspaper or butcher paper for this delicious but messy event.

Makes 8 to 10 servings

DEEP-SEA AVOCADO AND SHRIMP SPREAD

One of the delights of living in the tropics is being able to reach up and pluck a perfect avocado or two from a tree. Combined with tiny shrimp and molded into a fish shape (or any other you might like), avocados are here transformed into an elegant spread for crackers, toasted slivers of French bread, or melba toast rounds.

....

¼ cup olive oil
1 garlic clove, minced
¼ cup lime juice
2 large avocados
3 tablespoons cold water
1 envelope unflavored gelatin
¼ teaspoon salt
¼ teaspoon ground black pepper
⅛ to ¼ teaspoon hot pepper sauce, to taste
¼ cup mayonnaise
½ pound bay shrimp, rinsed and drained
1 cup heavy cream, whipped

....

GARNISH:
Lime slices
Orange slices
Watercress sprigs

....

Combine the olive oil, garlic, and lime juice in a bowl. Peel and dice the avocados, and marinate them in the oil mixture for 2 hours.

Put the water into the top of a double boiler. Sprinkle the gelatin over the water, then set the pan over boiling water. When the gelatin has dis-solved, remove the top of the double boiler from the heat, and let the mixture cool.

In a blender or food processor, purée the avocado and its marinade, the gelatin, the seasonings, the mayonnaise, and the shrimp. Fold in the whipped cream, taste the mixture, and add more seasonings, if you like. Pour the mixture into a 4- to 5-cup mold, cover the mold, and chill it for at least 6 hours.

Turn the mold out onto a serving platter, and garnish it with lime and orange slices and sprigs of watercress. Serve the mold with crackers or toast.

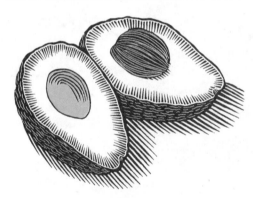

BAMBOOSHAY NUTS

During Carnival in the islands, you're likely to hear revelers saying, "Bambooshay!" which means "Enjoy yourself, have a great time!" That's what you and your guests will be doing as you nibble these nuts.

....

½ cup vegetable oil
8 cups whole dry-roasted peanuts
1¼ cups sugar
2 tablespoons ground cumin
1 tablespoon hot red pepper flakes
¼ cup sugar

. . . .

Heat the oil in a large skillet (if you don't have a large skillet, divide the oil, nuts, and sugar, and cook in two batches). Add the peanuts and 1 cup sugar, and cook over medium heat, stirring constantly, until the nuts are golden brown and the sugar has carmelized, about 3 to 4 minutes.

Remove the nuts to a large bowl, and add the cumin and hot pepper flakes. Toss to distribute the seasonings. Let the nuts cool, then toss them with the remaining sugar. Serve them immediately, or let them cool, and store them in a tightly covered tin.

A CARNIVAL OF SOUPS

A CARNIVAL OF SOUPS

CARIBBEAN BOUILLABAISSE

This special soup takes a French idea and gives it an island spin. With some bread and a big green salad, this soup makes a very satisfying meal.

....

1½ cups minced onions
¾ cup chopped leeks
½ cup olive oil
5 garlic cloves, mashed
2 cups peeled and seeded tomatoes
12 cups water
¼ cup minced parsley
2 tablespoons minced basil
¼ teaspoon fennel seeds
1 tablespoon Sazón seasoning (see page 4)
2 tablespoons grated orange zest
Salt and pepper to taste
4 pounds fish (whatever is available), cut into chunks
1 to 2 pounds shellfish (small crabs, shrimp, Caribbean lobster, whelks, etc.)
1½ pounds mussels

....

ROUILLE:
½ cup chopped red bell pepper, simmered for several minutes in salted water and drained, or
½ cup chopped pimiento
2 jalapeño peppers, chopped, or Tabasco sauce to taste

2 medium potatoes, cooked and peeled
8 garlic cloves, mashed
1 tablespoon minced basil
½ cup olive oil
10 slices garlic toast

....

In a large pot, sauté the onions and leeks slowly in the olive oil. Stir in the garlic and tomatoes, and cook 5 minutes. Add the water, herbs, and seasonings. Bring the mixture to a boil, reduce the heat, and simmer for about 30 minutes.

To make the *rouille*, put all the ingredients but the olive oil in a food processor or blender, and whirl until they form a very sticky paste. Add the olive oil very slowly, with the machine running. Set the mixture aside. At this point you can let the soup cool and then refrigerate it, if you'd like to serve it later.

About 20 minutes before serving time, bring the soup to a boil, and add the fish, shellfish, and mussels. Bring the soup back to the boil, and simmer it about 10 minutes. Beat 4 to 6 tablespoons of hot broth into the *rouille*. Place a piece of garlic toast in the bottom of each soup plate, and ladle in soup. Be sure each serving has plenty of fish, and mussels in the shells. Serve the *rouille* sauce in separate bowls.

Makes about 10 servings

MANGO SOUP WITH RASPBERRY PURÉE

A luscious fruit soup looks beautiful with a fragile spiderweb of raspberry purée on top. Chilled soups are one way we like to take advantage of our bounty of tropical fruits.

....

3 cups chopped ripe mango flesh
Juice of 1 lemon
¼ cup dry sherry
¼ cup dry white wine
1 pinch ground cloves
½ teaspoon ground ginger
½ teaspoon ground cinnamon
1 cup heavy cream

....

RASPBERRY PURÉE:
1 cup fresh or frozen raspberries
2 tablespoons rum

....

Put the chopped mango and lemon juice into a saucepan. Add the sherry and white wine, and bring the mixture to a boil. Lower the heat, and simmer until the fruit is soft. Let the mixture cool.

Pour the cooked fruit and liquid into a blender. Add the spices, and blend at low speed until the mixture is smooth. (You may have to do this in two batches.) Transfer the purée to a bowl, and stir in the heavy cream. Chill the soup well.

Purée the raspberries and rum in a blender, and strain the purée to remove the seeds.

When you are ready to serve, spoon the soup into chilled bowls. Put the raspberry purée into a pastry bag with a small round tip, or into a plastic bottle with a small tip (such as a bottle used for ketchup or mustard). Squeeze concentric circles of purée on top of the soup. With a knife, cut back and forth across the circles to create a spider-web effect.

Makes 4 servings

MANGO MADNESS

When the mango trees in Tortola are heavy with ripening fruit, there's a little madness in the summer air. Each year the first taste of this sensual fruit seems even better than memory recalls.

But eating a mango can be messy. One of our most treasured mango memories is of the summer afternoon a neighbor invited us for a swim in her pool. She passed around champagne in silver goblets and mangoes fresh from her trees. We paddled around the pool, mango juice dripping from our chins, and thought that we had, indeed, found paradise.

PEANUT PUMPKIN SOUP

With their green skins and rather lumpy complexions, Caribbean pumpkins don't make world-class jack-o'-lanterns, but they do make great soup. Sometimes we have our own Caribbean pumpkin patch growing right at the hotel, and guests are often curious to know the name of the peculiar-looking green fruit growing on the vines. When we tell them it's pumpkin, they sometimes give us one of those incredulous looks that implies we may have been in the tropical sun too long.

The flesh from common orange pumpkins, either fresh or canned, works just fine in this recipe.

....

¼ cup butter
4 cups cooked and puréed pumpkin
2 cups cooked and puréed sweet
    potatoes
1 cup smooth peanut butter
6 cups chicken broth
Salt and pepper to taste

....

GARNISHES:
Sour cream
Snipped chives
Chopped peanuts

....

Heat the butter in a large pot over medium heat. Stir in the pumpkin, sweet potatoes, and peanut butter. Add the broth, and season with salt and pepper. Stir until the soup is smooth. Reduce the heat, and simmer the soup for 20 minutes.

Before serving, garnish the soup with sour cream, chopped peanuts, and chives.

CURRIED ZUCCHINI SOUP

A soupçon of Caribbean curry enhances this soup, which is equally good served hot or cold.

....

5 tablespoons butter
2 onions, coarsely chopped
3 tablespoons curry powder
6 cups chicken broth
2 potatoes, peeled and cubed
Salt and pepper to taste
6 small zucchini (about 1 pound)
1½ cups heavy cream

....

GARNISH:
Snipped fresh chives

....

Melt 4 tablespoons of the butter in a heavy pot. Add the onions and curry powder, and sauté the onions until they are soft, about 15 minutes. Add the broth and potatoes, and bring the mixture to a boil. Reduce the heat, and simmer the mixture, uncovered, for 15 minutes.

Season the soup with salt and pepper. Slice five of the zucchini, add them to the soup pot, and simmer the soup 10 minutes more. Purée the soup in batches in a food processor or blender. While the machine is running, add the cream in a steady stream. Return the soup to the pot, and heat it gently (do not let it boil).

Cut the remaining zucchini into julienne strips. Heat the remaining 1 tablespoon butter in a skillet, and add the julienned zucchini. Sauté the zucchini over medium heat until it is just wilted, about 1 minute. Add the zucchini to the soup.

Serve the soup hot or chilled, garnished with the minced chives.

Makes 8 servings

CHILLED SPINACH AND OYSTER BISQUE

When fresh callaloo leaves are available, we often use them in this soup for a slightly different flavor.

. . . .

1 cup minced mushrooms
1 garlic clove, minced

2 tablespoons butter
1 tablespoon flour
2 cups milk
1 pound shucked oysters and their liquor
1 cup cooked, well-drained, and chopped spinach
2 cups milk
1 cup heavy cream
2 teaspoons Worcestershire sauce
½ teaspoon ground thyme
Salt and pepper to taste

. . . .

GARNISH:
Lemon slices

. . . .

In a saucepan, sauté the mushrooms and garlic in the butter until the mushrooms are soft. Sprinkle them with flour, and cook them, stirring, 3 minutes. Gradually add the milk, and cook the mixture until it is smooth and slightly thickened. In a blender or food processor, purée the mixture in batches with the oysters, their liquor, and the spinach.

Return the purée to the saucepan. Stir in the cream and seasonings, and heat the soup gently.

Remove the hot soup from the heat, and let it cool. Chill the soup, then adjust the seasonings to your taste. Serve the chilled soup garnished with lemon slices.

Makes 6 servings

GINGERED CARROT AND PEAR BISQUE

Although we don't grow pears in the Caribbean, they travel well and are almost always available in our markets. We like to combine them with carrots for a lovely golden soup with the island kick of ginger.

....

1 cup diced onion
2 tablespoons butter
1 tablespoon minced peeled
    gingerroot
2 cups chicken broth
1 pound carrots, peeled and cut into
    chunks
2 large unpeeled pears, coarsely
    chopped
½ cup cooked rice
1 bay leaf
1½ cups cream or half-and-half
Salt and pepper to taste

....

GARNISH:
Julienned carrot
Chopped fresh dillweed

....

In a large saucepan, sauté the onion in the butter until the onion is translucent and tender. Add the ginger, and sauté another minute or two. Add the chicken broth, carrots, pears, rice, and bay leaf, and simmer, partly covered, until the carrots are tender.

Remove the bay leaf. Purée the mixture in a blender or food processor, blending in cream or half-and-half to thin the soup to your taste. Season with salt and pepper. Reheat the soup gently and serve it hot, or let it cool completely, chill it well, and serve it cold with a garnish of julienned carrot and fresh dill.

Makes 4 servings

GINGER

....

The spice we call ginger is the root of a perennial plant with large, vivid yellowish flowers born on a spike. Ginger was brought to England before the Norman Conquest, and by the time Queen Elizabeth I took the throne ginger was so popular that the queen employed a gifted baker whose sole occupation was to fashion portraits of members of the court in gingerbread.

The ginger plant reached the Caribbean shortly after the New World was discovered. Today it is one of the most popular flavors in island cooking, and it is also highly regarded as a digestive aid.

We like to have fresh gingeroot always on hand, and we've found it keeps very well in a jar filled with sherry. When we've used all the ginger, the sherry has taken on a wonderful flavor that we enjoy using in marinades and stir-fries.

CRAB OR LOBSTER CHOWDER

All cooks who live near the sea develop their own interpretations of the ubiquitous fish chowder. We use our local lobster for this elegant rendition.

....

1 potato, peeled and diced
1 cup water
2 teaspoons butter
1 onion, minced
1½ teaspoons salt
½ teaspoon paprika
¼ teaspoon white pepper
3 cups milk
1 cup light cream
1½ cups flaked uncooked crab meat
     or chopped uncooked lobster meat
3 tablespoons cognac or dry sherry
Finely minced parsley or snipped
     chives

....

Put the potato, water, and ½ teaspoon salt into a small saucepan, and bring them to a boil. Reduce the heat, and simmer the potato until it is tender. Set the pan aside.

Heat the butter in a large saucepan, add the onion, and sauté it until it is translucent. Stir in the seasonings. Add the milk and cream. Bring the mixture to a boil, stirring constantly. Reduce the heat and simmer, uncovered, until the liquid is smooth.

Stir in the crab meat or lobster and the potato with its cooking liquid. Simmer the soup for 10 minutes more.

Stir in the cognac or sherry. Garnish the soup with the parsley or chives, and serve.

Makes 8 servings

CHILLED MELON AND CHAMPAGNE SOUP

A delightful soup with a celebratory splash of champagne, this is a cool inauguration for a special meal.

....

4 cups chopped honeydew melon,
     cantaloupe, or a combination
½ cup orange juice
1 tablespoon fresh lemon juice
1 tablespoon fresh lime juice
½ cup chilled champagne

....

GARNISH:
Fresh mint leaves

....

In a blender, purée 3½ cups of the melon. Blend in the juices and, just before serving, stir in the champagne. Garnish the soup with the remaining ½ cup chopped melon and the mint leaves, and serve.

Makes 6 servings

ISLAND STYLE: HAITI

Those who love Haiti find enchantment here that is difficult to describe. Perhaps it is the warmth and gentle spirit of the people or the rugged green beauty of the land. Some visitors may respond to the rich culture and art that the direst poverty and most difficult conditions have failed to obliterate.

Or maybe it's just the food. In Haiti, the robust flavors of the islands combine with subtle French refinements to create a special style of island cooking. Here fish is gently poached in Gallic fashion, then smothered in vegetables and hot peppers in a way that is distinctly Caribbean. Fish, pork, sweet potatoes, yams, plantains, and bananas, ingredients common to most Caribbean islands, often appear on Haitian plates, but local cooks seem to work some special alchemy on them, producing meals that linger in the memory. A juicy mango fresh from a nearby tree might find its way to the table in the company of chicken breasts poached with herbs.

Although the French influence is very strong in elegant Haitian restaurants, the local cuisine is as vivid and spicy as the country itself. Whereas almost all islands have

their own special rice-and-bean dish, Haiti's is particularly distinctive. Rice djon djon is made nowhere else in the Caribbean because it requires an ingredient found only on Haiti—small black mushrooms with earthy-tasting caps and inedible stems that produce a deep-black dye. The stems are used to color the water in which the rice is cooked; then they are discarded. The rice is combined with lima beans and the mushroom caps. Griot (glazed pork), served with a spicy sauce called ti-mal-ice, is a popular local dish. Tassot is an old recipe in which pork, beef, or poultry is dried in the burning sun on a hot tin roof before being marinated in spiced lime juice and then grilled. Food, always a measure of a nation's character, in Haiti easily juxtaposes the simplicity of the Caribbean with the savoir faire of France.

Haiti fetes the senses while it baffles the mind. How has its dark history and uncertain present failed to dim the spirit that pervades this singular country? For many visitors the lure of Haiti is simply magic, a voodoo spell that brings them back time and again to a place that is simply like no other on Earth.

GUADELOUPE SEASIDE CHOWDER

Dipping a net into the water just outside one's doorstep is often the first step toward dinner in the Caribbean. A variety of reef fish, called "pot fish" on some islands, make this spicy soup a full meal.

1/4 cup olive oil
2 onions, chopped

4 green onions, chopped

1 thyme sprig

10 cups cold water

3 pounds firm white fish, cut into
    1-inch cubes (reserve the
    trimmings)

3 garlic cloves, crushed

2 allspice berries

1 bay leaf

2 whole Scotch bonnet (or
    habanero) peppers, or other fresh
    hot peppers to taste

1 pound new potatoes, peeled and
    cubed

1 pound peeled, seeded, and chopped
    tomatoes

⅛ teaspoon annatto oil (see page
    7)

1 tablespoon Pernod liqueur

2 tablespoons drained
    capers

¼ cup julienne slivers of fresh
    basil

....

In a large pot, heat the oil. Add the onions, green onions, and thyme. Sauté until the onions are translucent. Add the fish trimmings, water, garlic, spices, and peppers, and bring the mixture to a boil. Reduce the heat, and simmer the mixture, uncovered, for 30 minutes.

Remove the peppers from the broth, and discard them. Strain the broth through a double layer of dampened cheesecloth, pressing lightly to extract as much liquid as possible. Discard the solids. Return the broth to a clean pot, and add the potatoes. Simmer for 10 minutes or until the potatoes are almost cooked. Add the tomatoes and annatto oil to the soup. Add the fish cubes, and simmer for 8 minutes or until the fish is opaque. Add the Pernod and capers, and simmer for 5 minutes more. Serve the soup immediately, sprinkled with the julienned basil.

Makes 6 to 8 servings

GROUPER QUENELLES IN SEAFOOD BROTH

A quenelle is an ethereal pleasure that appears on your plate for a fleeting moment and then dissolves like a cloud on your tongue. It's difficult to find words to describe perfectly made quenelles, but they are certainly much more than dumplings.

Until recently quenelles were part of that rarefied cuisine that emerges only from restaurants with the most ambitious kitchens. All that changed with the advent of the food processor. Where once the making of a quenelle was an exhausting project, too daunting for any moderately sane cook to attempt, today almost all of the work can be accomplished easily with the flick of a switch.

QUENELLES:

½ cup milk
¼ cup butter
½ teaspoon salt
⅛ teaspoon ground white pepper
½ cup flour
3 eggs
2 egg yolks
½ pound boned raw grouper, puréed
   in a food processor
¾ cup cold butter
1 tablespoon heavy cream
Salt and white pepper to taste
Fresh or dried dillweed

SEAFOOD BROTH:

4 pounds fish trimmings
2 onions, chopped
3 celery ribs, chopped
3 carrots, chopped
2 teaspoons dried thyme
1 bay leaf
12 black peppercorns
6 parsley sprigs
2 cups white wine

GARNISH:
Fresh dillweed

To make the quenelles, put the milk, butter, salt, and pepper into a small, heavy saucepan, and bring the mixture to a boil. Add the flour all at once, stirring rapidly, and continue stirring over high heat until the mixture forms a ball. Put the mixture into a food processor fitted with a steel blade. Add the whole eggs and egg yolks, and process until mixture is smooth. Add the grouper, and process again. Blend in the butter, cream, salt, white pepper, and dill, and chill the mixture for 2 hours.

To make the broth, put the ingredients into a large stockpot, and cover them with cold water. Bring the mixture to a boil, and reduce the heat to a simmer. Skim the stock, and continue to simmer it gently for 20 to 30 minutes. Strain the stock, let it cool, and refrigerate it.

When you are ready to serve, heat the broth to a simmer. Use a wet teaspoon to dip out a rounded mass of the quenelle mixture and another spoon to slip the quenelle into the simmering broth. Form the rest of the mixture into quenelles this way, and poach them for about 10 minutes. The quenelles are done when they have approximately doubled in size and they roll over easily. Fill each soup plate with broth and a portion of the quenelles, and serve the soup with a sprinkling of dill.

Makes 8 to 10 servings

ROASTED CORN SOUP

Sink your spoon into the dazzling flavors of mellow roasted corn and fiery peppers. This is a great opener for dinner cooked on the grill. If you like, add freshly cooked shrimp, lobster, or crab to the finished soup.

. . . .

8 ears fresh corn, with their husks
3 shallots, minced
½ Scotch bonnet (or habanero) pepper, or 2 jalapeño peppers, minced
1 cup white wine
1 cup water
1 celery rib, diced
2 cups half-and-half
1 cup chicken broth
1 to 2 teaspoons minced dillweed
1½ teaspoons salt
1 pinch cayenne
¼ teaspoon ground white pepper

. . . .

GARNISH:
Chopped fresh dillweed or snipped chives

. . . .

Put the unhusked ears of corn in cold water, and soak them for 20 to 30 minutes. You can roast the corn either on a grill or in the oven. If you'd like to grill the corn, prepare the fire. If you'd rather use the oven, preheat it to 400°.

To grill the corn, place it, still unhusked, on the hot grill. Roast it for 20 minutes, turning it often. If you are using the oven, place the soaked corn on the oven rack, and bake the corn until it is tender, about 20 minutes.

Cut the kernels from the cobs with a sharp knife, and set 1½ cups of kernels aside. Put the remaining corn, the shallots, and the pepper into a pot over medium heat. Add the wine and water. Bring the mixture to a boil, reduce the heat, and simmer until the vegetables are soft, about 10 minutes.

Purée the vegetables and liquid in a blender. Strain the purée, and put the liquid back into the pot over medium heat. Add the reserved corn kernels, celery, half-and-half, chicken stock, dill, salt, cayenne pepper, and white pepper. Cook the soup for 10 minutes. Serve it sprinkled with fresh dill or chives.

Makes 8 servings

Garden Party Lunch

. . . .

TROPICAL GAZPACHO
WITH CILANTRO CROUTONS

◆

TUNA SALAD
WITH TANGERINE VINAIGRETTE

◆

TOASTED COCONUT BREAD

◆

KIWI MOUSSE

TROPICAL GAZPACHO WITH CILANTRO CROUTONS

This is one of our favorite soups, perfect for the Caribbean climate. We like adding cilantro to the croutons, but you might prefer another herb, perhaps basil or rosemary.

....

6 medium tomatoes, peeled, seeded, and chopped
½ cup onions, chopped
½ cup chopped green onions
4 celery ribs, chopped
2 cucumbers, peeled, seeded, and chopped
1 green bell pepper, chopped
1 yellow bell pepper, chopped
¼ cup red wine vinegar

....

6 cups tomato juice
1 cup sliced black olives
Salt and pepper to taste
Hot pepper sauce to taste
Worcestershire sauce to taste

....

CILANTRO CROUTONS:
¼ cup butter
2 tablespoons chopped cilantro
2 cups ¾-inch cubes of whole-wheat bread

....

In a blender, purée two-thirds of the tomatoes, onions, celery, cucumbers, and peppers. Stir in the vinegar, tomato juice, olives, and remaining chopped vegetables. Season the soup with salt, pepper, hot sauce, and Worcestershire sauce. Chill the soup.

To make the croutons, heat the butter in a skillet, and add the cilantro and bread cubes. Cook the bread cubes over medium heat until they are crisp and golden brown. Let them cool. Serve them on top of the gazpacho.

Makes 10 servings

WILD MUSHROOM BISQUE

Although we don't have the famed black mushrooms that are found in Haiti, tasty edible mushrooms do grow on Tortola—or at least that is what is believed by those who have tasted the mushroom tea at Bomba's Shack. Not being trained mycologists, we leave mushroom hunting to others and play it safe with well-tamed fungi.

....

½ pound chanterelle or shiitake mushrooms
½ pound white mushrooms
Juice of 1 lemon
1½ tablespoons unsalted butter
2 medium shallots, minced
1 thyme sprig
1 bay leaf
Salt and pepper to taste
1½ cups chicken broth

1 tablespoon cornstarch stirred with
   ¼ cup water (optional)
2 cups heavy cream

....

GARNISH:
   Chopped thyme and parsley

....

Sprinkle all the mushrooms with the lemon juice. Slice one-quarter of the shiitakes or chanterelles, and reserve these. Cut the remaining mushrooms into small cubes. Heat the butter in a saucepan, and sauté the shallots. Add the mushrooms, thyme, and bay leaf, and cook until the liquid disappears.

Add the chicken broth, salt, and pepper. Simmer 20 minutes. Thicken the soup, if you like, with the cornstarch mixture. Simmer for 10 minutes more. Add the cream and reserved mushrooms, and simmer until the soup is heated through. Garnish it with chopped thyme and parsley, and serve.

Makes 6 servings

Vegetarian Pleasures

....

WILD MUSHROOM BISQUE

◆

CARROT SALAD VINAIGRETTE

◆

PUMPKIN, BLACK BEAN,
AND PARMESAN LASAGNA

◆

AMARETTO ORANGES WITH SORBET

CARIBBEAN BLACK BEAN SOUP

This is one of the most popular soups in the Caribbean. We add Italian sausage (either hot or mild) because we like the flavor it imparts. Serve the soup over cooked rice.

....

1 pound dried black beans, washed
   and picked over
½ pound Italian sausage
1 large onion, chopped
½ teaspoon ground cloves
Beef or chicken broth
Salt and pepper to taste
Dark rum or pepper wine (see page
   68)

....

GARNISH:
   Minced white onions
   Chopped avocado
   Chopped red or orange pepper

....

Soak the beans overnight in cold water. Drain them, and put them into a large saucepan. Remove any casings from the sausage, and cook the meat with the onions in a skillet until the sausage is no longer pink and the onions are limp. Add the sausage and onions to the beans in the saucepan, add the cloves, and cover the beans in water by about 2 inches. Bring the beans to a boil, lower the heat, and cover the pan. Simmer the beans 2½ to 3 hours, until they are very tender.

Drain the beans, measure the liquid, and add enough broth to bring the quantity to 8 cups. Purée the beans in a blender, in batches, with some of the liquid. Return the beans to the saucepan, add the remaining liquid, and add salt and pepper to taste. Simmer the beans gently for 15 minutes longer. Serve them in soup bowls with the garnishes.

Makes 6 servings

PEPPER WINE

In a jar, combine 20 bird peppers or other very small hot peppers, or 5 Scotch bonnet (or habanero) peppers, with 1 cup dry sherry. Close the jar tightly, and refrigerate it for several days. The sherry will gradually pick up heat from the peppers, becoming a lively addition for soups, stews, and other dishes.

SUGAR MILL CURRIED BANANA SOUP

The smooth sweetness of bananas and a gentle whisper of curry unite in this elegant but easy potage.

....

2 tablespoons butter
1 onion, chopped
1 garlic clove, minced
2 teaspoons curry powder
¼ cup raw rice
5 cups rich chicken broth
1½ cups half-and-half
½ cup heavy cream
2 bananas, peeled and cut into
    chunks
Salt and pepper to taste
2 tablespoons lemon juice

....

GARNISH:
    *Thinly sliced, fried banana, or
    toasted shredded coconut (see page
    69)*

....

Heat the butter in a large, heavy pan. Sauté the onion and garlic until the onion is limp. Add the curry powder, and stir it with the vegetables for about 2 to 3 minutes over low heat. Add the rice, and stir to coat it with butter. Pour in the chicken broth, bring the mixture to a boil, reduce the heat, and cover the pan. Cook the rice until it is very tender, about 25 minutes.

Put the mixture into a blender. Add the half-and-half, heavy cream, and bananas, and whirl until the soup is smooth. (You may have to do this in batches.) Season the soup with salt, pepper, and lemon juice. Serve it heated or chilled, garnished with banana chips or toasted coconut.

Makes 6 servings

TOMATO AND GINGER WINE SOUP

Popular in the Caribbean, Stone's Ginger Wine should be available from most well-stocked liquor stores elsewhere. If you can't find it, steep a 2-inch knob of fresh ginger in sherry for several days before making the soup, then substitute the sherry for the ginger wine.

....

3 cups chicken or beef broth
2 cups peeled plum tomatoes,
    cubed
2 tablespoons tomato purée
3 large onions, minced
3 tablespoons butter
3 tablespoons flour

¾ cup Stone's Ginger Wine
2 tablespoons lemon juice
1½ cups cream
Salt and pepper to taste

....

GARNISH:
Chopped fresh tomatoes
Basil or dill sprigs

....

Heat the stock in a saucepan. Add the tomatoes, tomato purée, and onions, and simmer 1 hour. Remove the pan from the heat and whirl the mixture in a blender. Heat the butter in the saucepan, stir in the flour, and cook the roux for about 1 minute, without browning. Gradually stir in the blended soup. Add the wine and lemon juice, and heat the soup for 5 minutes.

Remove the soup from the heat, and stir in the cream. Serve each bowl garnished with chopped fresh tomatoes and a sprig of fresh basil or dill.

Makes 6 servings

TOASTED COCONUT

To toast grated or shredded coconut, whether it is fresh or dried, spread it in a baking pan, and put it into a 350° oven for 10 to 12 minutes.

CALLALOO

Callaloo is the principal ingredient in the ubiquitous West Indian soup of the same name. Although each island has its own version, cooks throughout the Caribbean agree that young green callaloo leaves are essential in their soup pots. The edible root of the same plant is called dasheen, tannia, taro, malanga, or yautia, depending on which island it grows on. Confusing the issue further is another plant that also is called callaloo on some islands, but is elsewhere known as Chinese spinach or Indian kale. Dasheen leaves are rarely available in North America, but spinach or Swiss chard can be substituted.

. . . .

1 pound spinach or Swiss chard
3 cups water
3 garlic cloves, minced
1 onion, chopped
½ teaspoon dried thyme
2 tablespoons minced parsley
½ pound okra, sliced
1 peeled and cubed eggplant
1 cup cubed cooked ham
Hot pepper sauce to taste

. . . .

Put the greens in a pot with the water, garlic, onion, thyme, and parsley. Bring the ingredients just to a boil, reduce the heat, and simmer until the greens are tender.

Add the okra and eggplant, and cook the soup 10 minutes longer.

Remove the soup from the heat, and purée it in batches in a food processor or blender. Return it to the pot, add the ham, and season the soup with salt and pepper and hot pepper sauce. Simmer gently for 5 minutes.

Serve the soup immediately.

Makes 6 servings

BREADFRUIT VICHYSSOISE

The Sugar Mill has its own lush breadfruit tree that shades the hotel's entrance and provides us with bushels of cannonball-size fruit. We like to think our tree is related to those that Captain Bligh of the *Bounty* brought to St. Vincent in 1793 after surviving the notorious mutiny. In the Caribbean, breadfruit stands in for potatoes in many dishes, and nowhere more elegantly than in this island version of a French classic.

Fresh or canned breadfruit is available in markets specializing in Caribbean products. You can substitute potatoes for the breadfruit, if you like, and thereby return the dish to its French origins.

··············

¼ cup butter
1 cup minced onions
1 teaspoon minced garlic
1½ cups peeled, cored, and coarsely
    chopped breadfruit, or 4 slices
    canned breadfruit, coarsely
    chopped
4 cups chicken broth
1 cup heavy cream
Salt and pepper to taste

··············

GARNISH:
    Snipped chives or minced green
      onion

··············

Melt the butter over moderate heat in a large, heavy pot. Add the onions and garlic, and sauté them for about 5 minutes, until they are soft and transparent.

Stir in the chopped breadfruit and the chicken broth, and bring the mixture to a boil over high heat. Reduce the heat to low, cover the pot tightly, and simmer for about 20 minutes, until the breadfruit is tender enough to be easily mashed against the side of the pan.

In a blender or food processor, purée the soup, in batches, with the cream. Season the puréed soup with salt and pepper, and chill the soup for 3 hours.

Serve the soup cold, garnished with chives or green onions.

Makes 6 servings

SCALLOP SOUP

This delicious soup is so simple to prepare that we are a little reluctant to reveal the recipe. We often serve Scallop Soup at home before a gala holiday dinner, because it's festive but not filling, and it leaves us plenty of time to deal with more demanding courses.

··············

3 cups chicken broth
1½ cups beef broth
⅓ cup clam broth
⅓ cup white port
½ pound scallops, cut into thin strips

··············

GARNISH:
    Thinly sliced green onions or snipped
      chives

··············

Put the beef and chicken broths and port into a saucepan, and bring the mixture to a boil. Season the broth to taste with salt and pepper. Divide the scallops among individual serving bowls and ladle the broth over the top. The heat of the broth will cook the scallops while leaving them meltingly tender. Garnish the soup with green onions or chives, and serve.

Makes 6 servings

CHILLED CUCUMBER SOUP

Our climate makes cold soups very popular. This is one of our favorites, because it's light and refreshing and a great starter for any rich meal.

....

4 cucumbers, peeled, seeded, and cut into chunks
1½ cups chicken broth
1½ cups sour cream or plain yogurt
2 garlic cloves, minced
3 tablespoons white wine vinegar
Salt and pepper to taste

....

GARNISH:
Chopped tomato
Minced green onions or fresh dillweed

....

Combine the cucumbers, chicken broth, sour cream or yogurt, garlic, vinegar, and salt and pepper in a food processor or blender, and whirl until the mixture is smooth. Chill the soup thoroughly.

Pour the soup into serving bowls. Sprinkle it with chopped tomato and green onion or dill, and serve.

Makes 6 servings

SOUP SAVERS

Sometimes a soup needs just a little something to turn it from a flop into a success. Here are a few things that can perk up a dull potage.

GARLIC: Adds flavor to any soup.
LEMON JUICE: Its sharp citrus flavor sometimes adds just the right piquancy.
TOMATO PASTE: Adds both color and flavor to a lackluster soup.
CREAM: Smoothes and enriches.

HERBS

BASIL: Great with any tomato-based soup.
THYME: For a subtle smoky flavor.
CHIVES: Adds a nippy, oniony taste.
PARSLEY: Finely chopped, it adds color and a slightly peppery accent.
ROSEMARY: Imparts a woodsy, piney flavor.

SPICES

CAYENNE: Use sparingly to add a mellow, peppy flavor.
CURRY: Enlivens a dreary soup, but before adding it cook it in a bit of butter to remove its rough, raw flavor.
NUTMEG: A unique nutty flavor that is especially good in cream soups.

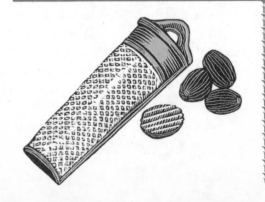

CONCH CHOWDER

Almost everyone has seen the lovely pink and orange shell of the conch, but not everyone has eaten this critter. Like the abalone, conch is tough as a boot if abused, but delicious when treated with care. Tenderize the conch by pounding it with a mallet until the tissue has broken down.

If you can't get conch, you can substitute clams in this recipe. Simmer the clam broth, water or wine, onion, celery, and peppers for 15 minutes, then add the clams and simmer 15 minutes longer. Finish the soup as directed.

....

1 pound tenderized conch, chopped
    into bite-size pieces
3 cups clam broth
3 cups water or dry white wine
Salt and pepper to taste
1 onion, diced
3 to 4 celery ribs, diced
1 red bell pepper, diced
1 green bell pepper, diced
4 tomatoes, peeled, seeded, and
    diced
2 large potatoes, peeled, cubed, and
    cooked until tender
1 teaspoon dried thyme
1 cup heavy cream or
    half-and-half

....

GARNISH:
    Chopped parsley

....

In a large saucepan, simmer the conch, clam broth, water, wine, and salt and pepper for 1½ hours.

Add the onion, celery, and red and green peppers. Continue simmering the soup for ½ hour longer.

Add the tomatoes, potatoes, thyme, and cream or half-and-half, and heat the soup through. Season with more salt and pepper, if you like. Garnish with chopped parsley, and serve.

Makes about 2½ quarts

CREOLE PEANUT SOUP

In the markets of the Caribbean one always finds big bags of peanuts in their shells. As men play dominoes under the shade of seagrape trees, they shell and eat peanuts while contemplating the next move.

1 medium onion, minced
2 tablespoons butter
2 tablespoons flour
4 cups chicken broth
¾ cup peanut butter
1 cup heavy cream
1 minced jalapeño pepper
Hot pepper sauce, celery salt, lemon
   juice, and salt and pepper to taste

GARNISH:
   Chopped roasted peanuts
   Minced green onions

Cook the onion in the butter until the onion is limp. Stir in the flour, and cook for 3 minutes, stirring constantly. Gradually stir in the broth. Stir in the peanut butter, and cook and stir the soup until it is smooth and slightly thickened. Cover the pan, and simmer the soup gently 15 to 20 minutes.

Stir in the cream, and season the soup to taste with the minced hot pepper, hot pepper sauce, and other seasonings. Garnish with peanuts and green onions, and serve.

Makes 6 servings

Calypso Salads and Side Dishes

CALYPSO SALADS AND SIDE DISHES

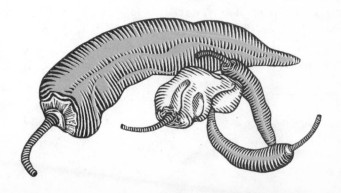

FLOWER POWER

A friend once expressed concern because we put red hibiscus flowers on the dining room tables every night. "But what if you run out of flowers?" she asked.

We explained that no one ever runs out of flowers in the tropics. The hibiscus is a favorite of ours since it blooms so profusely and all parts of the plant are edible. We use the leaves to adorn plates, the flowers to decorate the tables, and the petals to make tea.

"Bush teas," made from herbs and leaves, are very popular in the Caribbean, and recipes for these potions have been passed down through generations. Through the years we've learned about the curative properties of lemongrass, black wattle, wormgrass, lime, soursop, and other leaves when steeped in hot water for sipping.

But it wasn't until we met Doris Jadan, from St. John, that we discovered hibiscus tea. This brew makes no claim as a curative, but it's tasty and beautiful to look at. Doris suggests that about five blossoms make a 4-ounce cup of tea, which can be sweetened with honey and flavored with lemongrass or a slice of lime. Hibiscus tea doesn't have a strong flavor, but its color is beautiful, and when it is drunk either hot or cold, the tea is delightfully refreshing.

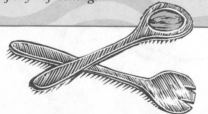

SWEET AND SOUR PEPPERS

Make these any time you have extra sweet peppers. They keep very well in the refrigerator and are terrific in salads, spooned over brie to serve with crackers, or simply on their own to brighten up an otherwise dull dinner plate.

....

3 cups water
½ cup sherry vinegar or champagne
    vinegar
⅓ cup honey
2 onions, thinly sliced
8 garlic cloves, sliced
2 bay leaves
½ teaspoon whole black peppercorns
2 pounds bell peppers (red, yellow,
    orange, or a combination), cut
    lengthwise into 1-inch-wide strips
4 thyme sprigs

....

Combine the water, vinegar, honey, onions, garlic, bay leaves, and peppercorns in a large pot, and bring the ingredients to a boil. Add the peppers and thyme, and simmer them for 15 minutes. Remove the pot from the heat, let the peppers cool, and refrigerate them, with their cooking liquid, in a covered container. They will keep for up to 2 weeks in the refrigerator.

Makes 6 servings

HEARTS OF PALM CARNIVAL

One day a visitor, one of those footloose types who roam the islands, dropped in at the Sugar Mill. He could weave hats and intricate birds out of dried grass, and he seemed to know a lot about living off the land. One night, after helping some of our staff take trash to the dump, he returned with the trunk of a Sabal palm tree that someone had discarded. He whacked away at it with a machete until he retrieved the tender heart, and then cooked it with salt pork. For us it was a terrific new taste experience, and when we said so he replied, "Well heck, it's nothin' but old swamp cabbage."

Alas, we've never again found such a treasure at the dump.

....

½ cup coarsely chopped Kalamata
    olives
3 coarsely chopped tomatoes
3 chopped green onions (both white
    and green parts)
1 garlic clove, minced
½ Scotch bonnet (or habanero)
    pepper or 1 to 2 jalapeño peppers,
    minced
¼ cup olive oil
Salt and pepper to taste
18 canned hearts of palm, cut in half
    vertically

Loose-leaf lettuce

....

In a bowl, gently mix together all the ingredients except the hearts of palm and the lettuce. Arrange the lettuce on individual salad plates. Place the hearts of palm in a fan shape on each plate of lettuce. Mound a portion of the chopped vegetables at each apex, and serve.

Makes 6 servings

Summer Lunch Buffet

....

FISH ESCABECHE

◆

RED BEAN AND RICE SALAD

◆

LEEK AND PEPPER SALAD
WITH TAPENADE

◆

GREEN BANANAS
IN OLIVE VINAIGRETTE

◆

KEY LIME PIE

LEEK AND PEPPER SALAD WITH TAPENADE

Peppers—hot and mild, green, red, orange, yellow, and purple—all grow in happy profusion in the islands, and we're always looking for new ways to use them. This colorful and sophisticated salad has become a real favorite.

....

12 leeks, trimmed
1½ cups olive oil
1 teaspoon fresh thyme leaves
1 garlic clove, minced
Grated zest of 1 orange
⅓ cup dry white wine
Salt and pepper to taste
1¼ cups pitted Kalamata olives
½ cup walnuts, toasted for 8 to 10
    minutes in a 350° oven and chopped
1 teaspoon minced rosemary
2 jalapeño peppers, stemmed and
    seeded, or 3 tablespoons canned
    diced jalapeño peppers
Zest and juice of 1 lemon
2 tablespoons armagnac or cognac
6 red bell peppers

....

Slit the green portion of the leeks with a knife, and wash the leaves thoroughly under running water to remove all grit. In a pot, simmer the leeks gently in salted water for about 10 minutes, until they are just tender when pierced with a knife.

Whisk together ½ cup of the oil, the thyme, the garlic, the orange zest, the wine, and the salt and pepper in a bowl. Set the marinade aside.

Drain the leeks on paper towels. While they are still warm, place them in a shallow dish and cover them with the marinade. Allow them to sit for 1 to 2 hours at room temperature, turning them occasionally.

In a food processor or blender, whirl the olives, walnuts, rosemary, hot pepper, lemon juice, zest, and brandy. Don't overprocess them; the mixture should have some texture. With the machine running, gradually add the remaining oil. Set the sauce aside.

Prepare a charcoal fire for grilling, or preheat the broiler.

Broil the leeks and peppers, or grill them over charcoal, until they are charred. Put the peppers in a plastic bag, and leave the bag in the freezer while you prepare the leeks. Discard the burned leek leaves, and cut any large leeks in half lengthwise. Arrange the leeks cut side down on a plate, fanning out the leaves. Remove the peppers from the freezer, and peel them under running water. Cut them in half vertically, and remove the stems and seeds. Lay the grilled pepper halves between the leeks. Season the vegetables with salt and pepper. Place some of the tapenade in the center of the platter, and garnish the plate with fresh rosemary. Serve the salad at room temperature, with the remaining sauce in a separate bowl.

Makes 6 to 8 servings

Papaya and Prosciutto with Ginger Vinaigrette

This can be served as a first course or as a salad. Either way, the sweet, salty, and tart flavors will dance on your taste buds.

. . . .

DRESSING:

> *½ cup Stone's Ginger Wine (see page 69)*
> *½ cup water*
> *¼ cup peeled and minced gingerroot*
> *2 tablespoons white wine vinegar*
> *5 tablespoons olive oil*
> *Salt and pepper to taste*

. . . .

SALAD:

> *3 papayas or 1 large melon, peeled and sliced ½ inch thick*
> *1 head loose-leaf lettuce*
> *3 ounces prosciutto, cut into slivers*
> *Watercress or parsley sprigs*
> *1 red bell pepper, cut into julienne strips*

. . . .

To make the dressing, put the wine, water, and ginger into a saucepan, and bring them to a boil over high heat. Reduce the heat, cover the pot, and simmer the ingredients ½ hour.

Uncover the pan, raise the heat, and reduce the liquid until only ¼ cup remains. Pour it into a bowl, and let it cool. Add the vinegar, and whisk in the oil, salt, and pepper.

Arrange the lettuce on a platter or on individual plates. Place the papaya or melon slices on top. Sprinkle the prosciutto on top, and spoon the ginger vinaigrette over all. Garnish with the watercress or parsley and red pepper, and serve.

Makes 6 servings

Curried Tomato Salad

If you have some of the wonderful tomatoes of summer so much the better, but even if your tomatoes are tasteless pink tennis balls, this treatment will give them a lift. We particularly like this dish as a prelude for barbecued, grilled, or roasted meat.

. . . .

> *3 tomatoes, peeled, seeded, and diced*
> *1 large red onion, chopped*
> *Salt and pepper to taste*
> *¾ cup mayonnaise*
> *¼ cup minced parsley*
> *1 tablespoon curry powder*
> *Loose-leaf lettuce*

. . . .

Combine the onions and tomatoes in a bowl. Add the salt and pepper, and chill the mixture well.

In a small bowl, mix together the mayonnaise, parsley, and curry powder. Add the curry dressing to the tomato mixture, and mix well. Spoon the tomato-onion mixture onto lettuce leaves, and serve immediately.

Makes 6 servings

GREEN PAPAYA SALAD

In the islands, we don't use papaya only when it's ripe; we also use it when it's green, much as you might use zucchini. Try this salad the next time your greengrocer is overloaded with underripe papayas. Select dark green papayas with no streaks of yellow, if possible.

....

3 green papayas, peeled and cut into
    1-inch cubes or julienne strips
2 tablespoons capers, rinsed
1 tablespoon celery seed
2 red bell peppers, chopped
4 green onions (all of the white parts
    and some of the green), chopped

....

MUSTARD DRESSING:
  1 whole egg
  1 tablespoon grated parmesan cheese
  ½ teaspoon salt

½ teaspoon ground black pepper
2 tablespoons Dijon mustard
3 tablespoons lemon juice
1 teaspoon Worcestershire sauce
1 cup olive oil
Green loose-leaf lettuce or spinach
    leaves

....

Cook the papaya in a covered pan with as little water as necessary, so all the moisture will be absorbed when the papaya is done. Simmer the papaya until it is tender, about 15 minutes. Let the papaya cool, then chill it.

In a bowl, toss the capers, celery seed, peppers, and onions with the chilled papaya.

In another bowl, whisk together all the dressing ingredients. Add just enough dressing to the salad to moisten it, and toss the salad. (Refrigerate any remaining dressing to use later on tossed green salads.) Spoon the papaya into a bowl lined with lettuce or spinach leaves, and serve.

Makes 6 to 8 servings

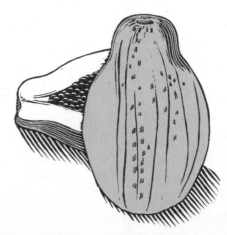

GREEN BANANAS IN OLIVE VINAIGRETTE

Cooking unripe bananas and then serving them cold in a vinaigrette may be a new idea to you, but we think you'll like the result.

....

4 pounds green bananas
2 quarts water
2 cups milk
1 tablespoon salt
½ cup balsamic vinegar
1 teaspoon salt
1 teaspoon coarsely ground black
  pepper
1¼ cups olive oil
1½ cups pitted Kalamata olives
4 bay leaves
½ cup minced fresh parsley

....

Trim the ends off each banana, and make two lengthwise slits in the peel, on opposite sides. Do not remove the peel or cut into the banana flesh. Put the water into a large pot, and add the milk and salt. Bring the liquid to a boil, and add the bananas. Reduce the heat, and simmer the bananas until they appear cooked through but are still firm, about 15 to 20 minutes. Drain the bananas, peel them, and cut them diagonally into 1-inch pieces.

To make the dressing, combine the vinegar, salt, and pepper in a glass bowl. Slowly whisk in the oil. Stir in the olives, bay leaves, and banana slices. Allow the salad to stand at room temperature at least 1 hour. Before serving, remove the bay leaves and stir in the minced parsley.

Makes 6 servings

CARROT SALAD VINAIGRETTE

This glorious golden salad, made with ingredients you're likely to have on hand, adds a bright note to any menu.

....

10 large carrots, peeled and cut into
  julienne strips or coarsely grated
4 green onions, minced
2 tablespoons minced parsley
2 tablespoons grated lemon zest
½ cup olive oil
3 tablespoons lemon juice
¼ teaspoon dry mustard
Salt and pepper to taste

....

Cook the carrots in a covered saucepan, in about 1 inch of boiling water, until they are barely tender (about 5 minutes). Drain them, and plunge them into cold water. Drain them again, and turn them into a serving bowl. Add the onions, parsley, and lemon zest, and mix. In a small bowl, whisk together the olive oil, lemon juice, mustard, and salt and pepper. Pour the dressing over the carrots, and toss until the carrots are coated with the dressing. Serve them at room temperature.

Makes 6 servings

TUNA SALAD WITH TANGERINE VINAIGRETTE

Although tangerines are not native to the Caribbean, we've planted a small tree in our home garden in Brewer's Bay. It has yet to bear fruit, but when it does, you can be sure we'll use some of it in this refreshing salad.

....

MARINADE:
1 tablespoon soy sauce
2 green onions (all of the white parts and some of the green), minced
⅓ cup olive oil
1 tablespoon crushed fennel seeds
1 teaspoon celery seed
1 tablespoon minced celery
½ teaspoon dried thyme
1 small bay leaf, crushed
1 tablespoon grated tangerine zest
1½ pounds fresh tuna steaks, about 1 inch thick
6 tangerines
Loose-leaf lettuce

....

TANGERINE VINAIGRETTE:
2 tablespoons balsamic vinegar
2 tablespoons red wine vinegar
1 teaspoon Dijon mustard
¾ cup olive oil
1 teaspoon grated tangerine zest
1 teaspoon crushed fennel seeds
Salt and pepper to taste

....

GARNISH:
¼ cup minced cilantro

....

Combine the marinade ingredients in a glass or ceramic bowl. Place the tuna in the marinade, and allow it to marinate in the refrigerator for about 30 minutes. Prepare a charcoal fire for grilling, or preheat the broiler.

Peel four of the tangerines, and pull them apart into sections. Put them into a bowl. Cut and squeeze the remaining two tangerines, and pour their juice over the sectioned tangerines.

Grill or broil the marinated fish until it is done to your liking (it should be cooked through and springy to the touch). Cut each piece of tuna across the grain into 3 to 4 slices. Drain the tangerine sections, reserving the juice. Arrange the lettuce on individual plates, top with the tuna slices and tangerine sections, and cover and chill the plates.

In a small saucepan, reduce the tangerine juice by one-fourth. Let the juice cool.

To make the vinaigrette, combine the vinegars, tangerine juice, and mustard in a bowl. Whisk in the oil, and season with the tangerine zest, fennel seeds, and salt and pepper. Just before serving, drizzle the dressing over the salad plates, and sprinkle with minced cilantro.

Makes 6 servings

CARIBBEAN BLACK BEAN AND SEAFOOD SALAD

W e've become devotees of Caribbean black beans, which we use often and in various preparations. This salad is a kaleidoscope of flavors and colors.

....

1½ cups (1 15-ounce can) cooked black beans, drained and rinsed
½ cup chopped red bell peppers
½ cup chopped yellow bell peppers
½ cup chopped green onions
1 cup fresh cut corn, or 1 10-ounce package frozen corn, thawed
½ cup minced basil

....

DRESSING:
½ cup cider vinegar
1 tablespoon Dijon mustard
1½ teaspoons ground cumin
1 teaspoon minced garlic
1 teaspoon freshly ground black pepper
½ teaspoon salt
1½ cups olive oil

....

1 head broccoli (about 2 pounds), broken into flowerets, steamed until just tender, and cooled
Loose-leaf lettuce
Poached or grilled fish, scallops, shrimp, or mussels, cooled

....

Combine the beans, peppers, celery, onions, corn, and basil in a bowl. In another bowl, whisk together the dressing ingredients. Add just enough dressing to the bean mixture to coat the ingredients, and toss. Put the broccoli into another bowl, add enough dressing to coat it lightly, and toss.

Place lettuce leaves on a plate, and mound the bean mixture in the center. Surround the bean mixture with cooked seafood and broccoli, and drizzle the fish with the remaining dressing.

Makes 6 servings

THE BOUNTIFUL BEAN

B eans are a staple of life in the Caribbean. Jessica Harris, whose books on Caribbean cuisine and history, Sky Juice and Flying Fish and Iron Pots and Wooden Spoons, are essentials for the library of anyone interested in island food or just good reading, points out that beans or peas and rice can be found on every island of the Caribbean.

Whether called rice and peas (as in Jamaica, the British Virgin Islands, and the other English-speaking islands), arroz con gandules (as in Puerto Rico), moros y cristianos (as in Cuba), or riz au pois (as in Haiti), this savory and nutritious dish fills plates all over the Caribbean.

ISLAND SHRIMP SALAD

Imagine sitting at a table where your feet are touching sand and the view is of pelicans diving into the bluest sea you've ever seen. That's the ideal setting for this fresh-flavored salad of tropical fruits and seafood. The lime, coconut, and ginger dressing is almost as good as a trip to the islands.

....

2 pounds cooked large shrimp, shelled and deveined
2 papayas, peeled and sliced
2 mangoes, peeled and sliced
½ fresh pineapple, peeled, cored, and cut lengthwise into spears
2 avocados, peeled and sliced
1 to 2 kiwis, sliced
Butter lettuce

....

DRESSING:

½ cup heavy cream
2 tablespoons fresh or dried grated coconut
2 tablespoons lime juice
1 tablespoon grated lime or lemon zest
2 teaspoons honey
1 teaspoon grated gingerroot
¼ cup mayonnaise

....

GARNISH:

Toasted fresh or dried grated coconut (see page 69)
Chopped macadamia or other nuts
Mint sprigs

....

Arrange the shrimp and fruit attractively over lettuce on a large platter or individual salad plates.

Combine all the dressing ingredients except the mayonnaise in a food processor or blender, and whirl until the mixture is fluffy. Fold the mixture into the mayonnaise. Place a dollop of dressing on each individual salad, or, if you're serving the salad on a platter, put the dressing into a small bowl to be served on the side. Garnish the salad with toasted coconut, nuts, and mint, and serve immediately.

Makes 4 to 6 servings

Cane Garden Bay Picnic

....

STONE CRAB CLAWS
WITH KEY LIME MAYONNAISE

◆

CHICHARRONE DE POLLO

◆

RED BEAN AND RICE SALAD

◆

CHOCOLATE TRUFFLE TART

DRESSING FOR SUCCESS

Here are a few of our favorite dressings for tossed green salads. Although a simple vinaigrette is always a good choice, something different is often nice for a change.

Creamy Dill Dressing

1¼ cups mayonnaise
½ cup sour cream
2 teaspoons chopped fresh dillweed,
    or ½ teaspoon dried dillweed
2 tablespoons grated parmesan cheese
1½ teaspoons coarsely ground black
    pepper
1 garlic clove, minced
Juice of ½ lemon
2 teaspoons Worcestershire sauce
1 teaspoon grated onion
1 teaspoon cider vinegar

....

Stir all the ingredients together, and chill the dressing before using it.

Lemon Mustard Dressing

1 egg
1 tablespoon grated parmesan cheese
½ teaspoon salt
¼ teaspoon ground black pepper
2 tablespoons Dijon mustard
3 tablespoons lemon juice
1 teaspoon Worcestershire sauce
½ cup vegetable oil

....

In a bowl, whisk all the ingredients until they are well blended. Refrigerate the dressing until you are ready to use it.

Curry Dressing

1⅓ cups vegetable oil
½ cup garlic-flavored wine vinegar
¼ cup dry white wine
¼ cup soy sauce
2 teaspoons sugar
2 teaspoons dry mustard
1 teaspoon curry powder
1 teaspoon salt
1 teaspoon ground black pepper

....

In a bowl, whisk all the ingredients together. This dressing is not only great on any salad greens, but also delicious as a dip for raw vegetables.

Parsley Dressing

¾ cup vegetable oil
3 tablespoons lemon juice
½ teaspoon Dijon mustard
½ teaspoon salt
¼ teaspoon ground black pepper
1 cup fresh parsley, loosely packed
1 garlic clove

....

Put all the ingredients into a food processor or blender, and whirl until they are well combined.

CHICKEN SALAD WITH MANGO MAYONNAISE

Almost everyone loves chicken salad in any form. We like the tropical twist of mango-flavored mayonnaise in this version. Separating the mango flesh from the pit can be difficult and messy unless you know the following trick. Cut through the mango on either side of the large pit, then score the flesh of each half in 1-inch crosshatched cuts. Turn each mango half inside out, and cut the flesh away from the skin. As we say in the islands, "No problem!"

. . . .

3 chicken breasts
2 ripe mangoes, peeled and cubed
2 egg yolks
¾ teaspoon salt
½ teaspoon ground black pepper
3 tablespoons lemon juice
½ cup olive oil
½ cup vegetable oil
1 head romaine lettuce
2 tablespoons minced parsley

. . . .

Poach the chicken breasts for about 10 minutes in enough simmering salted water to cover them. Set the pan aside, and let the breasts cool to room temperature in the liquid.

Remove the cooled meat from the bones, and cut it into strips about ½ inch wide.

In a food processor or blender, purée the mango, egg yolks, salt, and pepper. Add the lemon juice, and, with the machine running, pour in the oils in a thin stream to make a mayonnaise. Shred the lettuce, and put it on a platter. Place the chicken on top, and spoon the dressing over all. Sprinkle with parsley, and serve.

Makes 6 to 8 servings

RED BEAN AND RICE SALAD

Great with barbecues and a hit in the picnic basket, this salad offers a cool interpretation of the Caribbean's classic bean-and-rice combination.

. . . .

1 cup dried red beans (or pink beans or kidney beans), soaked overnight, drained, and rinsed
1½ teaspoons salt
Ground black pepper to taste
6 cups water
2 tablespoons vegetable oil
1 onion, chopped
1 garlic clove, minced
2 cups raw rice
1 bay leaf
1 green bell pepper, chopped
2 medium tomatoes, peeled, seeded, and chopped
½ cup minced fresh parsley

. . . .

DRESSING:
¾ cup olive oil
2 tablespoons red wine vinegar
1 tablespoon lemon juice
Salt and pepper to taste

....

In a heavy saucepan, combine the beans with ½ teaspoon salt, a little pepper, and the water. Bring the beans to a boil, reduce the heat, and simmer them, partially covered, for 1½ to 2 hours, until the beans are tender.

Drain the beans, reserving the cooking liquid. Add enough water to the liquid to make 4 cups. Let the beans cool.

Heat the oil in a large saucepan. Add the onion and garlic, and sauté them just until the onion is limp and translucent. Add the rice, and stir it over medium heat just until the grains turn milky and opaque. Add the bay leaf, the reserved bean liquid and water, 1 teaspoon salt, and some pepper. Cover the pan, reduce the heat to very low, and simmer the rice undisturbed for 20 minutes or until it is tender and has absorbed all the liquid. Let the rice cool.

When you are ready to serve, combine the rice and beans in a serving bowl, and add the green pepper, tomatoes, and parsley. In a small bowl, whisk together the olive oil, vinegar, and lemon juice. Add salt and pepper. Pour the dressing over the salad, toss lightly with a wooden spoon until the ingredients are well combined, and serve.

Makes 6 servings

SPINACH TIMBALES

This is another way we like our locally grown vine spinach. Although simple to prepare, the timbales look very impressive. We like the color contrast of the red pepper cut-out, which is placed in the bottom of the mold so that it tops the timbale when the timbale is turned out. For each timbale we cut a square of red bell pepper, trim about ¼ inch from the fleshy side so the pepper isn't too thick, and cut a flower-like shape with a small fancy cutter (if you don't have a small cutter, you can use a sharp paring knife to cut a small circle or strips). We place the cut pepper skin side down in the mold before adding the timbale mixture.

....

6 pimiento flowers, cut from
*   pimientos or red bell pepper*
¼ cup finely minced onion
1 tablespoon butter
¼ cup grated Swiss cheese
6 tablespoons soft bread crumbs
3 eggs, beaten
¼ cup milk
¼ cup cream
1½ cups cooked spinach, well
*   drained and chopped*
Salt and pepper to taste

....

Oil six small timbale molds (also called dariole molds) or custard cups.

Place a pimiento flower in the bottom of each mold. Preheat the oven to 325°.

In a small skillet, cook the onions in the butter until they are limp. Put them into a mixing bowl. Stir in the cheese, bread crumbs, and eggs. Heat the milk and cream together, and slowly beat the hot milk and cream into the egg mixture. Stir in the spinach, and season with salt and pepper.

Spoon the spinach mixture into the prepared molds. Place cake racks in a baking pan and put the molds on top. Pour boiling water into the baking pan until it comes halfway up the molds. Bake the timbales for about 20 to 30 minutes, or until a knife inserted in the timbales comes out clean. Allow the timbales to settle for 5 minutes, then turn them out onto plates, and serve.

Makes 6 servings

CORN TIMBALES WITH BASIL CREAM

Our locally grown basil has a smaller leaf than the Italian variety, but it is just as flavorful. Basil of any sort gives vitality to the sauce for these delicate timbales.

....

TIMBALES:
  1¾ cups cream-style corn

⅔ cup grated Swiss cheese
3 eggs, beaten
½ teaspoon salt
¼ teaspoon paprika
A few drops hot pepper sauce

....

BASIL CREAM:
  2 cups heavy cream
  ½ cup chopped basil, or ½ cup
    chopped parsley and 1 teaspoon
    dried basil
  6 basil sprigs

....

Preheat the oven to 325°. Stir together all the timbale ingredients. Oil or butter six small timbale molds or custard cups. Pour the mixture into molds. Place cake racks in a baking pan, and put the molds on top. Pour boiling water into the bottom of baking pan until it comes halfway up the molds. Bake the timbales for about 20 to 30 minutes or until a knife inserted in the timbales comes out clean.

While the timbales are baking, boil the cream until it is reduced by half. Stir the fresh basil (or parsley-and-dried-basil mixture) into the hot cream.

Remove the timbales from the oven, and allow them to settle for 5 minutes. Turn them out onto plates, and spoon on the Basil Cream.

Garnish each timbale with a basil sprig, and serve.

Makes 6 servings

ISLAND STYLE: ST. VINCENT AND THE GRENADINES

Piles of papayas, breadfruit, mangoes; heaps of exotic Caribbean vegetables such as christophenes, eddoes, and cassava; green coconuts sloshing with sweet coconut water, peanuts, sweet corn, ruby tomatoes—St. Vincent's market is a kaleidoscope of fruits and vegetables grown in the prolific Mesopotamia Valley, about which Vincentians say with great pride, "Even the rocks grow in Mespo."

In the lively seafood market handily close to this patchwork of produce is an equally colorful display of fish freshly pulled from local waters. Nearby, the charcoal ladies, slightly dingy from handling their product, provide fuel for the braziers used in most St. Vincent homes. St. Vincent may not have (or want) the glitter and glamour of some other Caribbean destinations, but it feeds itself and its neighbors very well indeed.

St. Vincent moors the northern end of the Grenadines, a necklace of island gems that is heaven for yachties, divers, and snorkelers.

In these stunning islands, simplicity is often just a few miles away from worldly sophistication. Elegant resorts like Petit St. Vincent and Mustique, holiday homes to royalty and rock stars, are just a short sail from Bequia, where your entertainment may be going to a boat christening or learning to catch and cook local lobster. Robinson Crusoe islands dot this area of the Caribbean: Canouan, Mayreau, Palm, and Union as well as the exquisite Tobago Cays, now a national park and naturally protected from cruise ships and even large yachts by patches of deadly coral heads.

The cuisine of the Grenadines reflects ideas and recipes borrowed from all who have come ashore. Restaurants in this group of lightly populated islands are usually small and highly personal, but menus featuring dishes such as curried conch, seafood cassoulet, and lobster crepes hint at the cosmopolitan cast of characters who have left a culinary legacy on St. Vincent and the Grenadines.

CURRIED CITRUS RICE

Rice is so popular in the Caribbean that some families buy it in 20-pound sacks. Enhanced by the flavors of curry and citrus, rice makes a perfect accompaniment to poultry or fish dishes.

....

¼ cup butter
1 medium onion, thinly sliced
2 teaspoons curry powder
1 cup raw rice
1 cup orange juice
1 cup chicken broth
1 teaspoon salt
1 bay leaf

....

Melt the butter in a heavy saucepan, and sauté the onion until it is limp and translucent. Stir in the curry powder and rice. Cook the mixture 2 minutes, stirring constantly.

Add the remaining ingredients, and stir. Bring the mixture to a boil, lower the heat, and cover the saucepan. Simmer the rice for 15 to 20 minutes, or until it is tender and the liquid has been absorbed. Remove the bay leaf before serving.

Makes 6 servings

Black Beans and Rice with Rum

Another classic rice-and-bean combination, this time accented by a dash of rum.

....

2 tablespoons olive oil
1 large onion, chopped
1 garlic clove, minced
1 celery rib, chopped
1 carrot, peeled and chopped
4¼ cups water
½ pound dried black beans, washed, picked over, and soaked overnight
¼ teaspoon ground black pepper
2 tablespoons minced fresh parsley
1 cup raw rice
2 tablespoons dark rum
½ teaspoon salt

....

GARNISH:
Minced cilantro

....

Heat the olive oil in a large pot. Sauté the onion, garlic, celery, and carrots for about 5 minutes, or until the onions are translucent. Add 2 cups water, and bring the mixture to a boil.

Drain the beans, and add them with the pepper and parsley to the pot. Cover the pot, bring the contents back to a boil, and reduce the heat until the water is just simmering. Cook the beans for 2½ hours or until they are tender. Stir the beans occasionally as they cook, and add more water if necessary.

While the beans are cooking, bring the remaining 2¼ cups water to a boil in a saucepan. Add the rice, reduce the heat to medium, and cover the pan. Simmer the rice 20 minutes, stirring occasionally.

When the beans are tender, stir in the rum and salt. Put the rice on a warm serving platter. Drain any excess liquid from the beans, and spoon the beans on top of the rice. Garnish the platter with minced cilantro, and serve.

Makes 6 servings

HOT STUFF

It is said that West Indian pepper sauce is tested by pouring a drop on the tablecloth; if the sauce fails to eat a hole through the fabric, it is rejected as too weak. We can't swear that anyone actually performs this test, but we know that tendermouths are wise to approach Caribbean hot sauces with respect.

Scotch bonnets and bird peppers, two of the most popular peppers in the islands, are hot enough to tingle your tonsils. The Scotch bonnet, a small pepper that looks like a miniature bonnet or lantern, comes in the rainbow colors of orange, red, yellow, and green. Don't be deceived by its innocent appearance; it is an incendiary device. (Some say the Mexican habanero is the same pepper, whereas others claim they are merely kissing cousins. Whatever the truth of the matter, habaneros can be used in any recipe calling for Scotch bonnets.) The small, slender bird pepper, which closely resembles the pepper used to make Tabasco sauce, also packs a wallop.

All hot peppers contain oils that can cause skin irritation or even burning, so it's always wise when working with these peppers to wear gloves and to avoid touching your face or eyes. If you feel a burning sensation anywhere on your skin, rubbing the affected area with sugar will help to neutralize the oil.

You can enjoy the flavor of hot peppers without all the heat by removing the seeds and veins before using the peppers. Remember, too, that a little goes a long way; except for those people who gobble down hot peppers competitively, moderation, we think, is usually the best policy.

PETE'S HOT SAUCE

This recipe was brought to us by our friend Pete Whims. To us, no cheeseburger is quite complete without Pete's sauce—and when we've been indulging a bit too much, it also does wonderful things for cottage cheese. Try it, too, on barbecued fish or meat, on salads, or on whole-wheat toast with cream cheese. Tendermouths can hold back a bit on the peppers.

....

½ cup chopped black olives

3 tomatoes, peeled, seeded, and chopped

3 green onions (both white and green parts), chopped

½ Scotch bonnet (or habanero) pepper, minced, or 2 to 3 jalapeño peppers, chopped

3 tablespoons olive oil

2 teaspoons garlic powder

....

Mix all the ingredients together. Store the sauce in a tightly sealed jar in the refrigerator. The sauce is best after the flavors marry for about 3 days.

MAJOR MORGAN'S MANGO CHUTNEY

Hot-pepper sauces, salsas, and chutneys are popular accessories to Caribbean main courses. The sweet, hot tang of chutney is a perfect accompaniment for all kinds of meat, fish, and even vegetables, and is a staple of most island pantries.

....

¾ cup brown sugar
1½ cups white wine vinegar
1 large onion, chopped
1 green bell pepper, chopped
1 garlic clove, minced
1 lime, thinly sliced
1½ teaspoons ground cinnamon
½ teaspoon ground cloves
½ teaspoon ground ginger
½ teaspoon chili powder
½ teaspoon ground coriander
1 pinch saffron (optional)
½ teaspoon ground allspice
¾ cup raisins
3 large mangoes, peeled and cubed
2 pounds peaches, peeled and sliced

....

In a large pot, combine all the ingredients except the mangoes and peaches, and bring the mixture to a boil, stirring occasionally. Reduce the heat, and simmer the mixture, uncovered, for an hour.

While the mixture is cooking, climb into the bathtub or pull on a wet suit, and peel and cube the mangoes (or see page 88 for advice on tidy mango dissection).

Add the fruit to the pot, and continue simmering until the fruit is tender, about 30 minutes.

Pour the mixture into hot sterilized canning jars, and seal the jars. Immerse the jars in a kettle of boiling water, the surface of which comes to at least an inch above the jar tops. Boil the jars for 5 minutes.

Remove the jars and allow them to cool. Test for a good seal by pressing down on the center of the lid after the jar has cooled. If it stays down all is well; the chutney can be put on the pantry shelf. If not, store it in the refrigerator.

Makes about 8 cups

TOMATO CHUTNEY

If you find yourself with a surplus of tomatoes, this is a dandy way to use them up. You'll congratulate yourself every time you dollop this chutney on a hamburger, a steak, or a bit of grilled fish, or serve it with curry.

....

4 cups tomatoes, peeled, seeded, and
*   chopped*
2 onions, chopped
1 lime, thinly sliced
1½ cups cider vinegar

1½ cups sugar
1 tablespoon salt
1 tablespoon ground ginger
3 garlic cloves, mashed
2 teaspoons chili powder
½ teaspoon ground mace
2 tablespoons minced gingerroot
1 tablespoon white mustard seed
½ teaspoon minced Scotch bonnet (or
    habanero) pepper, or 3 tablespoons
    minced jalapeño peppers

....

Put all the ingredients into a large
pot, and simmer them gently over low
heat, stirring occasionally, for 1½ hours

or until the chutney is thick and syrupy.
Pour it into hot sterilized canning jars,
and process the jars according to the directions for Major Morgan's Mango
Chutney (see page 94).

Makes about 6 cups

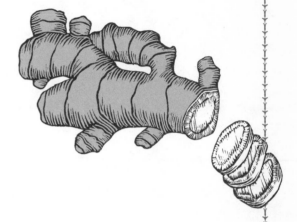

Pastas
under
the Palms

PASTAS UNDER THE PALMS

PASTA WITH CONCH IN PARSLEY CREAM

Pasta and shellfish are always a great alliance. We love this combination of conch, the queen of the Caribbean Sea, with bright peppers and delicate angel-hair pasta. If conch is not available, try the same recipe with shrimp, sautéing them briefly with the onion and peppers before adding the broth and cream.

....

2 tablespoons vegetable oil
1 onion
1 large garlic clove, minced
1 red bell pepper, cut into julienne
   strips
1 yellow bell pepper, cut into julienne
   strips
1 cup clam broth
1 cup heavy cream
1 to 1½ pounds peeled, tenderized,
   and cooked conch, cut into bite-
   size pieces
1 bunch parsley, finely minced
½ cup minced basil
Salt, pepper, and cayenne to taste

SHELL GAME

The queen conch (pronounced "konk"), royally dressed in an elegant shell touched by shades of pink, gold, and cream, moves at a stately pace through the clear green waters of the shallows. By extending her foot and digging her sickle-shaped operculum into the sand, she moves through the waving undersea grasses to find the algae she'll dine on today.

The conch is treasured as much for her meat as for her beautiful shell. Cleaning conch is a laborious and messy process that is best left to local experts, who do it with such skill that they almost make it look easy. In the kitchen, the meat is tenderized; many Caribbean kitchens have pressure cookers to make short work of this process. Rubbing the meat with a papaya leaf also helps to soften it. Once your conch has been tenderized, you can prepare it in numerous delicious ways,

from chowder to fritters, stews to conchburgers. Experiment with conch using recipes calling for scallops, abalone, or clams.

Conch is so popular in the islands that folklore has developed around it. Blowing the conch shell signals the setting of the sun in some parts of the Caribbean and southern Florida. Sailors keep a conch horn on their boat to use in fog or to signal that they need a bridge opened. Some claim aphrodisiac powers for conch meat (perhaps helping to explain its popularity), and dried conch is often called "Hurricane Ham," since it was much appreciated when other meats and fish were in short supply after storms. The conch even has taken its place alongside the Oscar and the Emmy: The Caribbean Hotel Association's annual award for Hotelier of the Year is a Golden Conch statuette.

1½ pounds spinach angel-hair pasta,
cooked and drained

....

In a skillet, heat the oil. Sauté the onion, garlic, and peppers very slowly until they are soft. Add the clam broth, cream, and conch, and simmer the mixture until it is thickened. Add the parsley and basil, and continue to simmer the sauce until the parsley has lost its raw taste. Season the sauce with salt, pepper, and cayenne. Serve it over the hot pasta.

Makes 6 servings

AVOCADO PASTA SAUCE

Avocados grow in profusion in the Caribbean, but they are seasonal. We seem to be always waiting for a new crop to ripen or fighting off a green tidal wave of fruit that threatens to engulf us. When avocados are dangling from every tree, this simple pasta is a great way to enjoy them.

....

¼ cup butter, melted
3 green onions, minced
1 garlic clove, minced
2 tablespoons minced fresh basil
1 cup dry white wine
¾ cup minced parsley
1½ cups ricotta cheese
3 ripe avocados, mashed

Salt and pepper to taste
1 pound linguine, cooked and drained

....

GARNISH:
Chopped fresh tomatoes
Pitted black olives (preferably Greek
or Italian)

....

Heat the butter in a skillet, and add the green onions, garlic, and basil. Cook until the onions are tender. Add the wine and parsley, and simmer for 5 minutes longer. Stir in the ricotta cheese; blend it well and heat it through. Stir in the mashed avocado, season to taste with salt and pepper, and immediately spoon the sauce over hot cooked linguine. Garnish with chopped fresh tomatoes and black olives, and serve.

Makes 6 servings

WHERE TO PUT YOUR PESTO

....

◆ *Dollop it on baked potatoes.*
◆ *Spread it under the skin of poultry before baking.*
◆ *Toss it with hot pasta for a quick meal.*
◆ *Blend it with butter, and spread it on grilled fish.*
◆ *Spread it on slices of toasted French or Italian bread.*
◆ *Spoon a bit into scrambled eggs or omelets.*

GARDEN PATCH PASTA

Most Caribbean homes have small gardens where eggplant, peppers, squash, and tomatoes are grown for family use. This delicious healthful pasta sauce takes advantage of fresh-picked (or freshly purchased) garden produce.

....

1 1-pound eggplant, peeled and cut into ½-inch slices
¼ cup olive oil
3 medium onions, diced
2 tablespoons minced garlic
1 cup diced red bell peppers
1 cup diced yellow bell peppers
2 zucchini, diced
2 yellow squashes, diced
12 mushrooms, sliced
4 cups (1 28-ounce can) peeled tomatoes
¼ cup minced fresh basil, or 4 teaspoons dried basil
4 teaspoons salt
2 tablespoons minced parsley
¼ cup dry red wine
2 teaspoons dried oregano
6 dashes hot pepper sauce
1 bay leaf
2 cups (1 16-ounce can) cooked garbanzo beans, drained
¼ cup pine nuts, lightly toasted in a skillet
Shaved or grated parmesan cheese
1 pound pasta, cooked and drained

....

Sprinkle the eggplant slices with salt. Place them on paper towels, and leave them for 20 to 30 minutes.

Pat the eggplant dry, and cut it into ½-inch cubes.

In a large skillet, heat the olive oil. Add the onions, garlic, peppers, zucchini, and yellow squashes, and stir-fry the vegetables over high heat for about 5 minutes. Rinse and dry the eggplant, and add it with the mushrooms to the pan. Reduce the heat, and sauté the vegetables for about 10 minutes, stirring them occasionally.

Add the tomatoes, tomato paste, basil, salt, parsley, wine, oregano, hot sauce, and bay leaf, and bring the mixture to a boil. Add the garbanzo beans, lower the heat, and simmer until the vegetables are tender but not too soft. Taste, and adjust the seasoning. Remove the bay leaf.

Spoon the vegetables over hot cooked pasta, and sprinkle the dish with toasted pine nuts and parmesan cheese before serving.

This sauce can be made ahead and refrigerated or frozen, and then reheated before serving.

Makes 6 to 8 servings

PLENTY OF PESTOS

What began as a simple preparation of basil, olive oil, pine nuts, and cheese has been taken up by the foodies and kicked around until some of its descendants wouldn't be recognized at a family reunion. We draw the line at pesto recipes featuring sardines or figs.

The first recipe here is for pesto as Italians usually make it. For a spinach pesto recipe, see page 124.

Classic Pesto

This freezes very well if you leave out the cheese, and add it just before serving. We like to freeze pesto in ice trays, which make handy little portions to use later.

3 cups basil leaves, loosely packed
¾ cup olive oil
¼ cup pine nuts (or walnuts)
3 garlic cloves
1 teaspoon salt
½ cup grated parmesan cheese

Whirl the basil, oil, nuts, garlic, and salt in a blender or food processor until the mixture is smooth.

Olive Pesto

This mixture takes considerable liberties with the original concept, but it is delicious on grilled fish, such as swordfish or tuna, and on toasted baguettes.

....

¾ cup Niçoise olives, pitted
½ cup basil leaves, loosely packed
¼ cup parsley leaves
2 shallots or green onions (white parts only)
2 tablespoons pine nuts
2 garlic cloves, mashed
¼ cup olive oil
¼ cup grated parmesan cheese

....

Whirl all the ingredients except the oil and cheese in a food processor or blender until the mixture is smooth. Add the oil and cheese, and blend thoroughly.

Makes about 1 cup

LINGUINE WITH SMOKED TUNA AND RED CAVIAR

Our chef Rick Buttafuso has a wonderful way with Caribbean ingredients, but his heart and his heritage require a bit of pasta from time to time. This is one of our favorites of his creations, in which he uses locally caught and smoked tuna.

....

1½ cups half-and-half

1 cucumber, peeled, halved
    lengthwise, and cut crosswise into
    ¼-inch slices

1 tablespoon minced dillweed

1 tablespoon cornstarch combined
    with ¼ cup water

12 ounces linguine, cooked with a
    good glug of olive oil and
    drained

¾ pound smoked tuna, sliced and cut
    into strips

....

GARNISH:

2 ounces red caviar
Chopped green onions
Minced parsley

....

In a saucepan, bring the half-and-half to a simmer with the cucumber and dill. Cook 3 minutes over medium-high heat. Drizzle and stir in the cornstarch mixture, and heat the sauce for another 2 minutes to cook out any starchy flavor. Add the tuna to the cream mixture, and spoon the tuna sauce over the hot pasta. Garnish with the caviar, green onions, and parsley, and serve.

Makes 4 servings

Poolside Pasta Party

....

PROSCIUTTO AND MANGO WITH
PEPPER-MANGO COULIS

◆

LINGUINE WITH SMOKED TUNA
AND RED CAVIAR

◆

LEEK AND PEPPER SALAD
WITH TAPENADE

◆

COCONUT CLOUD TART

LIME CREAM PASTA

Communications in the Sugar Mill kitchen can be amusing, since the workers come from all over the island chain, and their English, Spanish, or French is often frosted with a Creole patois. This recipe is a happy accident that occurred when one of our cooks, a wonderful woman from Santo Domingo, misread the recipe for lemon pasta and used lime instead. We loved the result and never looked back at lemons again.

....

1½ cups heavy cream
2 tablespoons chopped parsley
2 tablespoons grated lime zest
Salt and pepper to taste
1 pound plain or spinach fettuccine,
    cooked and drained

3 tablespoons butter
Grated parmesan cheese

....

GARNISH:
Red caviar

....

Pour the cream into a large skillet, and cook it over medium-high heat until it thickens slightly and big, shiny bubbles form. Add the chopped parsley, grated lime zest, and salt and pepper.

Toss the hot pasta with the butter, cheese, and lime-cream sauce. Garnish with red caviar, and serve.

Makes 6 servings

TORTELLINI WITH SPINACH AND WHELKS OR CLAMS

Whelks, known elsewhere as sea snails, are fun to catch, difficult to clean, and delicious to eat. They live in tidal pools or on rocks or ledges. The two rock jetties that protect the Sugar Mill beach are usually covered with whelks. To prepare whelks, boil them for 30 to 45 minutes in salted water, and then extract the meat from the shells using a needle or safety pin. Remove the operculum, or the "door," and all the innards, leaving only the small bit of tasty white meat. Clams are a tasty substitute.

....

2 tablespoons olive oil
3 tablespoons butter
1 large onion, chopped
2 garlic cloves, minced
¾ pound minced fresh spinach
    leaves, or 10 ounces frozen
    spinach, thawed, chopped,
    drained, and squeezed dry
¼ cup minced fresh parsley
1 pound pasta, cooked and
    drained
1 pound cooked and shelled whelks
    or baby clams, drained
Salt and pepper to taste
Grated parmesan cheese

....

Heat the oil and 2 tablespoons of the butter in a skillet. Add the onion and garlic, and sauté them over low heat until the onion is translucent. Stir in the spinach. Cover the skillet, and cook the mixture 15 minutes over low heat.

Toss the hot pasta with the remaining butter. Add the whelks or clams and salt and pepper to the spinach mixture, and spoon the sauce over the pasta. Sprinkle with parmesan cheese, and serve.

Makes 6 servings

"I DREAM OF THE ITALIAN WEST INDIES."

—CALVIN TRILLIN

RASTA PASTA

The Rastafarians on Tortola are gentle folk who are gifted farmers. This red, yellow, and green pasta honors their vegetarian tradition.

....

4 tablespoons olive oil
2 garlic cloves, minced
1 large onion, sliced
2 yellow or red bell peppers (or 1 of
  each), cut into julienne strips
1 pound fettuccine, cooked and
  drained
2 cups cooked and drained black
  beans
Salt and pepper to taste
2 cups cooked broccoli flowerets,
  without stems
¼ cup minced fresh basil, or 1
  teaspoon dried basil
2 teaspoons minced fresh oregano, or
  ½ teaspoon dried oregano
Grated parmesan cheese

....

Heat 3 tablespoons of the oil in a large skillet, and sauté the garlic, onion, and peppers just until they are limp. Stir in the black beans, and season the mixture with salt and pepper.

Cook the broccoli in rapidly boiling salted water for about 7 minutes, or until it is just tender. Drain it.

Toss the hot fettuccine with the remaining 1 tablespoon olive oil. Add the bean-and-pepper mixture, the broccoli, and the herbs, and toss again. Sprinkle generously with parmesan cheese. Serve the pasta at room temperature as a salad or main dish.

Makes 4 to 6 servings

PASTA WITH SUGAR SNAP PEAS AND ASPARAGUS

Alas, neither sugar snap peas nor asparagus grows in the Caribbean, but they are available from time to time for about the price you might expect to pay for one of the crown jewels. Budget considerations aside, we love both vegetables and indulge ourselves and our guests occasionally. One of our favorite treats is this delicious pasta, which is great in small portions as a first course and steps in with equal aplomb as a quick, easy, healthful, and elegant main course. Who could ask for anything more?

....

2 pounds asparagus, trimmed and
  cut crosswise into 1½-inch pieces
1 pound sugar snap peas or snow
  peas, trimmed
3 tablespoons olive oil
½ teaspoon minced garlic
Salt and pepper to taste
1 pound bow-tie or shell pasta,
  cooked and drained
½ cup grated parmesan cheese

....

Cook the asparagus in boiling water until it is tender but still crisp. Drain it, and put it into a bowl of ice water. Cook the peas in boiling water for about 2 minutes. Drain them, and put them in cold water, too.

In a skillet, heat 2 tablespoons olive oil. Briefly heat the garlic in it, then drain and add the cooked asparagus and peas, and toss the mixture. Season it with salt and pepper.

Toss the hot pasta with the remaining 1 tablespoon oil. Add the vegetable mixture, and toss again. Garnish with parmesan cheese, and serve.

Makes 6 servings

PENNE WITH HOT PEPPER-VODKA SAUCE

This is one of those recipes that require flaming to burn off the alcohol. No need to be frightened, but do take reasonable precautions. Roll up your sleeves, and use a long match. Do not shake the pan—that could intensify the flames. If you need to quench the flames in a hurry, just put the lid on the pan.

....

6 tablespoons butter
1 large onion, minced
½ cup vodka
1 Scotch bonnet (or habanero)
  pepper, or other hot pepper to
  taste, seeded and minced
½ pound prosciutto or smoked ham,
  slivered
1½ cups heavy cream
¾ cup grated parmesan cheese
Salt and pepper to taste
1½ pounds penne, cooked and
  drained

....

Heat the butter in a large skillet, and sauté the onion until it is limp and translucent. Warm the vodka in a small saucepan. Add the hot pepper and ham to the onion, pour on the heated vodka, and ignite the vodka. When the flame burns out, add the cream, and simmer the sauce until it is thickened. Add the cheese, and stir until the ingredients are well combined. Season the sauce with salt and pepper. Toss the hot pasta with the sauce, and serve.

Makes 6 servings

ISLAND STYLE: U.S. VIRGIN ISLANDS

*C*olumbus's discovery in 1493 of what are now called the U.S. Virgin Islands began a long diplomatic minuet over their fate and future among European powers as well as the Knights of Malta. Like three lovely sisters, St. Thomas, St. Croix, and St. John became the focus for many lustful suitors. The Danes held sway over these islands from the seventeenth through the nineteenth centuries, a time of pirates and privateers, sugar plantations, slave revolts, and liberation. The United States purchased the islands in 1917.

Today the sister islands have grown up, each in her own way. St. Thomas is the bustling, bawdy one with an eye for the main chance. Patrician St. Croix is more sedate, with picturesque Christiansted a visual reminder of her Danish heritage. St. John is the natural beauty, protected, as any great beauty should be, by a sympathetic patron. Laurance Rockefeller bought more than five thousand acres of undeveloped land on St. John during the fifties, and gave it to the U.S. as a national park. Since then more land has been acquired, and eventually the park will encompass two-thirds of the island, securing its wild loveliness for the future.

Because of their proximity to the mainland and the endless stream of vacationers, these islands have had their Caribbean patina rubbed down and sanitized for stateside consumption. You'll find Colonel Sanders's fried chicken here, although you'll also find local restaurants serving stewed chicken and rice.

On St. Thomas, new restaurants have proliferated. Many have hip young chefs who use local ingredients in entirely new ways. Others feature Chinese, Indian, French, or Italian food, or even Texas barbecue. Even West Indian food can be found if you know where to go.

St. Croix's Whim Great House, a beautifully restored mansion, is a visual reminder of this island's plantation days. The legions of servants are gone, but echoes of the balls and the splendid dinners linger. Separated from the main house in case of fire, the kitchen was then as now the heart of the plantation. Simple but effective equipment included brick ovens, iron pots, and a mortar and pestle for grinding spices. One of the mixtures the cooks might have ground is still popular: thyme, parsley, chives, black pepper, and sea salt. Cruzan seasoning, as this mixture is known, is used to spice up everything from salad to roast chicken or fried fish.

St. John has few restaurants but a wealth of unusual tropical fruits. Genip trees produce small green fruit with apricot-colored flesh and one large stone. Beloved for after-school snacks, genips also make a lovely jelly. The pink-orange flesh of the mammee apple is good either raw or stewed, and it makes excellent chutney. Passion fruit, which grows on a vine and resembles a thick-skinned plum, has yellow or orange translucent flesh with a tart, citrus-like flavor that is wonderful in sorbets, jams, and exotic drinks. The twisted, gnarled trunks of seagrape trees line most beaches on St. John. When the bunches of grape-like fruits ripen, cooks on St. John gather the grapes to make jelly with a flavor similar to that of true grapes.

The three U.S. Virgins, although yoked together by proximity, history, and government, have managed to retain their individuality. Even at table you can recognize subtle differences that mark each island's unique personality.

SEAFOOD LASAGNA

A perfect dish for the harried host or hostess, this elegant baked pasta can be made ahead and cooked just before the party. It also freezes well.

. . . .

1 dozen mushrooms, sliced
2 tablespoons butter

. . . .

SPINACH AND RICOTTA FILLING:

15 ounces ricotta cheese
1 cup chopped cooked spinach,
    squeezed dry
¼ cup chopped fresh basil, or
    1 tablespoon dried basil
Salt and pepper to taste
2 eggs, lightly beaten
½ cup grated parmesan cheese

. . . .

TOMATO BÉCHAMEL SAUCE:

½ cup butter
1 tablespoon minced garlic
½ cup flour
2 cups chicken broth
3 cups milk
¼ cup tomato paste
Salt and pepper to taste
1 dash hot pepper sauce

. . . .

1½ to 2 pounds seafood (shrimp,
    scallops, or fish cut into bite-size
    pieces, or a combination)
1 pound plain or spinach lasagna
    noodles, cooked and drained

1 cup each coarsely grated Swiss and
    cheddar cheeses

. . . .

Preheat the oven to 375°.

In a skillet, sauté the sliced mushrooms in the butter until they are tender. Reserve them.

In a bowl, combine the ricotta, spinach, basil, salt and pepper, eggs, and parmesan cheese. Mix them together thoroughly, and set the bowl aside.

To make the sauce, melt the butter in a saucepan, and briefly sauté the garlic. Add the flour, and, stirring with a wire whisk, cook the roux over medium heat for several minutes. Gradually add the chicken broth and milk to the butter-and-flour mixture, whisking constantly. Cook the sauce over medium heat until it is thickened. Stir in the tomato paste, and season the sauce with salt, pepper, and hot pepper sauce.

To assemble the lasagna, spread the bottom of a large rectangular pan (approximately 11¾ by 7½ by 1¾ inches) with some of the sauce, then add a layer of noodles. Top this with a layer of mushrooms, the seafood, and then the spinach-cheese mixture. Add another layer of noodles. Spoon on the remaining sauce, and top with a layer of grated Swiss and cheddar cheeses.

Bake the lasagna for 35 to 45 minutes, then cut it into pieces, and serve it hot.

Makes 10 to 12 servings

SCALLOP-FILLED PASTA FLOWERS

Most of our pasta recipes are quick and simple. This stunner is not. But when you are having an elegant dinner party and feel like pulling out all the stops, this is sure to wow your guests.

....

TOMATO SAUCE:

¼ cup butter

½ cup minced onion

2 pounds tomatoes, peeled, seeded, and chopped

2 garlic cloves, unpeeled

1 bouquet garni (a sprig of parsley, half a bay leaf, and ½ teaspoon dried thyme tied in cheesecloth)

1 4-inch strip orange zest

3 teaspoons sugar

Salt and pepper to taste

....

SCALLOP FILLING:

12 ounces small scallops, sliced or cut into bite-size pieces

6 mushrooms, sliced

1 cup milk

¼ cup butter

3 bacon slices, chopped

1 onion, chopped

1 garlic clove, chopped

3 tablespoons flour

3 tablespoons sherry

Salt and pepper to taste

Minced parsley

Lemon juice

....

PASTA:

1 egg

2 tablespoons minced parsley

1 tablespoon minced fresh oregano, or 1 teaspoon dried oregano

1 tablespoon fresh thyme leaves, or 1 teaspoon dried thyme

About 1 cup flour

¾ teaspoon salt

3 tablespoons olive oil

....

To make the tomato sauce, heat 2 tablespoons of the butter in a skillet, and cook the onion, covered, for 5 minutes over very low heat. Add the tomatoes, garlic, *bouquet garni*, orange zest, and sugar. Cover the skillet, and cook over medium heat for about 30 minutes.

Remove the garlic, *bouquet garni*, and orange peel. Purée the sauce by passing it through a sieve or the fine disc of a food mill. Season the sauce with salt and pepper, and reserve it.

To make the scallop filling, combine the scallops, mushrooms, and milk in a small saucepan. Place the pan over low heat, and heat until the milk begins to bubble around the edge. The scallops should be opaque but still very tender. Turn off the heat, and allow the scallops and mushrooms to steep.

Heat the butter in a heavy saucepan. When it has just begun to bubble, add the bacon, onions, and garlic. Sauté them, stirring, until the mixture is golden brown. Stir in the flour, and cook for

2 to 3 minutes, without allowing the flour to color. Strain the milk from the scallops into the saucepan, and cook over low heat, stirring, until the sauce has thickened. Add the sherry, salt and pepper, parsley, and lemon juice. Carefully stir in the scallops and mushrooms. Taste, and adjust the seasonings, if you like. Let the sauce cool.

To make the pasta, put the egg and herbs into a blender or a food processor fitted with a steel blade, and whirl until the herbs are chopped and completely combined with the egg. If you are using a food processor, add the flour, salt, and 1 tablespoon olive oil, and whirl until the contents are blended. Add just enough water to allow the dough to form a ball. If you will be rolling the pasta by hand, continue to work the dough in the processor for about 2 minutes.

If you are making the pasta entirely by hand, mix the flour and salt together, then mound them on a work surface. Make a well in the center, and pour in the egg-herb mixture. Stir the egg around and around, picking up flour from the edge each time. When the dough becomes too stiff to stir, flour your hands and begin kneading, adding just enough water to allow you to form a ball. Knead the dough until it is smooth and shiny, about 10 to 12 minutes.

If you are using a pasta machine, open the rollers to their widest, and put the dough through. Fold the dough in half, flour it, and repeat. Run the dough through the rollers on increasingly narrow settings until the pasta is the thickness you like. Place the rolled dough on a floured surface to dry slightly.

If you are forming the pasta by hand, divide the dough into six equal parts, and roll each into a thin 6-inch round. Allow the rounds to dry on a floured surface.

If you are using strips made by machine, cut them into 6-inch lengths, and stretch the strips with your hands so they are 6 inches wide as well as long.

Using a 6-inch round plate or bowl as a guide, cut the pasta into six circles. Cut the scraps into fettuccine-size strips, with a machine or by hand.

Drop the rounds into rapidly boiling salted water into which you have put 2 tablespoons olive oil. Carefully remove the rounds as they rise to the top, and flip them onto a counter or baking sheet. Cook the pasta strips, and drain them.

Preheat the oven to 425°.

When the pasta rounds are cool enough, spread them flat with your hands. Place a generous spoonful of the scallop filling in the center of each round, and draw up the edge to form a pouch. Pinch the top together, and secure it with a cocktail pick. Trim the top with a sharp knife, and wind one of the pasta strips around the top to resemble a flower. Make five more pasta flowers the same way.

Bring the sauce to a boil, and whisk

into it the remaining 2 tablespoons butter, cut into small pieces. Spoon the tomato sauce into six scallop shells or oven-proof dishes. Place a scallop-filled pasta flower on each shell or dish, and brush the flower with olive oil. Bake the flowers for 10 to 15 minutes, or until they are a light golden brown.

Serve them immediately.

Makes 6 servings

Pumpkin, Black Bean, and Parmesan Lasagna

The colors of this pasta dish are very handsome, showing what can happen when Caribbean ingredients infiltrate another cuisine—magic!

....

PUMPKIN FILLING:
  ¼ cup butter
  6 leeks, trimmed, rinsed, and minced
  4 cups cooked and puréed pumpkin
  ½ cup dry white wine
  Salt and pepper to taste

....

BEAN FILLING:
  2 tablespoons butter
  1 onion, chopped
  2 garlic cloves, minced
  2 cups (1 15-ounce can) cooked and
    drained black beans
  Salt, pepper, and cayenne to taste

....

BÉCHAMEL:
  ½ cup butter
  6 tablespoons flour
  2 cups chicken broth
  1 cup milk
  1 cup half-and-half
  1 cup grated parmesan cheese
  ½ teaspoon grated nutmeg
  Salt and pepper to taste
  3 large eggs, lightly beaten
  1¼ pounds lasagna noodles, cooked
    and drained
  2 cups lightly toasted walnut
    pieces
  1 cup grated parmesan cheese

....

Preheat the oven to 350°.

In a large saucepan, melt the butter, and sauté the leeks until they are soft. Add the pumpkin, white wine, and salt and pepper. Simmer the pumpkin filling until it is thickened, then remove the pan from the heat.

For the bean filling, heat the butter in a skillet. Sauté the onion and garlic until soft, and add the black beans. Season with salt, pepper, and cayenne. Remove the pan from the heat.

For the béchamel sauce, heat the butter in a saucepan, and stir in the flour. Cook the roux over low heat, stirring, for about 3 minutes. Gradually add the broth and milk. Cook gently for about 5 minutes.

Add the half-and-half, cheese, and nutmeg. Season the sauce with salt and pepper. Whisk in the eggs, and cook the sauce over very low heat until it is thickened. Remove the pan from the heat.

To assemble the lasagna, spread one-quarter of the béchamel over the bottom of a large baking dish (approximately 11¾ by 7½ by 1¾ inches). Layer one-third of the noodles, pumpkin filling, bean filling, and walnuts, and repeat this process two times, ending with the béchamel sauce. Sprinkle the lasagna with the parmesan cheese, and bake the lasagna for 1 hour or until it is hot and bubbly.

Cut the lasagna into pieces, and serve it immediately.

Makes 10 to 12 servings

Key Lime Pasta with Crab and Mustard Sauce

Although we love the special tart flavor of the small Key limes, the larger Persian or Tahitian limes are just fine for this dish.

. . . .

> 2 tablespoons olive oil
> 4 shallots, minced
> 2 tablespoons Dijon mustard
> 1 tablespoon grainy mustard
> 1 cup white wine
> 2 cups heavy cream
> 1½ pounds cooked crab or lobster meat
> ½ teaspoon cayenne
> Salt and pepper to taste
> 1½ pounds linguine, cooked and drained
> Grated zest of 1 lime

. . . .

In a saucepan, heat the olive oil, and add the shallots. Sauté them slowly for 1 minute; then add the two mustards and white wine. Cook, stirring, for 1 minute, then add the cream. Simmer the sauce until it has thickened.

Add the lobster or crab, cayenne, and salt and pepper to the sauce. Add the sauce to the hot pasta, and toss. Garnish with the lime zest, and serve.

Makes 6 to 8 servings

FAST PASTA SAUCES FOR TWO

....

Pasta with Tuna and Walnuts

Put 1 can drained tuna, 2 or 3 anchovy fillets, ¼ cup chopped walnuts, 1 garlic clove, 2 tablespoons olive oil, ⅓ cup heavy cream, and ¼ teaspoon ground black pepper in a blender or food processor. Whirl the sauce until it is smooth, then warm it gently over low heat. Toss it with hot pasta.

Pasta with Mushrooms and Blue Cheese

Sauté ½ cup chopped onions and 1 cup sliced mushrooms in 2 tablespoons butter. Stir in 2 teaspoons flour, and cook over low heat for 2 minutes. Add ½ cup crumbled blue cheese, ½ cup chicken broth, a dash of nutmeg, and 2 tablespoons heavy cream. Simmer the sauce until it has thickened. Toss it with cooked pasta, and top with additional crumbled blue cheese.

Hot Pepper and Broccoli Pasta

Boil 2 cups chopped broccoli in the same pot with the pasta (they will take the same length of time to cook). Drain the broccoli and pasta together.

While the broccoli and pasta are boiling, heat ¼ cup olive oil with 1 minced garlic clove and 1 teaspoon red pepper flakes. Toss the mixture with the pasta and broccoli. Sprinkle with grated parmesan cheese.

Pasta with Foie Gras

Sauté 8 sliced mushroom caps in butter. Add 4 ounces *foie gras*, and heat, stirring, until the *foie gras* is melted. Thin the sauce with cream, and toss it with cooked pasta. Add a few tablespoons minced parsley, and toss again.

Since this quick and elegant pasta is very rich, a crisp salad with vinaigrette makes a good counterpoint.

Pasta with Sweet Peppers and Pine Nuts

Heat 2 tablespoons olive oil and 1 tablespoon butter in a large skillet. Add 1 minced garlic clove, 2 chopped large sweet peppers (preferably 1 red and 1 yellow), and sauté over medium-high heat until the peppers are just tender.

In a small skillet, heat 1 tablespoon butter, and sauté ¼ cup pine nuts over low heat for about 2 to 3 minutes, or until they are golden.

Toss the pepper mixture with hot pasta, and sprinkle the pine nuts on top.

FROM THE FISH POT

FROM THE FISH POT

SPICED FISH WITH MINT-LIME BUTTER

The sizzling flavors of the bayous are kissing cousins to Caribbean seasonings. In this Cajun fish dish, the mint-lime butter provides a cooling balance of flavors. You can freeze the remaining butter in foil for future use (it's terrific on lamb chops).

. . . .

MINT-LIME BUTTER:
   ½ pound butter, softened
   1 bunch fresh mint, minced
   Juice and zest of 1 lime
   2 shallots, minced
   6 snapper, grouper, or mahimahi
      fillets (about 7 ounces each)
   2 tablespoons Cajun Seasoning (see
      "Cajun Seasoning")

. . . .

Melted butter

. . . .

Cajun Seasoning

. . . .

   2 TEASPOONS CAYENNE
   2 TEASPOONS SALT
   1 TEASPOON WHITE PEPPER
   1 TEASPOON BLACK PEPPER
   1 TEASPOON DRIED BASIL
   ½ TEASPOON DRIED THYME
   2 TEASPOONS PAPRIKA

To make the mint-lime butter, beat the butter in a mixer until the butter is light and fluffy. Beat in the mint, lime juice, zest, and shallots. Put the butter on a sheet of waxed paper, form it into a cylinder, and wrap the butter securely. Refrigerate or freeze it until it is firm.

Preheat the oven to 450°. Lay the fish in a large baking dish, sprinkle with the Cajun Seasoning, and drizzle on some melted butter. Bake the fish about 5 minutes for each ½ inch of thickness.

When the fish is ready, place a slice of mint-lime butter on top of each fillet, and serve.

Makes 6 servings

FISH WITH MANGOES AND GREEN PEPPERCORNS

In her book *Sky Juice and Flying Fish*, Jessica Harris relates the story of the mango's arrival in the West Indies. In 1872, a French vessel carrying a cargo of mangoes was captured off the coast of Jamaica, and the cargo was washed out to sea. The fruit floated to various islands, where the seeds sprouted, and mangoes became part of the islands' fruit basket.

. . . .

SAUCE:
   2 tablespoons butter

1 tablespoon whole drained brined
  green peppercorns
2 tablespoons crushed drained
  brined green peppercorns
½ cup heavy cream

. . . .

4 ½-inch-thick fillets of snapper,
  grouper, or other firm fish
Lime juice
Flour seasoned with salt and pepper,
  for dusting the fish
1 tablespoon vegetable oil
3 tablespoons butter
2 mangoes, peeled and sliced into
  16 wedges

. . . .

To make the sauce, heat the butter in a small saucepan. Add the whole and crushed green peppercorns, and cook for 1 minute. Add the heavy cream, and simmer for 3 minutes. Remove the pan from the heat, and keep the sauce warm.

Rub the fish with lime juice, and dust it with the seasoned flour. Heat the vegetable oil and 1 tablespoon of the butter in a skillet, and cook the fish over medium-high heat, turning it once, for 4 to 5 minutes or just until it is cooked through. While the fish cooks, heat the remaining 2 table-spoons butter in another skillet, add the mango slices, and cook them gently for 1 minute, turning them once.

Put the fish on serving plates, and spoon on a tablespoon or two of the sauce. Arrange four mango slices over each fillet, and serve.

A Fish Should Smell Fresh . . .

"It is perhaps impossible to say what 'fresh' smells like, except that it smells right, not dubious. It smells like new-cut grass, new-mown hay, an innocent brook, or a child emerging from his bath, or almost any happy clean thing for that matter.

But when a fish smells wrong, it is not for buying or for burning. It should be tossed away ruthlessly, where not even a fatalistic cat would deign to touch it."

—M.F.K. Fisher

Makes 4 servings

Dinner under the Stars

....

TROPICAL GAZPACHO
WITH CILANTRO CROUTONS

◆

GRILLED MARINATED SWORDFISH

◆

GREEN PAPAYA SALAD

◆

PIÑA COLADA CAKE

GRILLED MARINATED SWORDFISH

Swordfish is just one of the many firm, mildly flavored fish that are often called "steakfish" in the Caribbean. Others include tuna, kingfish, marlin, and mahimahi. All are excellent with this marinade.

....

MARINADE:

½ cup soy sauce
½ cup orange juice
¼ cup olive oil
¼ cup tomato paste
2 tablespoons minced fresh parsley
3 garlic cloves, minced
2 teaspoons lemon juice
1 teaspoon dried oregano
1 teaspoon ground black pepper

....

6 swordfish steaks

....

GARNISH:

Orange slices
Parsley sprigs

....

In a bowl, whisk together all the marinade ingredients. Place the swordfish steaks in a single layer in a shallow dish. Pour the marinade over, and allow the fish to sit in the refrigerator 1 hour.

Prepare a fire for grilling.

Remove the swordfish from the marinade, and grill the fish about 5 inches from the heat for 4 to 5 minutes on each side, or just until the fish is firm. Garnish it with orange slices and parsley, and serve.

Makes 6 servings

FISH IN PHYLLO WRAP

This is a very pretty party dish, and a convenient one. You can wrap the fish in phyllo and refrigerate it for several hours, then bake it just before serving time.

....

½ cup plus 2 tablespoons butter
12 sheets frozen phyllo dough, thawed
6 tablespoons dry bread crumbs
6 6- to 8-ounce fillets of snapper, grouper, or other firm fish
6 teaspoons Pernod liqueur
Salt and pepper to taste
Paprika

....

SAUCE:

 2 shallots or green onions, minced
 ¾ cup white wine vinegar
 3 tablespoons lemon juice
 ¾ cup unsalted cold butter, cut into
  bits
 3 tablespoons minced fresh parsley

....

Preheat the oven to 350°. Melt ½ cup butter.

Place one sheet of phyllo, its short side parallel to your body, on your work surface (cover the remaining sheets with a damp cloth to keep them from drying out). Brush the sheet with melted butter. Sprinkle it with 1 tablespoon bread crumbs. Top the phyllo with a second sheet, and brush with butter. Place one fish fillet about 1 inch from the short side of the phyllo and 2½ to 3 inches from both long sides (you may need to trim the fish to fit). Sprinkle the fish with 1 teaspoon Pernod, and season it lightly with salt and pepper. Cut the remaining 2 tablespoons butter into six pieces, and place one piece on the fish. Fold the phyllo around the fish as you would wrap a gift, making a neat rectangular packet. Place the packet seam side down on a baking sheet. Repeat the process to make six packets. Brush the tops and sides of the packets with the remaining melted butter, and sprinkle them with paprika. Bake the packets until they are golden brown, about 30 minutes.

When the packets are almost ready, make the sauce. Cook the shallot or green onion, vinegar, and lemon juice in a small saucepan over medium heat until the onion is softened, about 1½ minutes. Reduce the heat to medium-low. Whisk in the butter one piece at a time, incorporating the butter completely between additions. Stir in the parsley. When the packets are ready, drizzle each one with some of the warm sauce, and serve.

Makes 6 servings

PHYLLO FACTS

....

For many people, phyllo dough is very intimidating. It's true that to make it from scratch is a daunting enterprise and one that, frankly, we've steered clear of. Happily, though, there's no need to spend the rest of your life trying to roll a sheet of pastry thin enough to make a proper phyllo—not when your grocer likely has the dough in the freezer compartment.

Thaw frozen dough in the refrigerator overnight. You'll find that each package contains about 20 to 24 sheets of dough, but you should remove no more than four sheets at a time. Rewrap the rest, and cover them with a damp towel; uncovered, the fragile pastry dries out quickly and becomes too brittle to use.

With a soft-bristled brush, apply melted butter to each sheet of phyllo, and stack the sheets as you work.

If carefully wrapped, phyllo freezes well for up to three months.

FISH WITH CORAL SUNSET SAUCE

The heavenly color of this sauce reminds us of some of the spectacular skies we see as the sun sets behind our neighboring islands each evening.

....

1 cup heavy cream
⅓ cup clam broth
2 to 3 tablespoons tomato paste
Salt and pepper to taste
1 package Sazón seasoning (see page 4)
1 tomato, seeded and chopped
2 tablespoons chopped fresh basil, parsley, or a combination
6 6- to 8-ounce fillets of grouper, snapper, or other firm fish

....

To make the sauce, combine the cream, clam broth, tomato paste, and salt and pepper in a saucepan. Heat the mixture, without letting it boil, until it is reduced to ¾ cup, about 10 minutes. Stir in the Sazón seasoning, and set the saucepan aside.

Poach, bake, or sauté the fish fillets. Reheat the sauce gently, if necessary, add the chopped tomatoes and basil or parsley, and spoon the sauce over the fish. Serve at once.

Makes 6 servings

COOK YOUR FISH THE CANADIAN WAY

....

Canada's Department of Fisheries relieved us all of a lot of guesswork and angst when they discovered that fish should be cooked precisely 10 minutes per inch of its thickness, or 5 minutes per ½ inch, whether the fish is poached, baked, sautéed, or grilled.

When you add fish to a poaching liquid, wait until the liquid reaches its simmering point before you begin timing.

For baking, the rule assumes you'll set the oven at 450°. A delicate wrapping, however, may make a lower temperature, and a longer cooking time, preferable.

FISH WITH SUN-DRIED TOMATO VINAIGRETTE

Top the poached, grilled, baked, or sautéed fish of your choice with this delicious vinaigrette, the inspired creation of a former Sugar Mill chef, Jeff Oakley. Jeff's vinaigrette is also great on green salads, sausage, or steaks.

....

VINAIGRETTE:
    2 tablespoons minced peeled gingerroot
    2 large shallots, diced

Juice and zest of 3 limes
2 tablespoons raspberry vinegar
¼ cup Dijon mustard
3 tablespoons sugar
4 cups olive oil
2 cups julienned dried tomatoes
1 tablespoon cracked black pepper
Basil, thyme, parsley, or a
  combination, chopped

....

Cooked fish fillets

....

Put all the vinaigrette ingredients into a bowl or jar, and whisk or shake to blend them. Spoon some of the vinaigrette over the hot fish fillets, and refrigerate the remaining dressing for other uses.

GRILLED FISH WITH VEGETABLE JUMP-UP

In the islands a jump-up is a party of any kind. The lively and spirited carnival flavors of this fish dish make it a natural for any jump-up.

....

MARINADE:
2 garlic cloves, minced
1 tablespoon dried thyme
1 teaspoon salt
1 teaspoon ground black pepper
Juice of 4 limes
½ cup olive oil

....

TOPPING:
2 tomatoes, chopped
¾ cup sliced pitted black olives
3 tablespoons drained capers
¼ cup sliced green onions
¼ cup lime juice
¼ cup olive oil

....

6 6- to 8-ounce swordfish, tuna, or
  mahimahi steaks

....

Prepare a fire for grilling.

In a bowl, stir together the marinade ingredients. Place the fish in a single layer in a shallow dish. Pour the marinade over the fish, and turn the fish to coat it completely. Cover the dish, and refrigerate it for at least 1 hour.

Grill the fish. Combine the topping ingredients, and spoon them over the cooked fish. Serve at once.

Makes 6 servings

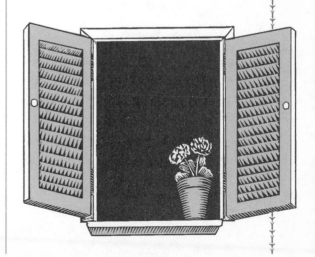

QUICK TOPPINGS FOR FISH

Fennel Butter

With a fork, beat together ½ cup softened butter, 2 teaspoons Pernod, 1 teaspoon crushed fennel seeds, 1 teaspoon lemon juice, 1 minced garlic clove, and ½ teaspoon dried thyme. Dot the fennel butter on fish, and grill or bake the fish until it is done. Garnish the fish with sliced lemon and a fresh fennel sprig.

Golden Souffléed Topping

Combine ¾ cup mayonnaise, ¼ cup grated parmesan cheese, 1 beaten egg white, and ¼ cup minced green onion tops or chives. Spoon the mixture onto fish, and bake the fish until it is done. The topping will puff into a fluffy crown.

Spinach Pesto

Combine ½ cup cooked, drained spinach, ½ cup minced parsley, ⅓ cup parmesan cheese, ¼ cup shelled walnuts, 2 garlic cloves, 2 teaspoons dried basil, ½ teaspoon fennel seeds, and salt and pepper to taste in a food processor or blender. Whirl until the mixture is smooth. With the motor running, add ⅓ cup olive oil in a slow stream, blending until the pesto is smooth. Serve the pesto on freshly cooked fish.

FISH CARNIVAL

This bright fish dish reminds us of the vivid colors of carnival, when troops of dancers take to the streets, bands boom forth with reggae and calypso compositions, and *mako jumbies* dressed in flashy satin outfits perch on tall stilt legs to tower over the crowds.

....

6 6- to 8-ounce fillets of grouper,
*   snapper, or other firm fish*
Juice of 2 lemons
¼ cup finely grated carrot
¼ cup chopped seeded tomato
¼ cup chopped green onion
⅓ cup mayonnaise
⅔ cup softened cream cheese
2 tablespoons minced parsley
Salt and pepper to taste
Lime wedges

....

Place the fish in a single layer in a baking dish. Squeeze the lemon juice over. With a fork, mash together the carrot, tomato, green onion, mayonnaise, cream cheese, parsley, and salt and pepper. Mound the vegetable mixture equally on top of each fillet. Bake the fish immediately, or cover and chill it until just before mealtime.

Bake the fish, uncovered, at 450° until it flakes when prodded with a fork, about 10 minutes. Serve it with the lime wedges.

Makes 6 servings

FISH WITH TOMATO AND BANANA

We think you'll be pleasantly surprised by the way the unlikely marriage of tomatoes and bananas works in this very simple fish preparation.

....

6 6- to 8-ounce fillets of grouper, snapper, or other firm fish
Salt and pepper to taste
½ cup lemon juice
½ cup olive oil
1 tablespoon minced garlic
2 teaspoons dried oregano
6 tomato slices
2 bananas or ripe plantains, peeled and sliced diagonally
2 tablespoons butter
Minced parsley

....

Preheat the oven to 450°. Pat the fish dry, and sprinkle it with salt and pepper. Combine the lemon juice, olive oil, garlic, and oregano in a shallow baking dish. Stir until the ingredients are well blended. Add the fish, and turn it to moisten both sides. Place the tomato slices on top of the fillets. Bake them for about 8 to 10 minutes, depending on their thickness.

While the fish bakes, sauté the banana or plantain slices in the butter. When the fish is ready, place it on serving plates. Lay the banana or plantain slices on top, sprinkle the parsley over, and serve immediately.

Makes 6 servings

FISH ESCABECHE

This is a popular dish in Puerto Rico and the Dominican Republic. Perfect for a warm-weather buffet, it can be made a day ahead.

....

2½ pounds firm white fish fillets (grouper or snapper are favorites)
2 cups milk
1 cup flour
Salt, pepper, and cayenne to taste
6 tablespoons olive oil
3 garlic cloves, minced
2 onions, cut into thin rings
3 tablespoons white wine vinegar
3 tablespoons drained capers
2 tablespoons dry white wine
1 to 2 teaspoons hot red pepper flakes
2 to 3 heads loose-leaf lettuce
3 tomatoes, sliced into wedges
3 lemons, sliced into wedges
Finely minced parsley

....

Cut the fish into finger-size pieces. Marinate them in the milk for 30 minutes.

Season the flour with salt, pepper, and cayenne. Drain the fish, and dredge the pieces in the flour. Heat ¼ cup olive oil in a skillet, and fry the fish, turning it once, until it is golden on both sides. Keep the fish warm.

Add the remaining 2 tablespoons oil to the skillet, and sauté the garlic and onion until the onion is limp. Add to the skillet the vinegar, capers, wine, and red pepper flakes. Cook over high heat until the liquid is reduced to 6 tablespoons. Pour the sauce over the fish. We like to serve this dish neither hot nor chilled but at room temperature, so all of the flavors are mellow and well combined. When you are ready to serve, mound the fish on lettuce-lined salad plates and garnish with tomato and lemon wedges. Sprinkle the fish with a drift of finely minced parsley.

Makes 6 servings

GRILLED OR BAKED FISH WITH WEST INDIAN CREOLE SAUCE

One of our talented chefs, Ivor Peters, prepares this traditional Caribbean dish with special flair.

....

6 *firm fish steaks (swordfish, tuna, or halibut), about 8 ounces each*
1 *teaspoon lemon juice*
3 *tablespoons olive oil*
1 *teaspoon salt*
½ *teaspoon ground black pepper*

....

CREOLE SAUCE:
2 *tablespoons melted butter*
1 *tablespoon minced garlic*
2 *medium onions, sliced*
1 *teaspoon minced thyme leaves*
2 *tomatoes, coarsely chopped*
2 *red bell peppers, cut into julienne strips*
2 *yellow or green bell peppers, cut into julienne strips*
1 *teaspoon hot pepper sauce*
1 *teaspoon lemon juice*
2 *cups tomato sauce*
Salt and pepper to taste

....

Prepare a fire for grilling, or preheat the oven to 450°.

Put the fish into a shallow dish. In a small bowl, whisk together the lemon juice, olive oil, salt, and pepper, and pour the mixture over the fish. Allow the fish to stand about 5 minutes to absorb the seasonings.

To make the sauce, heat the butter in a heavy skillet. Add the garlic, onion, and thyme, and sauté them over medium-high heat until the onions are limp. Reduce the heat to medium, and add the chopped tomatoes, peppers, hot sauce, and lemon juice. Cook the mixture for 4 minutes or until the peppers are tender. Add the tomato sauce, and simmer the sauce until it is thickened, about 5 minutes. Season it with salt and pepper, and keep it warm.

Remove the fish from the dish, and grill it over glowing ash-covered coals

or bake it for about 10 minutes for each inch of thickness.

To serve, place the fish on plates, and spoon the warm sauce on top.

Makes 6 servings

FISH BAKED IN BANANA LEAVES

We have dozens of banana plants growing at the Sugar Mill—not just for their fruit, but also for their leaves. If you're fresh out of banana leaves, parchment paper or foil will work just fine.

....

Banana leaves or parchment paper
Salt and pepper to taste
6 6- to 8-ounce fillets of grouper,
*   snapper, or other firm fish*
2 tomatoes, peeled, seeded, and
*   chopped*
¼ cup chopped green onions (some
*   of the green part and all of the*
*   white)*
½ cup coconut cream (see page 44)

....

Preheat the oven to 400°. Cut the banana leaves into rectangles large enough to be folded over the fish, or cut the parchment into similar pieces. Sear the banana leaves, if you're using them, over a gas flame until they are limp and pliable.

Place each fillet on a piece of banana leaf, parchment paper, or foil. Sprinkle the fish with the salt and pepper, chopped tomato, and chopped green onion. Spoon on some coconut cream. Fold the wrapping to enclose the fish and filling, and seal the edges by folding over twice. Fold over the ends in the same way. (When we are using banana leaves, we take the extra precaution of tying the packages with strands of tough local grass. String works as well.)

Bake the packets for 10 to 15 minutes, depending on the thickness of the fish. Allow your guests to open their own little bundles, which look like lovely gifts.

Makes 6 servings

COCONUT SHRIMP WITH VEGETABLES

We first enjoyed this exotic dish at Ginnie and John Morrell's home, overlooking Cane Garden Bay. We love the combination of flavors and the soothing coconut cream. By the way, Ginnie suggests that if you don't want to make coconut cream and can't find it in a store, you can combine equal parts of sweetened cream of coconut (such as Coco Lopez) and half-and-half.

....

½ cup vegetable oil
4 green onions, chopped
1 small onion, chopped
1 tablespoon minced peeled
    gingerroot
8 garlic cloves, minced
1¾ pounds shelled and deveined
    large shrimp
2 cups shredded head cabbage
1½ cups shredded Chinese cabbage
1 cup cubed peeled eggplant
1 cup peeled, sliced, and blanched
    carrots
1½ cups sliced zucchini
1 red bell pepper, sliced
1 bay leaf
Juice of 1 lime
1 teaspoon hot pepper sauce
½ cup coconut cream (see page 44)
1½ teaspoons arrowroot or
    cornstarch
Salt and pepper to taste

....

Heat ¼ cup of the oil in a large skillet or other heavy-bottomed pan. Sauté the onions, ginger, and garlic for about 5 minutes over medium heat. Add the shrimp, and cook, stirring continuously, until the shrimp turns pink. Remove the shrimp mixture to a bowl, and set it aside.

Add the remaining oil to the pan, and cook the cabbage, eggplant, carrots, zucchini, and pepper for 5 minutes over medium heat, stirring constantly. Add the bay leaf, lime juice, hot sauce, and coconut cream. Cover the pan, and simmer 10 minutes or until the vegetables are just tender.

Return the shrimp mixture to the pan, and cook an additional 5 minutes.

Combine the arrowroot with 2 tablespoons water. Stir this into the simmering mixture, and cook just until the mixture is thickened. Season with salt and pepper, and serve the mixture hot with white rice.

Makes 6 servings

SHRIMP SECRETS

....

♦ *When you buy shrimp, look for those with shells closely fitted to their bodies. Shrinkage is usually a sign that the shrimp are not fresh. Raw shrimp are usually grayish green (from some waters they may have a slightly pink tint).*

♦ *For a much deeper flavor when you boil shrimp, first wash the shells you've removed, place them in water, and bring the water to a boil. Let the shells boil for a few minutes, then strain the liquid and use it to cook the shrimp.*

♦ *If you're going to serve shrimp cold, remove them from the water when they're cooked and let them cool gradually at room temperature. Don't refrigerate them until they are cool, or they'll become tough.*

♦ *Unpeeled shrimp simmered in beer have an interesting flavor a little like lobster.*

CARIBBEAN CAJUN SHRIMP

The Caribbean-Cajun seasoning connection traces its roots to African cooks, who both transformed the tastes of the American South and also presided over the kitchens of Caribbean great houses. Their legacy is at work in this sprightly and very easy shrimp dish.

....

⅔ cup butter
2 tablespoons Worcestershire sauce

....

SHRIMP SEASONING:

1 teaspoon cayenne
1 teaspoon ground black pepper
2 teaspoons dried parsley
½ teaspoon garlic powder
½ teaspoon onion powder
½ teaspoon salt
1 teaspoon hot red pepper flakes
¼ teaspoon dried thyme
¼ teaspoon dried rosemary, crushed
¼ teaspoon dried oregano

....

3 pounds large shrimp, shelled and
    deveined, with tails on

....

Melt the butter with the Worcestershire sauce. Combine the ingredients for the shrimp seasoning. In a shallow baking dish, combine the melted butter, shrimp seasoning, and shrimp.

Cover the dish, and refrigerate it for 3 hours.

Preheat the oven to 350°. Place the baking dish in the oven, and bake the shrimp for 20 minutes or until they are pink. Serve the shrimp with rice.

Makes 6 servings

PIRATE'S SHRIMP IN PUFF PASTRY

If you have all the ingredients cut up and ready to go, the filling for this pretty party dish is as easy to put together as a quick stir-fry.

....

¼ cup butter
1 tablespoon vegetable oil
2 pounds large shrimp, shelled and
    deveined, with tails on
2 onions, chopped
2 cups sliced mushrooms
½ cup sherry
2 red, yellow, or orange bell peppers,
    chopped
2 tablespoons tomato paste
3 cups heavy cream
1 teaspoon chili powder
Salt and pepper to taste
Commercial puff pastry sheets, cut
    into 4-inch diamond shapes, baked
    according to package directions,
    and split in half

....

GARNISH:
*6 cooked shelled and deveined
shrimp with tails on
Minced parsley*

....

Heat 2 tablespoons butter and the oil in a skillet, and sauté the shrimp 2 to 3 minutes, depending on its size, until it is bright pink. Remove the shrimp to a bowl, and set it aside. Add the onions to the pan, and cook them over low heat until they are limp.

Add the remaining butter, and sauté the mushrooms until they are soft. Add the sherry and peppers, and cook gently for 2 minutes. Stir in the tomato paste, and then the cream, chili powder, and salt and pepper. Add the shrimp, and simmer gently for 2 to 3 minutes. Spoon the mixture into the split puff pastry diamonds, and garnish each with a shrimp and a drift of parsley.

Makes 6 servings

GINGER-LIME SCALLOPS WITH TOASTED WALNUTS

Sometimes an unusual combination of ingredients strikes just the right balance, as does this medley of smooth, tender scallops, crunchy walnuts, spicy ginger, and zingy lime. To toast the nuts, spread them on a baking sheet and heat them in a 350° oven until they are golden brown, about 3 to 5 minutes, shaking once or twice so they brown evenly. Toasting the nuts brings out their flavor and fragrance.

....

LIME-GINGER BUTTER:
*5 tablespoons softened butter
2 tablespoons grated lime zest
1 teaspoon ground ginger
Salt and pepper to taste*

....

*2 tablespoons olive oil
2 tablespoons butter
2 pounds scallops, patted dry
6 tablespoons fresh lime juice
⅔ cup walnuts, coarsely chopped and
toasted
Minced parsley*

....

With a fork, beat together the ingredients for the lime-ginger butter.

Heat the olive oil and 2 tablespoons butter in a skillet. Add the scallops, and sauté them until they are golden, about 2 minutes. Pour off the fat. Stir in the lime juice, and cook 1 minute. Lower the heat, and stir in the lime-ginger butter 1 tablespoon at a time. Cook just until a thick sauce forms.

Stir in the walnuts, sprinkle with parsley, and serve.

Makes 6 servings

ISLAND STYLE: PUERTO RICO

We wondered if our friend Gale had learned her driving technique while training for the Grand Prix. No, she's a New Yorker who had learned to drive in San Juan. Just when one of us was about to ask if eighty-five was the normal highway speed on the island, we realized that other cars were passing us, their drivers giving us disdainful looks.

We safely reached our destination, a mountain village where pork is king, and considered the trip well worth the damp palms it induced. Gale had brought us to visit one of her favorite lechonerías, one of a half dozen outdoor barbecue stalls in a town where wood smoke fills the air, and lechón asado (roast pig), pork ribs, sausage, and crispy cracklings are slowly cooked over hot coals. In Puerto Rico people travel miles to taste this marvelous meat on site. But that's not unusual on this island. Here food is so important that on weekends families drive across the island just to eat fresh fish caught and cooked in Cabo Rojo. So these culinary pilgrims don't run out of steam along the way, almost every main road is dotted with family-run stalls selling Puerto Rican fast food—including fritters filled with cheese, meat, codfish, or green bananas.

Such robust country specialties make up just one facet of Puerto Rico's culinary scene. Traditional champions of Spanish-Caribbean cooking, Puerto Rican chefs are now adapting traditional dishes to today's tastes. The trendiest restaurants have cut back on salt and rarely fry in lard, but the cornucopia of spices, herbs, and fresh ingredients still results in exciting dishes.

Sofrito, a potent combination of salt pork, onion, garlic, tomato, green pepper, ham, and annatto (achiote) seeds, is the backbone for many popular preparations. Island chefs sauté the seeds, once prized by the Taino Indians, in oil to turn it bright orange.

Asopao, a combination of chicken, rice, and perhaps twenty other ingredients, depending on the whim of the cook, has clear antecedents in Spain's paella, and could be called Puerto Rico's national dish.

With an active fishing industry, Puerto Ricans enjoy plenty of seafood: red snapper, marlin, sole, hake, octopus, conch, and Caribbean lobster as well as jueyes (land crabs). The island's oysters are tiny and exceptionally sweet.

With good fish, many local herbs, and a constant supply of exotic fruits and vegetables, today's Puerto Rican chefs are entering a new age. In just ten years the listings of restaurants in the Puerto Rican yellow pages has grown from four to fourteen pages. Visitors to Puerto Rico could, if they chose, spend their time simply eating their way across the island.

But with all this good food, something is needed to wash it down. Nowhere have we found such imaginative fresh fruit drinks. Mango, pineapple, fresh coconut, passion fruit, tamarind, and soursop are all blended together in various thirst-quenching, icy combinations. And, of course, there is rum. Puerto Rico produces many varieties of the region's trademark beverage, and this island claims to have invented the drink that has lifted many a weary traveler's spirit: the piña colada.

SHRIMP AND SCALLOP TIMBALES WITH DILL SABAYON

Elegant but easy, this dish benefits from just a few drops of Caribbean hot sauce, which add a dash of gusto. Although sabayon is usually a dessert sauce, we've made it savory with lemon juice and dill to complement the shellfish timbales. This dish will serve twelve if you offer it as a first course rather than a main course.

....

TIMBALES:

    1 pound medium shrimp, shelled and deveined
    ¾ pound sea scallops, rinsed and patted dry
    1½ teaspoons salt
    ¼ teaspoon hot pepper sauce
    ½ teaspoon freshly grated nutmeg
    Whites of 2 large eggs
    2½ cups heavy cream

....

GARNISH:

    Thin carrot slices, blanched just until limp and cut into decorative designs
    Green onion tops, blanched for 30 seconds and cut into thin strips

....

SAUCE:

    8 egg yolks
    3 tablespoons lemon juice
    ½ teaspoon salt
    1 pinch ground black pepper
    ¼ cup water
    2 tablespoons snipped fresh dillweed, or 2 teaspoons dried dillweed

....

To make the timbales, whirl the shrimp, scallops, salt, hot sauce, and nutmeg in a food processor (in two batches, if necessary) until the mixture is smooth, scraping down the side of the bowl several times. The machine should run for about 1½ minutes.

With the machine running, add the egg whites and cream, and whirl until the contents are well blended. The mixture should be thick and fluffy.

Preheat the oven to 350°.

Oil 12 ½-cup molds, and arrange the carrots and green onions in the bottoms in a pretty design. Carefully fill the molds with the timbale mixture. Place them in a baking pan, and fill the pan one-third of the way up the sides of the molds with boiling water. Put the pan into the hot oven, and bake the timbales for 30 minutes.

To make the sauce, put the egg yolks into the top of a double boiler over simmering water. Whisk until they are thickened and doubled in volume. Beat in the lemon juice, salt, pepper, and water, and continue whisking until the sauce again thickens. It should be thick enough to coat a spoon. Add the dill, and adjust the seasonings, if you like.

When the timbales are ready, re-

warm the sauce over low heat, if necessary. Spoon some of the warm sauce onto serving plates, unmold the timbales on top, and serve.

Makes 6 servings

PAN-SEARED SCALLOPS WITH TOMATO-MANGO SALSA

The tart tomatoes form a happy marriage with the sweet mangoes in this salsa. Try it with other seafood or grilled chicken breasts. It also makes a great dip with plantain chips.

....

SALSA:
    3 medium tomatoes, peeled, seeded,
        and chopped
    2 cups finely chopped mango
    ½ cup chopped red onion
    ⅓ cup chopped basil, loosely packed
    6 tablespoons red wine vinegar
    3 tablespoons capers

....

SCALLOPS:
    3 tablespoons olive oil
    36 sea scallops
    ¾ teaspoon salt
    ¾ teaspoon pepper

....

GARNISH:
    1 avocado, sliced
    Basil sprigs

....

Combine the salsa ingredients in a bowl. Cover the bowl, and refrigerate it for at least an hour.

Heat the olive oil in a large skillet. Add the scallops, and cook them, turning them once, until they are firm, about 3 minutes. Remove the scallops from the skillet, and sprinkle them with salt and pepper. Arrange the scallops on a plate, top them with salsa, and garnish them with avocado slices and basil. Serve at once.

Makes 6 servings

SCALLOPS IN PUFF PASTRY WITH ROASTED RED PEPPER SAUCE

We use a real scallop shell as a template for cutting out the puff pastry. If you don't have a scallop shell handy, you can draw a facsimile on paper, and use that as a cutting guide. Simple squares or circles of puff pastry are fine, too.

....

SAUCE:

2 red bell peppers or 3
  pimientos
3 tablespoons minced onion
1 cup dry white wine
½ cup clam broth
½ cup water
2 cups heavy cream
2 tablespoons cold butter
2 tablespoons lemon juice
Salt and pepper to taste
Commercial puff pastry

....

2½ pounds scallops
½ bay leaf
1 pinch thyme
¼ teaspoon salt
1 cup dry white wine
2 tablespoons cold butter

....

If you are using fresh peppers, turn them over a low flame, using a long fork, until the skins are black and charred. Put the peppers into a plastic bag, seal the bag, and let the peppers steam for 20 minutes. Peel off the skins, remove the seeds, and slice the peppers.

Boil together the roasted peppers or pimientos, onion, white wine, clam broth, and water in a heavy pan until the liquid is reduced to about 3 tablespoons. Add the cream, and simmer until the mixture is thickened. Put it into a blender or food processor, and whirl the mixture until it is smooth. Season it with the lemon juice and salt and pepper, and reserve the sauce.

Cut six scallop-shell shapes from the puff pastry, and bake the pieces according to the directions on the package until they are puffed and golden brown. Split them in half horizontally, and keep them warm.

Put the scallops into a saucepan with the bay leaf, thyme, salt, white wine, and enough water to cover the scallops. Bring the water to the boiling point, immediately lower the heat, and poach the scallops in barely simmering water, covered, until they are tender, about 3 to 4 minutes (boiling the scallops would toughen them).

Drain the scallops, and fill the warm puff pastry shells with them. Reheat the sauce, stir the butter into it, and spoon some of the sauce over the scallops. Serve immediately.

Makes 6 servings

Seaside Supper

....

CHILLED CURRIED ZUCCHINI SOUP

◆

GREEN SALAD WITH PARSLEY DRESSING

◆

SCALLOPS IN PUFF PASTRY
WITH ROASTED RED PEPPER SAUCE

◆

SPINACH TIMBALES

◆

GINGER-POACHED SPICE ISLANDS PEARS

SHRIMP ETOUFFÉE WITH CAJUN OYSTERS

Many trips to one of our favorite cities, New Orleans, and many conversations with one of our favorite people, Paul Prudhomme, reinforced our understanding of the intimate connections between Caribbean and Cajun and Louisiana Creole cuisines. This double shellfish recipe mirrors that relationship. Paul also explained that the literal meaning of *etouffée* is "smothered," but in Louisiana kitchens the word usually applies to dishes cooked with a roux and then covered with liquid.

....

7 tablespoons vegetable oil
¾ cup flour
½ cup chopped celery
½ cup chopped onions
¼ cup chopped red bell peppers
¼ cup chopped green bell peppers
1 tablespoon Cajun Seasoning (see page 118)
Liquor from the oysters (see right column)
Fish stock or clam broth
1 cup chopped green onions
2 tablespoons butter
1 pound shrimp, shelled, deveined, and diced

....

CAJUN OYSTERS:
18 to 24 oysters, shucked
1 cup flour
2 eggs
1 cup dry bread crumbs
1 teaspoon Cajun Seasoning (see page 118)
2 to 4 tablespoons butter

....

Heat the oil in a heavy (preferably cast-iron) skillet over high heat until the oil begins to smoke. Add the ¾ cup flour, and continue to heat, stirring, until a dark red-brown roux is formed, about 3 to 5 minutes. Remove the skillet from the heat, and add the chopped celery, onion, and bell peppers, and the 1 tablespoon Cajun Seasoning. Stir the mixture until it is cool.

Add enough fish stock or clam broth to the oyster liquor to make 2½ cups. In a pot, bring 2 cups of the liquid to a boil, and gradually add the roux-vegetable mixture. Heat, stirring, until the roux is dissolved.

In a skillet, sauté the green onions in the butter, and add the diced shrimp. When the shrimp is pink, firm, and cooked through, combine the shrimp and green onions with the *etouffée* and adjust the consistency of the *etouffée*, if you like, with the remaining stock. Keep the *etouffée* hot.

To prepare the oysters, dip them into the flour, then into the beaten egg, and finally into the bread crumbs seasoned with the 1 teaspoon Cajun Seasoning. In a skillet, sauté the oysters in the butter until they are crisp and golden brown, about 2 minutes on each side.

Serve the *etouffée* over white rice surrounded by the oysters.

Makes 6 servings

LOBSTER CREOLE

There are many views about the appropriate way to dispatch lobsters. Some favor a quick, clean kill using a knife. Others plunge the lobsters into boiling water. Soft-hearted souls put them into room-temperature water and bring it slowly to a boil, and those with the most tender sensibilities add a glug or two of vodka to the water to be sure the lobster passes into lobster heaven in tipsy bliss.

Sofrito, the basis of the sauce for this dish, was brought centuries ago from Spain to the Caribbean, where today its savory influence can be tasted on many islands. Make it ahead, if you like; it will keep in a covered container in the refrigerator for up to two weeks.

....

SOFRITO:
   1½ cups finely chopped salt pork
   1 teaspoon annatto oil (see page 7)

1½ cups minced onions
2 teaspoons minced garlic
½ cup chopped green bell peppers
3 ounces lean boneless ham, cut into ½-inch cubes
½ cup peeled, seeded, and chopped tomatoes
1 teaspoon dried oregano
2 tablespoons minced cilantro or parsley

....

2 1½- to 2-pound live lobsters, or an equivalent amount of lobster tails
3 tablespoons annatto oil (see page 7)
1 cup dry white wine
Minced cilantro or parsley
Lemon wedges

....

Sauté the salt pork in a heavy skillet over moderate heat, stirring often, until the salt pork is crisp and brown. Pour off all but 2 tablespoons fat. Add the annatto oil to the pan. Add the onions, garlic, and peppers, and sauté the vegetables for 5 to 10 minutes, until they are soft but not brown.

Add the ham, and stir until the mixture is well covered with oil. Stir in the chopped tomatoes, oregano, and cilantro or parsley. Reduce the heat to low, cover the pan tightly, and simmer for 30 minutes, stirring the mixture occasionally to prevent the vegetables from sticking to the bottom of the skillet. Let the *sofrito* cool, and reserve it.

Kill each lobster by plunging a knife into its back between the body and head, or by dropping it into rapidly boiling water and letting it cook for 1 minute. (Believe us, you'll feel worse about this step than the lobster does.)

Remove and discard the gelatinous sac in each head, and the long intestinal vein attached to the sac. Wash the lobsters well, and, with a sharp, heavy knife or heavy shears, cut the tail into medallions. Cut the body in half, clean it, and save the tomalley (liver) and any coral (roe) for the sauce. If you are using lobsters with claws, remove them.

Cook the head in rapidly boiling water for about 4 to 5 minutes, or until the shell turns red. Let the head cool, and reserve it for garnish.

Heat the annatto oil over high heat in a heavy skillet or wok. Add the lobster pieces, and fry them for 3 to 4 minutes, turning constantly, until the shells turn pink. Transfer them to a platter.

Pour all but a thin layer of oil from the skillet, add the wine, and bring it to a boil over high heat. Stir in the *sofrito*, and return to the skillet the lobsters and any liquid that has accumulated around them. Cover the skillet tightly, and simmer the lobster for 8 to 10 minutes, basting from time to time with a large spoon.

Arrange the lobster pieces on a large platter, over rice or on their own, and garnish with the lobster head, cilantro or parsley, and lemon wedges. Serve the lobster hot.

Makes 2 to 4 servings

LOBSTER AND CHRISTOPHENE CURRY

A vegetable of many names, the christophene is known as mirliton in Louisiana and chayote in Latin America. It's a green, pear-shaped vegetable from a West Indian vine of the cucumber family. The seed is edible and delicious cut up in salads. If you can't get christophenes, you can substitute Jerusalem artichokes or fresh water chestnuts in this recipe.

½ cup minced shallots

2½ cups dry white wine

¾ cup brandy

About 5 teaspoons curry powder, to taste

1 cup coconut cream (see page 44)

2 cups heavy cream

Salt, pepper, and cayenne to taste

3 cups cooked lobster meat, cut into chunks

¾ pound asparagus, trimmed, blanched, and cut into bite-size pieces

¾ pound christophene (chayote), peeled, cut into bite-size pieces, and cooked until just tender

Combine the shallots, wine, brandy, and curry powder in a saucepan, and reduce the mixture over medium heat to about ¾ cup. Strain the mixture, and return the liquid to the pan. Add the coconut cream and heavy cream. Reduce this mixture to 2½ cups over medium heat.

Season the sauce with salt, pepper, and cayenne. Add the lobster, asparagus, and christophene. Heat the curry, and serve it in lobster shells or on a bed of white rice.

Makes 6 servings

BIRDS OF PARADISE

BIRDS OF PARADISE

TRADE WINDS CHICKEN WITH PINEAPPLE SALSA

We've adapted this from a super salsa recipe given to us by one of our guests, Jaqueline Higuera McMahan, who has written three sizzling cookbooks, *California Rancho Cooking*, *Salsa*, and *The Red and Green Chile Book*. (All are published by The Olive Press, P.O. Box 194, Lake Hughes, California 93532.)

....

MARINADE:

3 garlic cloves, minced
1 teaspoon salt
¼ cup olive oil
1 tablespoon malt vinegar
1 teaspoon garlic powder
1 tablespoon paprika
2 tablespoons lime juice
1 packet Sazón seasoning (see page 4) or ½ teaspoon turmeric or 1 pinch saffron
Vegetable oil, for frying

....

4 chicken breast halves

....

PINEAPPLE SALSA:

2 cups diced fresh pineapple
½ peeled and diced christophene (chayote)
½ cup minced red onion
½ cup diced red bell pepper
1 jalapeño pepper, seeded and diced
2 teaspoons minced gingerroot
1 tablespoon raspberry vinegar
Salt to taste

....

GARNISH:

Cilantro sprigs

....

Purée all the marinade ingredients in a blender. Place the chicken in a baking pan, pour the marinade over, and marinate the chicken in the refrigerator overnight.

To make the pineapple salsa, combine all the ingredients, and taste. You might like to add some chopped fresh cilantro or more peppers.

Preheat the oven to 400°. Bake the marinated chicken for 30 to 40 minutes, until its juices run clear.

Remove the pan from the oven, and let the chicken cook in its marinade.

Just before serving time, drain the chicken well, and fry it for 3 minutes in ⅛ inch of oil.

Serve each chicken piece with a dollop of pineapple salsa (on the top or side) and a sprig of fresh cilantro.

Makes 4 servings

ISLAND CHICKEN

These make-ahead stuffed roast chicken breasts with honey-sesame glaze are a great dish for entertaining.

....

6 boned chicken breast halves, with
  their skins on, patted dry
Salt and pepper to taste
2 slices firm white bread
¼ cup heavy cream
1 small onion, minced
12 fresh water chestnuts, coarsely
  chopped
¼ pound ground beef
¼ pound ground pork
1 egg
1 tablespoon soy sauce
½ teaspoon finely minced peeled
  gingerroot
1 teaspoon salt
2 tablespoons vegetable oil
2 tablespoons honey
Sesame seeds

....

Preheat the oven to 325°. Sprinkle the chicken pieces with salt and pepper. Soak the bread in the cream for 5 minutes, then break the bread into small pieces. Put the pieces into a bowl with the onion, water chestnuts, beef, pork, egg, soy sauce, ginger, and salt. Stir the ingredients together until they are well combined.

Put one-sixth of the stuffing on the skinless side of each chicken piece. Fold the ends of the chicken over the stuffing, and secure them with toothpicks. Place the chicken pieces in a baking dish, and brush them with the oil. Bake them for 45 minutes or until the meat is tender.

Brush the chicken with honey, and sprinkle it with sesame seeds. At this point you can refrigerate the chicken, if you like, for later use.

Preheat the oven to 425°. Bake the chicken for 10 minutes, until the tops are brown and crisp. Remove the toothpicks before serving.

Makes 6 servings

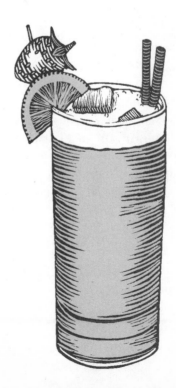

CHICKEN BREASTS ENSALADA

Crisp and crunchy cornmeal-crusted chicken breasts are topped by a colorful vegetable relish that is almost like a salad. This vivid dish is great for a special lunch or dinner.

....

SALAD:

    3 tomatoes, halved and squeezed to
        remove seeds and juice, then
        diced
    3 green onions (all of the white
        parts and some of the green),
        chopped
    2 garlic cloves, minced
    ½ cup olive oil
    Salt and pepper to taste
    2 tablespoons lemon juice
    1 teaspoon sugar
    2 cups chopped fresh basil (or a
        mixture of basil and parsley,
        arugula and parsley, or basil and
        spinach)
    24 Niçoise or Kalamata olives,
        pitted

....

    2 cups stone-ground cornmeal
    2 teaspoons salt
    ½ teaspoon ground black pepper
    ½ teaspoon chili powder
    ¼ teaspoon cayenne
    3 eggs, lightly beaten

    1 tablespoon water
    3 boned, skinned whole chicken
        breasts
    Olive oil, for frying

....

Put the tomatoes into a nonreactive bowl. Add the green onions, garlic, and olive oil, and stir. Season with salt and pepper, and stir in the lemon juice and sugar. Let the mixture stand, loosely covered, in a warm spot for several hours.

Chop the basil, spinach, or arugula into slivers; mince the parsley, if you're using it. Toss the greens with the tomato dressing, coating them well. Stir in the pitted olives. Set the salad aside.

Combine the cornmeal, salt, pepper, chili powder, and cayenne in a shallow bowl, and stir to mix the contents well. In another bowl, stir together the eggs and water.

Cut each chicken breast in half along the breastbone line. Pound each breast half thin between layers of waxed paper. Heat ⅛ inch olive oil in a large, heavy skillet. Dredge the chicken breast halves in cornmeal, then dip them into the egg mixture and again in the cornmeal. Fry the chicken pieces, turning them once, just until they are cooked through, about 2 to 3 minutes.

To serve, place the chicken on plates, and top each portion with some of the salad mixture.

Makes 6 servings

ISLAND STYLE: TRINIDAD AND TOBAGO

Trinidad, just seven miles off the South American coast, owes its cosmopolitan culture and eclectic cuisine to the mixture of people who have made this island their home. Trinidadians are descended from African slaves, Portuguese and Syrian merchants and sailors, East Indian sugar workers, English and Irish settlers, Arawak Indians, French planters, Chinese shopkeepers, and Spanish privateers. They mixed, they mingled, and they all contributed something to the savory stew that is Trinidad.

Whereas other islands have carnivals, Trinidad and Tobago have Carnival. This season begins in January and continues for six weeks, until the frenzy at dawn on J'ouvert Monday begins two days of utter chaos and celebration. For this occasion calypsonians work all year on new songs, while designers at a fever pitch of creativity come up with eye-snapping costumes for the marching groups, and steel drum bands practice the music that was invented on this island. Although the biggest festivities are in January and February, it seems that whenever you are in Trinidad everyone is planning for a new fête or recovering from one just completed.

If Trinidad is the island of worldly pleasure, then Tobago is her innocent sister. This small island, governmentally yoked with Trinidad, enjoyed wealth and luxury when sugar was king. "Great houses" dotted the island, and in London wealthy men were described as being "as rich as a Tobago planter."

The island's economy collapsed in the late nineteenth century, when the ruling sugar monopoly declared bankruptcy, and never since then has the island enjoyed such opulent days. Today Tobago lures nature lovers with its secluded beaches and forests of breadfruit, mango, cacao, and citrus.

Trinidad, and especially Port of Spain, the island's largest city, provides a bounty of eating experiences, probably the most eclectic in all the Caribbean. Indian flavors abound in dishes such as the curry-filled roti. Chinese cooks put a uniquely Trinidadian spin on their ancient cuisine with sultry spices and local vegetables.

It would be almost impossible to go hungry in Trinidad, where the roadside is dotted with clean, well-run stalls selling portable food. Here take-out is a passion, and the variety of foods-to-go is intriguing. We like to dip our spoons into callaloo, a swampy green soup popular throughout the Caribbean but especially loved here, where it is made with spinach-like dasheen leaves and flavored with crab or pork, okra, and coconut. Even the names of local dishes are enough to whet your appetite. Who could resist coocoo, steamed breadfruit and cornmeal pudding served with a topping of steamed fish? On our visit we skipped the tatoo (wild armadillo) and manicou (opossum) both of which often find their way into the stewpot here, but we happily ate cascadura, a local fish said to guarantee that those who eat it will return to Trinidad.

CHICKEN SHAPES AND SIZES

....

Selecting the proper chicken for whatever dish you're making will assure success.

....

BROILER-FRYER: *Ranges in weight from 1 to 3½ pounds. Although this bird is best for broiling or frying, a large one makes a good roaster, too.*
CAPON: *A male bird, desexed in its infancy so it will grow into a tender, meaty morsel for your table. Weights range from 4 to 8 pounds. Delicious roasted.*
ROASTER: *Larger than the broiler-fryer, it ranges in weight from 4 to 5 pounds.*
STEWING CHICKEN: *These birds range in weight from 3 to 5 pounds. Because of their . . . well, to put it politely, their maturity, they are best slowly braised until they are tender.*

CARAMBOLA-GLAZED BARBECUED CHICKEN

Carambola is also known as "star fruit," because its five wings create a star shape when it is sliced crosswise. We have carambola trees at the hotel and at our home, and we love the fruit's golden yellow, glossy skin and juicy, slightly citrus-like flesh. Carambola makes a wonderful garnish for fruit salads, desserts, and drinks. In this recipe it flavors a handsome glaze for grilled chicken.

....

2 3- to 3½-pound chickens, quartered
1 cup vegetable oil
¾ cup white wine vinegar
½ cup dry sherry
1 teaspoon minced garlic
½ teaspoon poultry seasoning
2 teaspoons Caribbean seasoning (see page 29)
2 carambolas, sliced
¼ cup lime juice
¼ cup honey
2 tablespoons white wine vinegar
1 tablespoon soy sauce
1 tablespoon minced garlic
1 dash hot pepper sauce

....

GARNISH:
3 to 4 carambolas, sliced

....

Place the chicken quarters in a shallow dish. In a bowl, stir together the oil, vinegar, sherry, garlic, and poultry seasoning, and 1 teaspoon of the Caribbean seasoning. Pour off 1 cup of this mixture, and set it aside. Pour the remaining mixture over the chicken. Cover the chicken, and refrigerate it for 2 to 3 hours.

Prepare a fire for grilling.

Put the carambolas into a blender or food processor. Add the lime juice, honey, vinegar, soy sauce, garlic, hot pepper sauce, and remaining 1 teaspoon Caribbean seasoning. Whirl until the mixture is smooth, stopping to scrape down the sides. Blend in the reserved marinade.

Grill the chicken over medium coals for about 30 minutes, turning it occasionally and basting with the carambola mixture after each turn. The chicken is done when it reaches 170° to 175° on a meat thermometer. Remove it from the heat, and allow it to stand for 10 minutes before serving.

Makes 6 to 8 servings

GRILLED CHICKEN BREASTS WITH PAPAYA-CILANTRO VINAIGRETTE

The clear, fresh flavor of this fruit sauce is a perfect counterpoint to the grilled chicken.

....

½ cup vegetable oil
¼ cup lime juice
1 teaspoon Caribbean seasoning (see page 29)
6 boned and skinned chicken breast halves

....

PAPAYA-CILANTRO VINAIGRETTE:
2 papayas, peeled and cut in chunks
2 green onions, trimmed and cut in 1-inch pieces
½ cup rice wine vinegar
2 teaspoons sesame oil
½ teaspoon ground black pepper

....

GARNISH:
Lime wedges

....

Combine the oil, lime juice, and Caribbean seasoning in a dish large enough to hold all the chicken in a single layer. Turn the mixture to coat the meat. Cover the dish with plastic wrap, and marinate the chicken in the refrigerator for 30 minutes.

Prepare a charcoal fire for grilling.

Drain the chicken well, and grill it 3 to 4 minutes on each side, until its juices run clear. While the chicken is cooking, put the ingredients for the papaya-cilantro vinaigrette into a food processor or blender. Whirl until the mixture is smooth and creamy. Spoon the sauce on the cooked chicken breasts, garnish with lime wedges, and serve.

Makes 6 servings

Chicken Breasts with Spinach Mousse and Pinot Noir Sauce

You can take the cooks out of California, but you can't take California out of the cooks. Occasionally we celebrate our roots by creating a recipe that honors the food and wine of our native state.

....

6 boned and skinned chicken breast
   halves
1 bunch spinach, blanched, drained,
   and squeezed to remove excess
   moisture
2 egg whites
1 pinch nutmeg
Salt and pepper to taste
¼ cup heavy cream
¼ cup toasted pine nuts

....

SAUCE:
1 cup pinot noir wine
2 bay leaves
1 tablespoon chopped shallots
4 whole black peppercorns
1 cup rich chicken broth
¼ cup butter
Salt and pepper to taste

....

Preheat the oven to 400°. Trim four of the chicken pieces, and pound them lightly between layers of waxed paper to an even thickness. Refrigerate them.

Cut the two remaining chicken breast halves into 1-inch cubes. In a food processor, chop the cubes fine. Add the spinach, and process 30 seconds. Add the egg whites, nutmeg, salt, and pepper, and process another 30 seconds. Add the cream, and process about 1 to 2 minutes, until the mousse is light yet firm in consistency. Fold in the toasted pine nuts, and adjust the seasonings.

Place the chicken breast halves on individual pieces of buttered foil. Spread a thin layer of mousse on each breast half, and roll the meat around the mousse. Tightly wrap the rolled chicken in the foil, and crimp the ends to seal them. Bake the chicken for 15 to 20 minutes, until the center reaches 140° and the chicken is firm and not spongy to the touch.

While the chicken bakes, make the sauce. Combine the wine with the bay leaves, shallots, and peppercorns in a saucepan. Boil the mixture to reduce it by three-quarters. Add the chicken stock, and reduce the mixture to 1 cup. Whisk in the butter, strain the sauce, and season it with salt and pepper. Keep the sauce warm.

Remove the chicken from the oven, and allow it to rest 5 minutes. Remove the foil, and slice each breast half into five pieces. Spoon a small pool of pinot noir sauce onto each plate, and fan the chicken slices on top. Serve immediately.

Makes 4 servings

CHIC WINE CHOICES

Whereas most meats dominate the flavor of a dish, chicken tends to defer to the tastes that accompany it. Because of this, it's important to consider the seasonings and preparation of any poultry dish when choosing a wine.

Creamy ingredients are often best set off by a fruity white, whereas a chicken dish seasoned with only a few light herbs suggests a light white wine. Tomato sauce or other robust sauces go well with red wine.

We've enjoyed roast turkey with a bottle of richly rounded chardonnay, but have been equally pleased on other occasions to escort the holiday bird with a light red wine. The richness of duck is enhanced by a tart young cabernet or zinfandel, whereas game birds are perfectly matched with a silky old burgundy, cabernet, or pinot noir.

GRILLED CHICKEN BREASTS WITH GAZPACHO SALSA

Salsamania seems to have taken over the world. Everyone loves the bright colors and flashy flavors of these sensational side dishes. This one takes its inspiration from the cold soup that is a favorite on all the Spanish islands of the Caribbean.

SALSA:
> 2 tablespoons olive oil
> 1 garlic clove, finely minced
> 1 tablespoon red wine vinegar
> 2 tablespoons water
> ¼ teaspoon ground cumin
> Hot pepper sauce to taste
> 1 slice firm white bread, crust removed, torn into pieces
> 2 tomatoes, seeded and finely chopped
> ½ cup peeled, seeded, and chopped cucumber
> ½ cup chopped green bell pepper
> ¼ cup chopped red onion
> 2 tablespoons chopped cilantro or parsley
> Salt and pepper to taste

> 4 boned whole chicken breasts, with their skins on
> Olive oil
> Salt and pepper to taste

Prepare a fire for grilling.

To make the salsa, put the olive oil, garlic, vinegar, water, cumin, hot sauce, and bread, and half the chopped tomatoes, into a blender or food processor. Blend the contents until smooth, and scoop them into a bowl. Stir in the remaining tomatoes, and the cucumber, pepper, onion, and cilantro or parsley. Season the mixture with salt and pepper. Cover the salsa, and refrigerate it.

Brush the chicken with olive oil, and season it with salt and pepper. Grill the chicken about 5 minutes on each side, or until it is cooked through. Cut the chicken diagonally into 1-inch slices, and serve them hot with the gazpacho salsa.

Makes 4 servings

Chicken and Papaya Stir-Fry

We once asked one of the Sugar Mill's kitchen staff to tell us about typical dishes from her island of Trinidad. We were amazed when one of the dishes she mentioned was chow mein. Caribbean chow mein? It was only later that we learned that on many islands the cuisine has been influenced by Chinese immigration. This dish uses island ingredients, but the stir-fry technique is strictly Chinese.

....

2 tablespoons vegetable oil
1 onion, chopped
1 garlic clove, minced
1 tablespoon minced peeled
  gingerroot
1 red bell pepper, chopped
1 yellow, orange, or green pepper,
  chopped

2½ pounds boned, skinned chicken
  breasts, cut into 1-inch cubes
1 teaspoon salt
¼ teaspoon ground black pepper
½ teaspoon cayenne
1 teaspoon paprika
¼ cup minced parsley
1 teaspoon white wine vinegar
¼ teaspoon ground cumin
1 cup 1-inch papaya cubes

....

In a wok or large skillet, heat 1 tablespoon oil over medium-high heat. Add the onion, garlic, ginger, and peppers, and stir-fry for 3 to 4 minutes, or just until the peppers and onion are tender. Remove the vegetables with a slotted spoon, and set them aside.

Add the remaining 1 tablespoon oil to the pan. Add the chicken and all of the remaining ingredients except the papaya. Stir-fry until the chicken is cooked through and lightly browned. Add the vegetables and papaya, and continue to stir-fry for 3 minutes. Serve the mixture over hot white rice.

Makes 6 servings

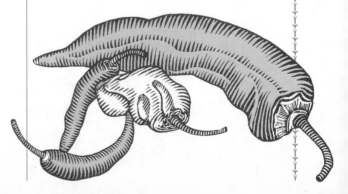

CHICHARRONE DE POLLO

In this Puerto Rican dish, chicken is marinated with a bouquet of seasonings, then baked and fried for a deeply flavored, crisp skin.

....

MARINADE:
   ¼ cup minced garlic
   1 tablespoon salt
   4 tablespoons garlic powder
   2 tablespoons onion powder
   2 tablespoons ground black pepper
   2 tablespoons dried oregano
   ¼ cup paprika
   ¼ cup ground coriander
   ¼ cup Sazón seasoning (see page 4)
      or ½ teaspoon turmeric or 1 pinch
      saffron
   1 cup olive oil
   ½ cup white vinegar
   1 cup chicken broth
   1½ cups lime juice

....

   5 to 6 pounds chicken legs and thighs
   Vegetable oil, for deep frying

....

In a blender or food processor, purée all the marinade ingredients to make a thin paste. Pour the marinade over the chicken, cover the chicken, and refrigerate it for 2 to 12 hours.

Preheat the oven to 400°.

Put the marinated chicken into a lightly greased baking pan, and bake the chicken, uncovered, for 30 minutes, turning and basting it halfway through the cooking. (At this point you can refrigerate the chicken for later use. Bring it to room temperature before proceeding.)

Heat the oil to 350° in a large, heavy pot. Deep-fry the chicken pieces, a few at a time, for about 3 minutes, or until they are golden. Serve them hot.

Makes 8 servings

ROAST CHICKEN WITH POACHED GARLIC

Don't be frightened of the garlic—the poaching tames it.

....

   6 chicken quarters (legs and thighs)
   1 garlic head (about 25 cloves)
   ⅓ cup butter
   1 tablespoon crumbled rosemary
   Salt and pepper to taste
   ½ cup dry white wine
   1½ cups chicken broth
   ¼ cup lemon juice
   Salt and pepper to taste

....

Separate the garlic cloves, but do not peel them. Drop them into a small saucepan of boiling water, and simmer them 2 to 3 minutes. Drain them, and slip off their skins. Set the peeled garlic aside.

Preheat the oven to 425°. Melt the butter in a roasting pan. Roll the chicken pieces in the butter, and arrange them in the pan. Sprinkle them with the rosemary, salt, and pepper. Roast the chicken 15 minutes.

Turn the chicken pieces over, and scatter the garlic on top. Baste with the butter in the pan. Continue roasting the chicken until it is golden, about 30 minutes.

Remove the chicken to warm plates, reserving the garlic. Pour off the fat from the roasting pan. Add the wine to the pan, and bring it to a boil on the stove top, stirring in the reserved garlic and scraping up any browned bits. When most of the wine has evaporated, add the stock and lemon juice, and boil rapidly until the sauce thickens slightly. Season it with salt and pepper. Pour some of the sauce and distribute some of the garlic cloves over each serving of chicken.

Makes 6 servings

CHICKEN CURRY

This is a gentle curry, suitable for those who aren't great fans of rambunctious seasoning.

. . . .

⅓ cup butter
2 onions, chopped
2 garlic cloves, minced

2 tablespoons minced peeled gingerroot
About 2 tablespoons curry powder, to taste
¼ cup flour
4 cups rich chicken broth
2 cups coconut milk (see page 44)
3 whole boned chicken breasts, poached and cut into 1-inch cubes
2 apples peeled, cored, and cut into chunks
Salt and pepper to taste

. . . .

CONDIMENTS:
Chopped bananas
Toasted fresh coconut (see page 69)
Chopped green onions
Crumbled cooked bacon
Chopped tomatoes
Yogurt with chopped cucumbers
Chopped peanuts
Chutney

. . . .

Heat the butter in a skillet. Sauté the onions, garlic, and ginger. Stir in the curry powder and flour, and cook gently, stirring constantly, for 5 minutes. Add the chicken broth and coconut milk, and cook, stirring constantly, until the mixture thickens (5 to 10 minutes). Strain it.

Add the chicken and apples to the curry sauce, and cook them gently until the chicken is heated through. Serve the curry on rice, accompanied by the condiments.

Makes 6 servings

Some Like It Hot!

There are those who believe no curry is worth the name unless it singes the taste buds and brings tears to the eyes. They gleefully trade stories about a curry in Trinidad that ate through a wooden bowl, or a dish in Delhi that melted their molars. To have lived through the experience at all, they imply, suggests a superhuman achievement.

Curries such as this exist, it's true, and once or twice we've been victims of such culinary arson. But the curries we've most enjoyed were much subtler, with a sophisticated balance of complex flavors.

The British, when introduced to the exotic and sophisticated dishes of India during the three centuries of the Raj, managed to reduce them to a single preparation: a virulent yellow sauce that flowed like the Ganges over sordid bits of gristled mutton. And that, for some people, is still what comes to mind when curry is mentioned.

Curry's BTU level varies with geography. The hottest curries are found in torrid climes, but even these curries are mellow and balanced, with no single flavor predominating.

Curry first arrived on the shores of Trinidad with the Indians who came there to live. From Trinidad this sultry sauce has made its way through the islands, changing and evolving along the way, but always served with a delicious chutney, which is often made from the juicy mangoes that are piled in local fruit stands each summer.

Garden Roasted Chicken

Stuffed under the skin of this roast chicken are vegetables and herbs that flourish in Caribbean gardens, as well as goat cheese. When we saw goats roaming the hills of Tortola, our first thought was "Ah, chèvre!" No such luck. Our goats are used strictly for meat. We promised ourselves that we'd try to make our own chèvre, but so far that project remains fairly far down the list. Until we make our own, we'll just have to use imported cheese.

....

1 cup minced onions
3 tablespoons olive oil
1½ cups freshly grated vegetables
   (christophene, zucchini, eggplant,
   carrots, or a combination)
3 garlic cloves, minced
2 tablespoons minced fresh basil, or
   1 teaspoon dried basil
2 tablespoons minced chives or green
   onion tops
1 tablespoon minced fresh oregano,
   or ½ teaspoon dried oregano
½ teaspoon ground black pepper
Melted butter
8 ounces cream cheese
4 ounces chèvre or feta cheese
½ cup grated parmesan cheese
1 egg
1 egg yolk
1 whole roasting chicken

....

In a large skillet, sauté the onions in the oil over medium heat for about 5 minutes, until they are translucent. Add the grated vegetables, garlic, herbs, and pepper. Turn up the heat, and briskly toss the vegetables in the pan. Keeping the vegetables as dry as possible, cook them just until they are tender, about 5 to 10 minutes. Remove the vegetables to a strainer, and allow them to drain for about 1 hour. Press them to remove any remaining liquid.

Combine the cheeses, egg, and egg yolk in a mixing bowl, and beat them together. Add the vegetable mixture to the cheese mixture, and blend thoroughly. Refrigerate the vegetable-cheese mixture 1 to 24 hours.

Remove the giblets, liver, and extra fat from the chicken's cavity, and wash the bird. Using your hands, gently separate the skin from the flesh of the breast, thighs, and legs. Put the stuffing mixture into a pastry bag fitted with a large round tube, and insert the stuffing by placing the point under the skin. Stuff the breast, thighs, and legs, but not the wings. Place the chicken in a roasting pan skin side up. (If you like, you can refrigerate the chicken at this point for later roasting.)

Preheat the oven to 375°.

Bake the chicken for 1 hour and 10 minutes, basting often with the melted butter.

Remove the pan from the oven, and allow the chicken to rest 3 to 5 minutes before you slice it. With its crisp skin and savory stuffing, this bird needs no sauce.

Makes 6 servings

Rum-Glazed Roast Turkey Breast with Plantain and Mango Stuffing

Don't save this sumptuous dish just for holidays; it's a tasty treat any day of the year.

....

¼ *cup butter*
2 *ripe plantains (or 3 to 4 underripe bananas), sliced into ½-inch-thick rounds*
4 *slices firm white bread, crusts removed, cut into ½-inch cubes*
Juice and grated zest of 1 orange
Juice and grated zest of 1 lime
1 *cup chopped walnuts*
1 *mango, peeled and coarsely chopped, or 1 cup chopped drained canned mango*
2 *teaspoons salt*
1 *boned turkey breast*
Butter
Salt and pepper to taste

....

Rum Glaze:
> ¼ cup sugar
> ¼ cup lime juice
> 3 tablespoons dark rum

....

Melt the butter, and fry the plantains, turning them once, until they are golden. Reserve the melted butter, and chop the fried plantains coarsely. Combine the orange and lime juices, and soak the bread in this mixture. Mix the butter, plantains, soaked bread, any remaining juice, walnuts, mango, and seasonings. If the mixture is too dry, add more citrus juice. If the mixture seems too loose, add fresh bread crumbs or ground walnuts.

Preheat the oven to 350°. Spread the turkey breast skin side down on your work surface, and cover the breast with the stuffing mixture. Roll up the breast, and tie it securely with string to ensure the stuffing does not escape. Stick skewers in each end of the roll for good measure. Dot the roll with butter, and sprinkle it with salt and pepper. Put the turkey into a baking pan, and put the pan into the hot oven.

Mix the sugar, lemon juice, and rum, and stir until the sugar is dissolved. After the meat has cooked for 1 hour, spoon on the glaze. Cook the turkey until it reaches 170°, basting with the pan juices every 15 minutes. The glaze should become thick and the roast a glossy brown. Remove the pan from the oven, and allow the meat to rest for 10 to 15 minutes before slicing it.

TURKEY TIPS

....

- ◆ An ideal turkey for roasting is about 10 pounds. It will serve 12 people.
- ◆ Use dental floss instead of thread to sew up a stuffed turkey. Floss holds better and won't tear the skin.
- ◆ Thick rubber gloves make it easy to pick up or turn a turkey in the roasting pan.
- ◆ You can broil a young turkey just as you would a chicken. Since turkey has less fat, though, you should oil it well and baste it frequently. Use medium heat, and plan to cook it for a longer time. Add a few tablespoons of water to the broiler pan after you turn the turkey to help keep the meat from scorching.

CORNISH GAME HENS WITH MANGO-CURRY BUTTER

As chutney aficionados know, mangoes and curry are a great combination. Spreading the mango-curry butter under the skin of the birds perfumes the flesh beautifully.

Mango-curry butter can be made several days ahead and refrigerated; return it to room temperature before you use it. Extra butter freezes well, and is delicious spread on hot grilled fish or grilled chicken breasts.

....

MANGO-CURRY BUTTER:

> 1 cup cold butter, cut into cubes
> 2 tablespoons grated lemon zest
> 2 tablespoons grated orange zest
> 1 shallot, minced
> 1 tablespoon minced garlic
> About 1 tablespoon curry powder
> 2 tablespoons unsweetened orange
>   juice concentrate
> 1 cup fresh or canned and drained
>   mango flesh

....

> 4 Cornish game hens
> 2 tablespoons softened butter

....

Put all of the ingredients for the mango-curry butter into a food processor. Whirl until the mixture is smooth. Spoon it into a container, and refrigerate it until you're ready to use it.

Preheat the oven to 450°. Put the hens breast side up on your work surface. Gently loosen the skin over the flesh of each breast, starting at the neck end; take care not to tear the skin. With your hand or a small spatula, spread 2 tablespoons of the seasoned butter under the skin of each breast, and pat the skin back into place. Truss the hens. Spread the unseasoned butter over the skins.

Put the hens on a rack in a roasting pan, and place the pan in the preheated oven. Immediately reduce the heat to 350°, and roast the hens until their internal temperature reaches 175°, about 45 minutes. Serve them hot.

Makes 4 servings

TROPICAL CITRUS GAME HENS

The honey we use for this dish comes from the nearby island of Virgin Gorda, where the bees must feast on ambrosial tropical flowers. Different honeys will impart different flavors to this dish, so do a little experimenting.

....

> 6 Cornish game hens
> ⅔ cup honey
> 1 tablespoon grated lemon zest
> 1 tablespoon grated orange zest
> 1 tablespoon lemon juice
> 1 tablespoon Dijon mustard
> 1 teaspoon curry powder
> 1 teaspoon ground ginger
> 2 large unpeeled oranges, cut in half
>   lengthwise, then cut crosswise into
>   ¼-inch slices

....

Preheat the oven to 450°. Put the hens on a rack in a roasting pan.

In a small bowl, mix together the honey, lemon and orange zests, lemon juice, mustard, curry powder, and ginger. Brush half the mixture over the game hens. Tuck the orange slices around the birds. Put the pan in the preheated oven, and immediately reduce the heat to 350°.

After about 20 minutes, baste the hens with the remaining honey-spice mixture. Roast them until their internal temperature reaches 175°, about 45 minutes total. Serve them hot.

Makes 6 servings

HONEY-LIME DUCK

Deciding how many ducks to buy for a party is tricky. Will you need a quarter or half a duck for each guest? At the Sugar Mill we serve half a small duck per person. If you are using large birds (about 4½ to 5 pounds), you can cut them into quarters. If a quarter duck per person seems too little, cook an extra duck and add some slices from it to each plate.

This recipe is particularly nice because the ducks can be cooked ahead and finished at the last moment.

....

2 to 3 ducks
2 cups water
1 tablespoon minced peeled
 gingerroot
2 tablespoons butter
½ cup lime juice
½ cup honey
1 tablespoon soy sauce

....

GARNISH:
 Orange slices
 Lime slices

....

Preheat the oven to 375°. Remove extra fat from each duck's cavity. Place the birds on a rack in a roasting pan, and pour the water into the pan. Bake the ducks on their sides for 30 minutes, then turn them onto their opposite sides and bake them 30 minutes more. Place them breast side up, and bake them another 30 minutes.

Let the ducks cool, then cut them into quarters and return them to the roasting rack. About 15 minutes before serving, raise the oven heat to 450°. Sauté the ginger in the butter for 2 to 3 minutes, and add the lime juice, honey, and soy sauce. Bring the mixture to a boil. Spoon the honey-lime mixture over the ducks, and bake them until they are crisp and brown.

Spoon a little of the liquid from the pan over each baked duck quarter, garnish with orange and lime slices, and serve.

Makes 6 servings

An Elegant Duck Dinner
....

CHILLED CUCUMBER SOUP

◆

ROASTED GINGER DUCK WITH
PORK-AND-ALMOND STUFFING

◆

SPINACH TIMBALES

◆

PLANTAIN CHIPS

◆

COLD AMARETTO SOUFFLÉ

MAHOGANY-GLAZED DUCK BREAST WITH SESAME-PEANUT NOODLES

This dish is another that reflects the Asian influence in the Caribbean. Duck breasts are becoming increasingly available in supermarkets these days, but if you can't find any you can substitute chicken breasts.

....

MARINADE:
½ cup soy sauce
½ cup ketchup
3 tablespoons honey
2 tablespoons vegetable oil
1 large garlic clove, minced
1 tablespoon crumbled dried rosemary

....

3 whole duck breasts, trimmed of excess fat
Lemon juice
Salt and pepper to taste
1 egg yolk
¼ cup sesame oil
¼ cup vegetable oil
2 tablespoons soy sauce
½ teaspoon finely minced garlic
2 tablespoons peanut butter, at room temperature
1 teaspoon chile oil (available in Asian markets)

8 ounces fine noodles, cooked and drained

....

GARNISH:
Minced green onion tops or chives
Chopped peanuts

....

Combine all the marinade ingredients in a bowl. Sprinkle the duck breasts with lemon juice and salt and pepper, and marinate the breasts for 1 to 2 hours.

Preheat the oven to 450°. Remove the breasts from the marinade, and reserve it. Put the breasts on a rack in a roasting pan, and roast them 15 minutes.

Remove the breasts from the oven, and reduce the oven temperature to 300°. Trim the fat from the breasts, and paint them with the marinade. Cook them 10 minutes more.

While the duck breasts cook, put the egg yolk into a blender or food processor, and, with the machine running, slowly add the sesame and vegetable oils. Add the soy sauce, garlic, peanut butter, and chile oil. Process the contents until they are thoroughly combined. Combine some of the sesame-oil mixture with the hot cooked noodles. (Extra sesame mixture makes a delicious dip or sauce for vegetables.)

To serve, place a bed of noodles on a warm plate, cut the duck breasts in thin diagonal slices, and fan the slices on the noodles. Sprinkle with green onions or chives and peanuts, and serve.

Makes 6 servings

LOVELY WEATHER FOR DUCK

Through the ages, duck, both wild and tame, has been a cause for celebration at the table. The Egyptians salted and dried ducks so they could be assured of a constant supply. To domesticate the birds, the Romans put eggs from wild duck nests under setting hens. When hatched, the lucky ducklings were fed on figs and dates to sweeten their flesh.

It was the Chinese, always clever about things gustatory, who brought these web-footed wonders out of the wild. The Japanese prefer semi-wild birds, and keep them in pens covered with netting to prevent them from escaping.

The ducks most of us eat are grown on Long Island and are all descended from three ducks and a drake brought from China in the late eighteenth century.

ROASTED GINGER DUCK WITH PORK-AND-ALMOND STUFFING

The Spanish introduced ginger to the islands from the Far East in the sixteenth century. Ginger has been grown here ever since, and it turns up in everything from cakes and cookies to ginger beer.

....

MARINADE:
>   4 ounces gingerroot, chopped or
>   grated
>   ¼ cup finely chopped garlic
>   ½ cup honey
>   2½ cups soy sauce
>   ¼ cup sesame oil
>   3 whole 4-pound ducks

....

STUFFING:
>   1 pound trimmed boneless pork
>   6 ounces almonds, lightly toasted
>   and minced
>   2 tablespoons chopped green
>   onion
>   2 teaspoons chopped garlic
>   ¼ cup honey
>   2 teaspoons chopped gingerroot
>   Salt and pepper to taste
>   4 eggs, beaten
>   ½ cup heavy cream
>   2 cups dry bread crumbs

....

Whisk together the marinade ingredients, and marinate the ducks for 24 hours.

Mix together all the stuffing ingredients except the cream and bread crumbs. Run the mixture through a meat grinder, using the fine die, or whirl the mixture in a food processor. Put the mixture into a bowl, and stir in the heavy cream and bread crumbs.

Preheat the oven to 375°. Fill the

ducks' cavities with the stuffing, and sew up the openings. Place the ducks on racks in roasting pans. Roast the ducks for 1 hour, skimming off fat as necessary.

Makes 6 servings

GRILLED QUAIL WITH MANGO-PAPAYA SAUCE

When one of our suppliers called with word that he could get quail for us, we were delighted. We wanted to give these little birds a Caribbean interpretation, so we paired them with a tropical fruit sauce.

. . . .

12 boned quail or 6 Cornish game
   hens

. . . .

MARINADE:
   1 cup vegetable oil
   ¼ cup sherry vinegar or cider
      vinegar
   ¼ cup orange juice
   1 garlic clove, minced
   1 tablespoon minced fresh tarragon,
      or 1 teaspoon dried tarragon
   1 tablespoon minced fresh basil, or
      1 teaspoon dried basil
   Salt and pepper to taste

. . . .

SAUCE:
   1 large mango, peeled and minced
   1 large papaya, peeled and minced
   1 teaspoon hot red pepper flakes
   ½ jalapeño pepper, seeded and
      minced
   Juice of 2 limes
   Salt and pepper to taste

. . . .

Whisk together all the marinade ingredients in a bowl, and marinate the quail or game hens for 2 to 3 hours at room temperature or overnight in the refrigerator.

Prepare a fire for grilling.

Grill the quail or game hens for 3 to 6 minutes on each side, until they are done to your liking.

While the birds cook, stir together all the sauce ingredients. Serve the sauce cold with the hot birds.

Makes 6 servings

TROPICAL
MEAT
WAVES

TROPICAL MEAT WAVES

FILET OF BEEF WITH WALNUT AND PORT STUFFING

This special-occasion dish was inspired by the British heritage of our island. In England you'd expect to enjoy walnuts and port after dinner, but we like them as part of the main course.

....

WALNUT STUFFING:
2 tablespoons butter
¼ cup minced onion
¼ cup minced walnuts
1 egg, beaten
½ bunch parsley, minced
1 teaspoon finely grated orange zest
2 tablespoons port
About ⅓ to ½ cup soft bread crumbs

....

1½ pound fillet of beef
Dijon mustard
Salt and pepper to taste
Melted butter, for basting

....

To make the stuffing, melt the butter in a skillet, and sauté the onions until they are limp. Remove the pan from the heat, and add the walnuts, beaten egg, parsley, orange zest, and port. Stir in enough bread crumbs to make the mixture hold together.

Preheat the oven to 500°. Cut any fat and sinew from the fillet with a sharp knife. Cut a horizontal slit about halfway through the fillet. Rub the in-side and outside of the fillet with a little Dijon mustard, and season with salt and pepper. Fill the fillet with the stuffing, and tie the fillet with string to retain its shape.

Roast the meat for about 25 minutes, basting every few minutes with the melted butter. For a very rare fillet, the temperature should reach 120°.

Remove the fillet from the oven, and allow it to rest 5 minutes. Serve it in ½-inch-thick slices.

Makes 6 servings

ROAST PRIME RIB WITH CRACKED PEPPER CRUST

In the British Caribbean, old traditions die hard, and one of these is roast beef and Yorkshire pudding. It may seem strange in a tropical clime to tuck into a huge meal more appropriate to a foggy day in London, but expatriots cling so tenaciously to old home ties that roast beef remains a favorite in the British Virgin Islands. We've seasoned ours with some sassy peppercorns to give it a Caribbean kick.

....

1 8- to 9-pound beef rib roast with bones
3 tablespoons Dijon mustard
1 tablespoon cracked black peppercorns

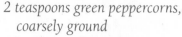

2 teaspoons green peppercorns,
    coarsely ground
1 teaspoon white peppercorns,
    coarsely ground
4 whole allspice, coarsely ground
½ teaspoon dried thyme
1 teaspoon salt

....

SAUCE:
1 cup dry red wine
4 cups beef broth
⅔ cup sherry
2 tablespoons cornstarch
¼ cup water
¼ cup Dijon mustard
Salt and pepper to taste

....

Preheat the oven to 425°. Place the beef in a roasting pan. Spread the mustard on the beef. Combine the peppers, allspice, thyme, and salt, and rub the seasonings into the beef. Roast the beef for 45 minutes.

Cover the beef loosely with foil, and continue roasting it until a meat thermometer inserted straight down from the top into the center registers 125° (for rare meat), about 1 hour. Remove the pan from the oven, and let the roast stand for 30 minutes before carving it.

To make the sauce, skim the fat from the pan juices, add the red wine, and deglaze the pan over medium heat, scraping up the brown bits. Boil the liquid until it is reduced by half, and transfer it to a saucepan. Add the broth and sherry, and boil the mixture 5 min-

utes. In a small bowl, stir together the cornstarch and ¼ cup water. Add this mixture to the pan, whisking to prevent lumps. Bring the sauce to a boil, and boil it for 1 minute. Season it with salt and pepper, and remove it from the heat.

Spoon a little sauce over each serving of meat. Serve the roast with Creole Horseradish Cream with Pecans (recipe follows).

Makes 8 servings

CREOLE HORSERADISH CREAM WITH PECANS

....

1 cup sour cream
¼ cup prepared horseradish
2 tablespoons white wine vinegar
4 teaspoons Creole-style or other
    grainy mustard
½ teaspoon sugar
Salt and pepper to taste
1 cup heavy cream
⅓ cup minced pecans, toasted 8 to 10
    minutes in a 350° oven

....

Stir together the sour cream, horseradish, vinegar, mustard, sugar, salt, and pepper in a large bowl. Refrigerate the mixture for at least 2 hours.

Just before serving, beat the cream to soft peaks. Whisk the sour cream mixture to soften it, then fold in the whipped cream and toasted pecans. Serve the horseradish cream with sliced roast beef.

Makes about 3 cups

CHRISTOPHENE AND SAUSAGE-FILLED FLANK STEAK

If you can't find christophene, zucchini makes an excellent substitute.

....

1 2- to 3-pound flank steak

....

MARINADE:
1 garlic clove, minced
2 tablespoons red wine vinegar
1 tablespoon Dijon mustard
¾ cup vegetable oil
1 teaspoon ground black pepper
½ teaspoon ground nutmeg

....

CHRISTOPHENE FILLING:
½ pound Italian sausage meat
(remove any casing)
1 large onion, chopped
1½ cups grated christophene
(chayote)
½ teaspoon salt
1 egg, lightly beaten

½ cup soft bread crumbs
¼ cup slivered almonds

....

GARNISH
Parsley sprigs
Cherry tomatoes

....

Score the steak, and pound it slightly. Mix together the marinade ingredients. Place the steak in a shallow dish, and cover it with the marinade. Allow the meat to marinate in the refrigerator for at least 4 hours, turning it often.

To make the filling, put the christophene in a sieve, and lightly salt it. Allow it to stand for about 20 minutes, and then squeeze it to remove excess moisture.

In a large skillet, cook the sausage meat over medium-low heat, stirring occasionally, for 5 to 6 minutes. Pour off all but 1 tablespoon fat. Add the onion, and sauté another 5 minutes. Remove the skillet from the heat, and add the salt, egg, bread crumbs, almonds, and 3 tablespoons of the steak marinade.

Preheat the oven to 450°. Remove the steak from the marinade, reserving the remaining marinade. Place the steak on a large cutting board. With a sharp knife, split the meat horizontally from a long side, leaving about ½ inch at the opposite edge intact. Open the steak as you would a book. Place the steak between two layers of plastic wrap, and pound it with the flat side of a mallet to a uniform thickness.

Spread the christophene filling to within 1 inch of each side. Roll the steak jelly-roll fashion, and tie it with string to secure it. Place the meat in a shallow roasting pan, and baste it with some of the marinade. Roast it, basting and turning it occasionally, 20 minutes for rare meat, 35 minutes for medium-rare.

Allow the meat to rest for 20 to 30 minutes before cutting it into ½-inch slices. Arrange the slices on a warm platter, and garnish them with parsley and cherry tomatoes.

Makes 6 servings

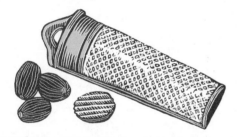

CHRISTOPHENE

Mirliton, chocho, xuxu, vegetable pear, chayote—this green, pear-shaped vegetable has as many names as a miscreant on the run. Increasingly available in the United States, it grows on a tropical vine that is related to the cucumber.

Christophene is a popular vegetable in the West Indies, and it can be used in almost all recipes that call for zucchini. When cut in julienne slices, christophene is a crisp punctuation for green salads.

BEEF IN COCONUT CREAM

We like to serve this dish on a deep-green bed of fresh spinach leaves that have been stir-fried briefly with oil, garlic, and minced ginger.

....

3 tablespoons vegetable oil
2 garlic cloves, minced
6 green onions, chopped
2 red, yellow, or orange bell peppers, cut into thin strips
½ teaspoon minced Scotch bonnet (or habanero) pepper, or other minced hot pepper to taste
2 pounds sirloin steak, sliced across the grain into ¼-inch strips
¼ cup minced fresh cilantro
¾ cup coconut cream (see page 44)
Salt and pepper to taste

....

GARNISH:
Thinly sliced red onions

....

Heat the oil in a skillet, and sauté the garlic, green onions, and peppers for 2 minutes. Add the meat and spices, and brown the meat over high heat. Add the cilantro and coconut cream, season with salt and pepper, and simmer for 5 to 7 minutes. Do not overcook the meat, or it will toughen. Garnish with sliced red onions, and serve.

HURRY CURRY

Most serious curry cooks prefer to create their own curry powders, mixing together different spices until the final product suits their tastes. Usually such mixtures include cumin, dried hot peppers, coriander, turmeric, ginger, and cardamon.

We've found the fresh-ground mixture produced by our own island spice shop, Sunny Caribbee, suits our taste perfectly and saves us a good deal of time in the kitchen. If you are interested in receiving Sunny Caribbee's catalog, which contains a selection of unusual island spices as well as items suitable as gifts, write or call—

Sunny Caribbee Spice Company
P.O. Box 286
Road Town, Tortola, BVI
809-494-2178

HER MAJESTY'S WEST INDIAN REGIMENTAL BEEF CURRY

We named this recipe for the West Indian troops who fought valiantly in World War II. It would have been "His Majesty" then, but we've updated the name in deference to the current queen.

....

5 pounds lean beef
¼ cup butter

1½ cups chopped onions
¼ cup minced peeled gingerroot
1 teaspoon sugar
1 tablespoon salt
¼ teaspoon ground black pepper
5 to 6 tablespoons curry powder
4 cups milk
1 cup coconut cream (see page 44)
1 cup grated fresh coconut (or dried
    coconut, soaked in milk for 15
    minutes, then drained)
1 cup lime juice
1 cup heavy cream

....

CONDIMENTS:
Chopped hard-boiled eggs
Chutney
Chopped tomatoes
Chopped roasted peanuts
Toasted coconut (see page 69)
Chopped green onions
Crumbled cooked bacon

....

Cut the beef into cubes, removing the fat and bones. Melt half the butter in a large, heavy pot. Add the onions and sauté them until they are tender, about 5 minutes. Remove them with a slotted spoon to a paper towel. Add the remaining butter to the pan, and brown the beef cubes. Return the onions to the pan, and add the ginger, sugar, salt, pepper, curry powder, and milk. Mix well. Cover the pot, and simmer the mixture over low heat 1 hour.

Add the coconut cream and grated coconut. Cover the pot, and cook the curry 5 minutes. Gradually stir in first the lime juice and then the cream. Simmer for 10 to 15 minutes or until the beef is tender. Serve the curry on fluffy rice with the condiments.

Makes 10 servings

TAMARIND AND ORANGE BRAISED BRISKET

Tamarind pods are about 3 to 6 inches long and contain large seeds surrounded by a thick date-like pulp. The pulp is used to make tamarind nectar, and is a principal ingredient in Worcestershire sauce. This tamarind-flavored brisket, delicious served hot or at room temperature, makes a great picnic dish when thinly sliced and served on lettuce, as a salad, or on crusty rolls.

Tamarind fruit-drink concentrate is available in many Caribbean, Indian, and Latin American markets.

. . . .

3 garlic cloves, minced
½ teaspoon ground cumin
½ teaspoon ground cloves
½ teaspoon minced Scotch bonnet (or habanero) pepper, or other hot pepper to taste
1 tablespoon fresh tamarind pulp, packaged tamarind paste,
tamarind fruit-drink concentrate, or 1 tablespoon prune juice plus 1 teaspoon Worcestershire sauce
Salt and pepper to taste
3 pounds beef brisket
2 tablespoons olive oil
2 cups beef stock
1 cup orange juice
1 onion, sliced
1 bay leaf

. . . .

GARNISH:
Watercress sprigs
Orange slices

. . . .

Make a paste by mixing together the garlic, cumin, cloves, hot pepper, and tamarind or prune juice and Worcestershire. Using the point of a sharp knife, cut slits all over the brisket, and stuff the paste into the holes.

Heat the olive oil in a large, heavy casserole or Dutch oven. Sprinkle the meat with salt and pepper, and brown it quickly on both sides in the hot oil. Drain off the oil, and add the beef stock, orange juice, onion, and bay leaf. Cover the pan, and cook the brisket over low heat for about 3 hours, or until the beef is tender. Skim off the fat. Slice the meat, and serve it garnished with watercress and orange slices.

Makes 8 to 10 servings

CARIBBEAN KEBOBS

Because it contains an enzyme capable of digesting protein, papaya is used as a meat tenderizer and as a digestive aid. Using papaya pulp in this marinade assures that your meat will be tender.

....

3 pounds beef, cut into 1½-inch cubes

....

MARINADE:
2 tablespoons peanut or other vegetable oil
2 onions, chopped
2 to 3 garlic cloves, chopped
½ cup puréed papaya or papaya nectar
3 tablespoons curry powder
3 tablespoons white wine vinegar
3 tablespoons brown sugar
Salt and pepper to taste

....

4 to 5 firm ripe bananas, or 3 to 4 ripe plantains, cut crosswise into 1-inch-thick rounds
18 1- to 1½-inch cubes fresh pineapple
18 1- to 1½-inch cubes fresh papaya

....

Heat the oil in a skillet, and sauté the onion and garlic over low heat until they are tender. Add the papaya purée or nectar, curry powder, vinegar, brown sugar, and salt and pepper, and mix well. Remove the skillet from the heat, and let the mixture cool. When the marinade is cool, put the meat into a shallow dish, and pour the marinade over. Marinate the meat for 4 to 8 hours.

Prepare a charcoal fire for grilling, or preheat the broiler. Drain and reserve the marinade. Thread the meat and fruit on skewers, and grill or broil them, basting often with the reserved marinade.

Remove the meat and fruit from the skewers, and serve them hot on a bed of fluffy rice.

Makes 6 servings

STEAKMANSHIP

*G*iving precise instructions for cooking steak is difficult, since broilers and grills differ widely, but a few general rules apply.

Be sure your steaks are at room temperature before you broil or grill them, and don't try to broil a steak that's less than 1 inch thick. Generally speaking, a boneless steak will take slightly longer to cook than one with a bone. A 1½-inch steak will take about 25 minutes (for rare meat) to 35 minutes (for well-done), but a meat thermometer will be your best guide.

You can marinate steak before cooking it or flavor it afterward with a seasoned butter such as the ones on these pages. Although steak is always special, you'll find it tastes even better when given this little extra attention.

STEAK BUTTERS

In the Sugar Mill dining room we never serve our steaks nude except by special request. We like to enhance them with butters and sauces in such intriguing flavors that even a devout meat-and-potatoes diner will appreciate them. By the way, all of these butters work equally well on hamburgers, and the Lemon Butter is delicious on grilled fish and on chicken breasts.

After you've mixed your butter, put it on a piece of waxed paper, and form the butter into a cylinder, wrapping it in the waxed paper. Refrigerate or freeze the butter until it is firm. When you are ready to serve, slice the butter into ½-inch rounds, and set one on top of each just-cooked steak.

Tarragon Butter

2 medium shallots, chopped
2 tablespoons chopped parsley
4 teaspoons tarragon vinegar
1 teaspoon dried tarragon
½ teaspoon ground pepper
½ cup chilled butter, cut into small
    pieces

. . . .

Combine the shallots, parsley, vinegar, tarragon, and pepper in a food processor, and mince them by turning the machine on and off several times. Add the butter, and blend well.

Blue Cheese–Mustard Butter

1 cup Madeira
3 tablespoons minced shallots
1½ cups heavy cream
¾ cup beef broth
¾ cup chilled butter, cut into pieces
8 ounces blue cheese
3 tablespoons Dijon mustard
Hot red pepper flakes

. . . .

Combine the Madeira and shallots in a heavy saucepan. Boil them over high heat until the liquid is reduced to 3 tablespoons. Add the cream and stock, and boil until the mixture is reduced to 1½ cups. Blend the butter, blue cheese, and mustard in a food processor. Whisk the butter mixture into the hot Madeira mixture about 2 tablespoons at a time. Simmer the mixture until it is creamy, about 3 minutes. Strain it, and season it with salt and hot red pepper flakes. Let the butter cool to room temperature, then spoon it onto your steaks.

Tomato-Basil Butter

1 cup chilled butter, cut into bits
¼ cup tomato paste
½ cup minced basil
2 teaspoons minced garlic
2 tablespoons grated lemon zest
Salt and pepper to taste

. . . .

Put all the ingredients into a food processor, and whirl them until they are well combined.

Spice Butter

½ cup chopped parsley, loosely
  packed
¼ cup drained capers
¼ cup chopped chives or green onion
  tops, loosely packed
1 teaspoon grated nutmeg
2 teaspoons grated lemon zest
1 teaspoon salt
½ teaspoon ground black pepper
1 cup chilled butter, cut into small
  pieces

. . . .

Put all the ingredients except the butter into a food processor, and whirl them until they are well minced. Add the butter, and continue processing until the mixture is smooth.

Lemon Butter

1 cup chilled butter, cut into small
  pieces
Juice of 2 lemons
1 teaspoon grated lemon zest
¼ teaspoon cayenne
1 teaspoon salt
½ teaspoon ground black pepper

. . . .

Blend all the ingredients, by hand or in a food processor.

Tournedos with Roasted Pepper Sauce and Avocado Butter

Avocados were once known around the Caribbean as "midshipman's butter" or "poor man's butter" because they are so abundant here in the islands. No one would ever call this a poor man's dish, however, although it takes advantage of our profusion of both avocados and peppers.

Roast the peppers over a grill, in a 450° oven, or over a gas flame until the skins blacken and blister. Put the peppers into a plastic bag, and refrigerate them for 30 minutes. Then peel off the peppers' skins.

. . . .

ROASTED RED PEPPER SAUCE:
  3 roasted and peeled red bell
    peppers
  2 shallots, minced
  ¼ cup tomato paste
  1 cup white wine
  ½ cup heavy cream
  1 teaspoon sugar
  Salt and pepper to taste

. . . .

AVOCADO BUTTER:
  ½ cup chilled butter, cut into small
    pieces
  1 tablespoon minced fresh oregano,
    or 1 teaspoon dried oregano

*1 tablespoon minced fresh basil, or 1
  teaspoon dried basil*
*1 teaspoon minced fresh thyme, or ¼
  teaspoon dried thyme*
2 teaspoons shallots
1 teaspoon lime juice
Salt and pepper to taste
½ cup cubed avocado
12 4-ounce beef fillets
Salt and pepper to taste

Prepare a fire for grilling.

Put the peppers into a saucepan with the shallots, tomato paste and white wine. Over high heat, reduce the mixture by half. Transfer the mixture to a blender or food processor, and purée it. Return it to the saucepan, and add the heavy cream, sugar, and salt and pepper. Boil the mixture until it is reduced to a sauce consistency.

To make the avocado butter, blend the butter with the herbs, shallots, and lime juice in a food processor until the contents are well combined. Add the avocado cubes, and continue processing until the mixture is smooth. Form the butter into a cylinder, wrap it in waxed paper, and refrigerate or freeze it until it is firm.

Season the meat with salt and pepper, and grill it until it is done to your taste. Spoon the sauce onto plates, place the tenderloins on top, and add slices of avocado butter. Serve immediately.

Makes 6 to 12 servings

PEELING PEPPERS

An easy way to remove the skins from roasted bell peppers is to place them in plastic bags after roasting them and then to put them in the freezer for up to 10 minutes. This stops the cooking and makes the skins slide off easily.

ORANGE VEAL SCALOPPINE

Oranges, both sweet and sour, grow luxuriantly in our tropical climate. When buying oranges, choose those that are heavy for their size and have a thin rather than thick peel, as they will be juicier.

6 3-ounce, thinly sliced veal cutlets
½ cup flour, for dredging
Salt and pepper to taste
1 tablespoon vegetable oil
3 tablespoons butter
1 cup strained orange juice
*1 teaspoon minced fresh sage, or 1
  generous pinch dried, crumbled
  sage*
Minced fresh sage or parsley

Put the cutlets between two layers of plastic wrap, and pound them with the flat side of a mallet to a uniform thickness. Season the flour with the salt and pepper. Heat the oil and 2 tablespoons of the butter in a heavy skillet over high heat. Dredge the veal in the seasoned flour, and shake off the excess. Add the cutlets to the pan (do not crowd them), and cook them 30 seconds on each side.

Discard the pan drippings. Add ¼ cup orange juice to the skillet, and boil it, scraping up the browned bits, until it is reduced to a glaze, about 1 minute. Add the remaining orange juice and sage. Season with salt and pepper. Boil the mixture until it thickens and just coats a spoon, about 1 minute. Remove the pan from the heat and swirl in the remaining 1 tablespoon butter. Pour in any juices accumulated from the veal. Transfer the veal to heated plates, spoon the sauce over, and sprinkle with fresh sage or parsley. Serve immediately.

Makes 6 servings

SOUR ORANGES

Also known as Seville or bitter oranges, these deep-orange fruits have thick, rough peels. In England sour oranges are used in making marmalade, but in the Caribbean they have many and varied uses.

Fresh sour oranges or bottled sour orange juice can often be found in Latin American markets.

VEAL SCALOPPINE WITH JULIENNE OF VEGETABLES

A bouquet of bright vegetables tops tender slices of veal in this dish. Substitute chicken breasts or turkey for the veal, if you like.

....

1 cup each 3-inch julienne strips of carrot, leek, cabbage, and celery or christophene
6 3-ounce, thinly sliced veal cutlets
½ cup flour
Salt and pepper to taste
6 tablespoons butter
1 pinch dried marjoram
2 tablespoons tomato sauce
6 thin slices Swiss cheese
Paprika

....

Preheat the oven to 400°. Blanch the vegetable strips in boiling salted water for 5 to 8 minutes. Drain the vegetables, and rinse them in cold water.

Season the flour with the salt and pepper, and dust the cutlets with the mixture. Melt 4 tablespoons of the butter in a large skillet, and cook the cutlets over high heat for about 30 seconds, until they are golden brown. Arrange them side by side on an ovenproof platter, and keep them warm.

In a bowl, mix the vegetables with the marjoram, the remaining 2 tablespoons butter, the tomato sauce, and salt to taste. Arrange some of the julienne strips on each cutlet. Cover each cutlet with a slice of cheese, and sprinkle with a little paprika. Put the platter in the oven for 5 minutes, or until the cheese melts. Serve at once.

Makes 6 servings

VEAL SCALOPPINE

Veal scaloppine is always delicious, but its cost can sometimes give one pause. If you want to try a scaloppine recipe without bending the budget, use turkey scallops instead. Available in most markets, turkey scallops are a perfect inexpensive substitute for special-occasion veal.

BASIL AND PARMESAN–CRUSTED VEAL CHOPS

Basil grows like crazy in the Caribbean, and we raise several types in our shadehouse at the hotel. Beyond the broad-leafed common type, we also like lemon basil, with its crisp lemon fragrance; sacred basil, with its purple flowers and slight clove scent; Mexican spice basil; and opal basil, with its handsome ruby leaves.

....

½ cup butter
¼ pound ground veal
2 egg yolks
2 cups firmly packed basil leaves
½ cup grated parmesan cheese
1 tablespoon coarse-grained mustard
1 teaspoon salt
½ teaspoon ground white pepper
½ cup olive oil
6 loin veal chops, patted dry
Salt and pepper to taste
½ cup dry bread crumbs

....

To make the crust mixture, blend together the butter, veal, egg yolks, basil, parmesan cheese, mustard, salt, and pepper in a food processor, turning the machine on and off until the mixture is smooth. Chill the mixture, covered, until you're ready to roast the chops.

Preheat the oven to 400°. In a large, heavy skillet, heat the olive oil over moderately high heat. Season the veal chops with salt and pepper. Brown the veal chops in the skillet, then transfer them to a broiler pan. Coat one side of each chop with some of the crust mixture, smoothing the top. Sprinkle the bread crumbs evenly on the crust mixture, and roast the chops on the middle rack of the oven for 12 to 15 minutes (for medium-rare meat). After removing the chops from the oven, preheat the broiler, if you like, and brown the chops for 1 to 2 minutes, or until the crust is golden. Serve them immediately.

Makes 6 servings

ISLAND STYLE: THE FRENCH ISLANDS

The menus in Martinique, Guadeloupe, St. Martin, and St. Barts are filled with so many seductive dishes that it's always hard to make a choice. The blend of Gallic and Creole cooking is made in heaven, especially when it is matched with fine French wines. As departments of France, each of these islands lives up to what is expected: four-hour lunches, six course meals, free flowing wine, and romance.

Most meals begin with le 'ti punch, a deadly little concoction of white rum, sugar syrup, lime, and ice. From there the choice is stupefying. Will it be crabes farcies, land crabs stuffed with French bread crumbs and herbs? Or would you rather try blaff, spanking fresh fish poached in wine flavored with lime, garlic, onions, bay, thyme, and peppers? Blood sausage fanciers will find spicy boudin créole a new taste treat. And let's not forget what happens when France meets India in colombo, a Gallic version of curry. Accras, tender and crisp little salt cod fritters, are a delicious way to start any meal.

Because of its dual nationality, St. Martin (French)/ St. Maarten (Dutch) provides a wide variety of dining experiences. On this go-go isle of condos and casinos, food is still a serious business, and on the French side the competition among restaurants is vigorous. Whether in an elegant restaurant or a waterside bistro, the standards must be able to withstand the fierce scrutiny and culinary expectations the French always bring to the table.

On Guadeloupe, one of the biggest holidays is the Fête des Cuisinières in mid-August, when the best of the women cooks prepare their finest dishes as offerings to Saint Lawrence. Dressed in traditional madras costumes and headdresses that reflect the East Indian influences on the island, they carry their baskets to the cathedral in the main city of Pointe-à-Pitre. After the food is blessed at a high mass, the women parade through the streets to a school yard. Upon arrival, they join those lucky enough to have purchased the highly prized tickets for the celebration, in a full day of eating, drinking, and dancing the beguiling beguine, which began here, no matter what Cole Porter would have you think.

St. Barts is certainly one of the most chic islands in the Caribbean, combining an irresistible mix of savoir faire and quaint charm. It is the playground of the rich and famous who don't have to worry where their next franc is coming from. But, despite the need for smelling salts when l'addition arrives, diners are rarely disappointed in any of the meals they eat here.

If you can imagine Paris with a calypso beat you have conjured up a fair idea of the French islands.

VEAL APPLE BAY

The Sugar Mill is located at Little Apple Bay, the small inlet for which this dish is named. Although we grow sugar apples (sweet, custardy tropical treats), our climate doesn't favor true apples. Happily, they travel well.

....

6 loin veal chops, patted dry

....

APPLE-RAISIN SAUCE:
2 apples, sliced
1 large red bell pepper, sliced
2 tablespoons butter
½ cup raisins
½ cup chopped walnuts
2 cups veal broth
½ cup heavy cream
Salt and pepper to taste

....

GARNISH:
½ cup chopped parsley

....

Preheat the oven to 400°. Sear the veal chops on a grill (or in a very hot skillet). Place the chops on a baking pan, and finish cooking them in the oven, about 10 to 12 minutes.

While the veal is cooking, sauté the apples and pepper in the butter until they are slightly softened. Add the raisins and walnuts, and toss. Add the veal stock, and reduce the liquid by half over high heat. Add the cream and salt and pepper. Spoon the hot sauce over the chops, garnish with chopped parsley, and serve.

Makes 6 servings

VEAL RAGOUT IN EMERALD SPINACH OR CALLALOO SAUCE

We make this succulent veal, in a sauce as green as grass, with our local vine spinach or with callaloo leaves as season and availability dictate.

....

6 tablespoons butter
3 pounds boneless veal for stewing, trimmed and cut into 1½-inch cubes
3 tablespoons flour
Grated nutmeg
Salt and pepper to taste
3 carrots, peeled and sliced diagonally
2 cups coarsely chopped onions
1 pound spinach or callaloo leaves, stemmed
¼ cup minced fresh dillweed, or 1 tablespoon dried dillweed
3 to 4 cup chicken broth
¾ cup heavy cream
Hot buttered noodles

....

GARNISH:

> Chopped fresh tomatoes or red bell
>   peppers
> 1 dill sprig

....

Preheat the oven to 350°. Melt the butter in a heavy pot. Add the veal, and cook it over medium-low heat, turning it often, until it is firm but not brown, 5 to 10 minutes. Stir the flour, nutmeg, and salt and pepper together in a small bowl, and sprinkle the mixture over the veal. Continue to cook the veal over low heat, stirring, for 5 minutes. Do not let the meat brown.

Add the carrots, onions, and enough broth to just cover the meat and vegetables. Raise the heat to medium, and bring the mixture just to a boil. Cover the pot, transfer it to the oven, and bake the veal mixture for 1½ hours.

When you are ready to serve, chop the spinach very fine in a food processor or by hand, adding a little of the veal sauce, if necessary. Stir the chopped spinach and dill into the veal mixture. Add the cream, and heat the ragout through. Taste it, and adjust the seasonings, if you like.

Serve the ragout on a bed of buttered noodles, garnished with chopped tomatoes or peppers and a dill sprig.

Makes 6 servings

VEAL RAGOUT WITH WILD MUSHROOMS AND FRESH BASIL

As we planted our garden, we learned that many plants that thrive in the rocky, sun-baked soil of southern Italy do equally well in our situation. We've had basil plants that grew to the size of baby buggies. This is one way we like to use the harvest.

....

> ¾ cup butter
> 3 pounds boneless veal for stewing,
>   trimmed and cut into 1½-inch
>   cubes
> ¼ cup flour
> Salt and pepper to taste
> 2 cups coarsely chopped onions
> 3 to 4 cups chicken broth
> ½ pound wild or fresh mushrooms, or
>   a combination, sliced
> ¾ cup heavy cream
> ½ cup minced basil
> 2 tablespoons lemon juice

....

Preheat the oven to 350°. Melt ½ cup butter in a heavy pot. Add the veal, and cook it over medium-low heat, turning it often, until it is firm but not brown, 5 to 10 minutes. Stir the flour and salt and pepper together in a small bowl, and sprinkle the mixture over the veal. Continue to cook the veal over low heat, stirring, for 5 minutes. Do not let the meat brown.

Add the onions and enough broth to just cover the meat and onions. Raise the heat to medium, and bring the mixture just to a boil. Cover the pot, transfer it to the oven, and bake the veal mixture for 1½ hours.

Heat the remaining ¼ cup butter in a skillet, and sauté the mushrooms. When you are almost ready to serve, add the cream, cooked mushrooms, and minced basil to the veal. Heat the ragout thoroughly. Add the lemon juice and, if you like, more salt and pepper. Serve the ragout hot.

Makes 6 servings

OLIVE AND ORANGE ROASTED VEAL

In the garden at our home on Tortola we have what we call "the citrus walk," along which we have planted a sweet orange tree, a blood orange, a tangerine, and a grapefruit. Although newly planted, one tree last year bore two—count them—*two* oranges. We're patiently waiting for the trees to mature so we can use our very own citrus in this dish.

....

OLIVE RELISH:
   ¾ cup pitted black olives
   1 teaspoon minced garlic
   1 tablespoon drained capers

   ¼ cup olive oil
   1 tablespoon chopped parsley

....

VEAL ROAST:
   1 3- to 3½-pound veal loin
   ¼ cup chopped sun-dried tomatoes, or 2 tablespoons dried tomato paste
   2 tablespoons orange marmalade
   ¾ cup dry red wine
   ¾ cup water
   About ⅓ cup chicken broth
   Greek or Italian black olives
   1 tablespoon cornstarch combined with 2 tablespoons water

....

GARNISH:
   Red and yellow cherry tomatoes lightly sautéed in garlic-flavored butter
   Cooked broccoli spears

....

Preheat the oven to 350°.

To make the olive relish, put the olives, garlic, and capers into a food processor, and process for a few seconds. With the motor running, slowly drizzle in the olive oil, and process until the mixture is smooth. Transfer it to a bowl, and stir in the parsley.

If the roast is in netting, remove it. Cut eight to ten slits ½ inch deep in the surface of the roast. Combine ¼ cup of the olive relish, the sun-dried tomatoes or paste, and the marmalade in a small bowl. Spread the mixture over the roast, pressing it into the slits. Retie the roast with string.

Place the veal in a roasting pan, and pour in the wine and water. Roast the veal for about 1½ hours, basting every 15 minutes and adding water if necessary. Remove the roast from the oven when its internal temperature reaches 165° to 170°. Allow the roast to sit at room temperature, tented with foil, for 15 minutes before you slice it.

While the roast is resting, pour the pan juices, plus enough chicken broth to make 2 cups, into a small saucepan. Stir in the olives, orange zest, and 1 tablespoon olive relish. Heat the mixture to a simmer. Whisk the cornstarch mixture into the sauce, bring the sauce back to a simmer, and simmer it until it is thickened. Slice the veal very thin, and serve it with the sauce. Surround the slices of veal with the sautéed cherry tomatoes and cooked broccoli spears. Serve at once.

Makes 6 servings

PORK CHOPS MARTINIQUE

Martinique's cooks, inspired by the rich cultural mix of their island, have long been touted as the best in the Caribbean. French cuisine, of course, is their touchstone, but they also borrow freely from Spain, Africa, India, and Asia.

Juice of 4 limes
4 garlic cloves, minced
Salt and pepper to taste
1 jalapeño pepper, minced
8 6- to 8-ounce loin pork chops
¼ cup sugar
3 tablespoons vegetable oil
1 packet Sazón seasoning (see page 4)
6 parsley sprigs
6 green onions, chopped
2 teaspoons dried thyme
½ cup hot water

Combine the lime juice, garlic, salt, black pepper, and jalapeño. Add the pork chops, and turn them to coat them well. Marinate them in the refrigerator, covered, for at least 40 minutes.

Combine the oil with the Sazón seasoning. Heat a skillet until it is very hot, and carefully add the sugar. Let it melt and turn golden brown (no darker), then pour in the oil mixed with Sazón seasoning. When this becomes bubbly, add the pork chops, and brown them. Cook them on each side for about 2 minutes.

Add the parsley, green onions, and thyme to the skillet, and stir. Slowly add the hot water. The water may splatter and sizzle for a few seconds, so be careful, and stand back! Let the sauce simmer over low heat until it is thick and the chops are cooked through, about 8 to 10 minutes, then serve the pork chops with the sauce spooned over them.

Makes 8 servings

Ginger

The his knotty rhizome of a tropical or-
chid-like plant is a favorite flavoring
in the Caribbean. But ginger had a long
and colorful history before reaching our
island shores.

It's said that Confucius enjoyed the
flavor of ginger, and, indeed, it was Chinese traders who carried the spice to the
Greeks and Romans. Trading brought the
spice north in Europe. In the Middle Ages,
one of the spice markets in Switzerland
was called Ginger Alley.

When ginger finally arrived in the
Caribbean, it became an instant favorite,
and found its way into many spicy dishes
as well as the much-beloved ginger beer.

Pecan-Crusted Pork Cutlets with Ginger Aïoli

Pork has been a popular meat in
the islands since the Arawak Indians hunted hogs, introduced by the
Spanish, and smoked and dried the
meat on wooden grills. We'll bet this
standout dish is considerably more
toothsome than Arawak jerky.

....

2 pounds boneless pork cutlets,
trimmed

⅓ cup sherry
⅓ cup soy sauce
4 green onions, minced
3 tablespoons minced peeled
 gingerroot

....

Ginger Aïoli:
 1 1-inch piece gingerroot, peeled
 1 large garlic clove
 2 egg yolks
 4 teaspoons sherry vinegar or cider
  vinegar
 ¼ teaspoon salt
 1 cup vegetable oil
 1½ tablespoons sesame oil
 4 drops hot chile oil
 1 tomato, seeded and diced
 1 green onion, minced
 2 cups fine dry bread crumbs
 1 cup minced pecans
 Flour, for dredging
 2 eggs, beaten lightly with 3
  tablespoons vegetable oil

....

Pound the pork between sheets of
waxed paper to ¼-inch thickness. Blend
the sherry, soy sauce, green onions, and
ginger in a glass or ceramic baking dish.
Add the pork. Cover the dish, and refrigerate it 2 hours.

To make the ginger aïoli, finely
mince the ginger and garlic in a food
processor. Add the egg yolks, vinegar,
and salt, and blend until the mixture
is smooth. Combine the oils. With the
food processor running, add the oil
mixture in a slow stream, and mix until the aïoli is thickened, about 1½ min-

utes. Transfer it to a bowl, and stir in the diced tomato and chopped green onion. Cover the dish, and refrigerate it at least 1 hour.

Drain the pork, and pat it dry. Mix the bread crumbs and pecans. Dredge the pork in flour, shaking off the excess. Dip it into the beaten eggs, then coat it in the bread-crumb mixture, pressing so the coating adheres to the meat.

In a large skillet, heat the oil. Cook the pork over medium-high heat, turning it once, until the coating is crisp and brown, about 3 minutes per side.

Arrange the cutlets on plates with dollops of aïoli on the side, and serve at once.

Makes 8 servings

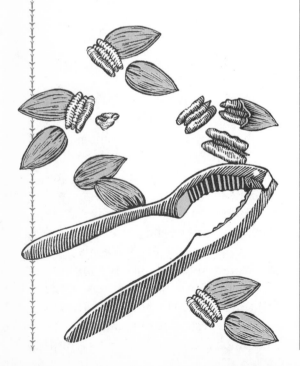

PORK MEDALLIONS WITH PEANUT SATE SAUCE

Peanuts and pork have always been a wonderful combination, and this smooth, rich sauce with faint fiery underpinnings is an especially welcome partner to the often bland taste of pork.

. . . .

PEANUT SATE SAUCE:
    2 tablespoons oil
    ¼ cup chopped green onions
    1 teaspoon minced garlic
    2 cups chicken broth
    ½ cup peanut butter
    1 tablespoon strained lime juice
    ¼ teaspoon minced peeled gingerroot
    ¼ teaspoon hot red pepper flakes
    2 pounds boneless pork tenderloin,
        cut into 1½-inch pieces

. . . .

    Flour, for dredging
    Salt and pepper to taste
    2 tablespoons butter
    1 tablespoon vegetable oil

. . . .

GARNISH:
    Chopped roasted peanuts
    Chopped green onions

. . . .

To make the sauce, sauté the green onions and garlic in the oil for 3 to 4 minutes, until the onions are soft and transparent but not brown. Pour in the chicken broth, and bring the mixture to a boil over high heat. Add the peanut butter, lime juice, ginger, and red pepper flakes. Simmer the sauce, uncovered, for 10 minutes, or until it is thick enough to coat a spoon heavily. Strain the sauce; reserve it.

Place the pork pieces cut side down on a work surface, and pound them until they are about ¼ inch thick. Season the flour with the salt and pepper, and dip each piece of pork in the mixture. In a large skillet, heat the butter and oil over medium-high heat. Cook the pork pieces, turning them once, until they are golden brown.

If the sauce has thickened too much while standing, thin it with chicken broth or water. Reheat it. To serve, spoon a ribbon of sauce over the pork medallions, and garnish with a sprinkling of chopped roasted peanuts and chopped green onions.

Makes 8 servings

Pork Roast Calypso

The island zest of ginger, nutmeg, cloves, bay leaves, and rum give this pork a distinctly Caribbean flavor.

....

1 5- to 6-pound pork loin roast
½ teaspoon ground black pepper
1 teaspoon salt
1 teaspoon ground ginger
½ teaspoon grated nutmeg
½ teaspoon ground cloves
2 garlic cloves, minced
¼ cup brown sugar
2 bay leaves, crumbled
¼ cup lime juice
1 cup dark rum
1 cup orange juice
2 cups (or more) chicken broth
2 teaspoons arrowroot combined
    with 1 tablespoon water

....

Preheat the oven to 325°.

Cut the fat on the pork in a diamond pattern. Mix together the pepper, salt, ginger, nutmeg, cloves, and garlic, and rub the mixture into the meat. Sprinkle on the brown sugar, and sprinkle the crumbled bay leaves on top. Place the pork on a rack in a roasting pan, and pour into the pan the lime juice, rum, orange juice, and 2 cups chicken broth. Roast the pork for 30 minutes per pound, adding more broth to the pan as necessary.

When the roast is done, remove the bay leaves. Spoon off the fat from the pan juices, and add more broth if it is needed to make enough sauce. Add the arrowroot paste to the pan, and stir constantly until the sauce has thickened. Season the sauce with salt and pepper, and serve it with the sliced pork.

Makes 6 to 8 servings

Sugar Mill Plantation Pork Roast

A favorite at the Sugar Mill restaurant, this is a creation of our head chef, Rick Buttafuso, who was inspired by our wealth of Caribbean ingredients.

....

Juice of 4 sour oranges, or juice of 4
    sweet oranges and 1 lime
2 garlic cloves, minced
2 tablespoons soy sauce
½ cup pineapple juice

....

FILLING:
2 ripe plantains, finely chopped
1 egg white
½ cup diced ham
¼ cup sliced green onions
½ cup soft bread crumbs
Salt and pepper to taste

....

BLACK-BEAN SAUCE:
1 tablespoon vegetable oil
½ cup chopped onions
2 garlic cloves, minced
1 red bell pepper, diced
2 cups cooked, drained, and rinsed
    black beans
Chicken broth or water
Salt and pepper to taste
1 teaspoon sugar

1 teaspoon Worcestershire sauce
A few drops hot pepper sauce

....

2 tablespoons clarified butter (see
    page 185)

....

Remove all the fat and the thin membrane that covers the pork. Slice the tenderloins horizontally from one long side, three-quarters of the way through. Pound each tenderloin into a rectangular shape.

In a shallow dish, combine the marinade ingredients. Place the tenderloins in the marinade, and pour the liquid over the meat. Refrigerate the dish for 2 to 3 hours.

Preheat the oven to 400°.

To make the filling, blend the plantains and egg white in a food processor. Put the mixture into a bowl, and stir in the remaining filling ingredients. The filling should be a thick, oatmeal-like consistency. Refrigerate it until you are ready to use it.

To fill the tenderloins, place them on a work surface, and spread the filling over them, leaving a 1-inch margin at the edges. Roll the meat from a long side like a jelly roll. Tie each roll with kitchen string.

Place the rolls on a rack in a roasting pan, and brush them with the clarified butter. Roast them until they become firm to the touch, about 30 minutes.

To make the black-bean sauce, heat

the oil in a skillet. Sauté the onion and garlic until the onion is limp, then add the diced red and yellow peppers, and sauté until the peppers are tender. Add the black beans, and heat the mixture through. Add enough broth or water to yield a consistency you like. Season the sauce with the salt, pepper, sugar, Worcestershire sauce, and hot sauce.

When the tenderloins are done, remove the string, and let them rest about 10 minutes. Then slice them into medallions, and serve them on the black-bean sauce.

Makes 4 servings

CLARIFIED BUTTER

Clarified butter can be heated to a higher temperature than regular butter without burning. To clarify a stick (½ cup) of butter, melt it over low heat in a small, heavy saucepan. Remove the pan from the heat, and allow the melted butter to sit for 5 minutes. Then skim off any white foam that has risen to the top, and discard it. Spoon off the clear liquid, leaving behind the solids on the bottom. Clarified butter will keep for several weeks in the refrigerator.

CITRUS MARINATED PORK

Our sunny islands have the perfect climate for growing oranges, which marry so well with pork. Our homegrown oranges often have a green tinge when they are fully ripe. This is natural; oranges that come from professional growers are often treated with a dye. In neither case is the flavor affected.

....

2 8- to 10-ounce pork tenderloins
2 teaspoons grated orange zest
*1 tablespoon fresh thyme leaves, or 1
    teaspoon dried thyme*
½ teaspoon ground black pepper
2 garlic cloves, minced
2 cups orange juice
*2 tablespoons rice vinegar or white
    wine vinegar*
2 tablespoons honey

....

GARNISH:
    Watercress
    Orange slices

....

With a mortar and pestle, grind together the orange zest, thyme, pepper, and garlic to a paste. Rub the paste into the pork. Put the pork into a dish, combine the orange juice and vinegar, and pour the mixture over the pork. Cover the meat, and refrigerate it for 2 to 8 hours.

Preheat the oven to 425°. Oil a baking pan lightly. Heat the pan in the oven for 4 minutes. Set the pork in the pan, and drizzle it with 1 tablespoon honey. Roast the pork 10 minutes. Turn the pork, and spoon any exuded juices over it. Drizzle the pork with the remaining 1 tablespoon honey. Roast the pork 20 to 25 minutes longer (for medium meat), basting it once or twice with the pan juices.

Remove the pork from the oven, and let it stand at room temperature 5 minutes. Cut it into ¼-inch slices, and serve it garnished with watercress and orange slices.

Makes 4 to 6 servings

BARBECUED PORK IN BANANA LEAVES WITH SULTRY SALSA

Cooking in banana leaves is an old Caribbean tradition. Occasionally the leaves are available in temperate climes from florists or flower markets, but, happily, a similar result can be obtained by cooking the roast in foil. This is a delicious dish for a casual party or picnic.

....

1 4½- to 5-pound pork loin

....

PASTE:

  1 tablespoon annatto oil (see page 7)
  2 garlic cloves
  1 tablespoon whole black peppercorns
  2 allspice berries
  1 tablespoon salt
  2 fresh jalapeño peppers, seeded and chopped
  ¾ cup sour orange juice, or ⅔ cup sweet orange juice and the juice of 1 lime
  1 tablespoon dried oregano
  1 teaspoon ground cumin

....

1 banana leaf, or aluminum foil

....

SULTRY SALSA:

  ½ cup olive oil
  1 onion, chopped
  2 garlic cloves, minced
  2 red bell peppers, coarsely chopped
  2 yellow, orange, or green bell peppers, coarsely chopped
  6 green olives, pitted and chopped
  12 Greek or Italian black olives, pitted and chopped
  1 to 2 hot peppers, finely minced
  ½ cup golden raisins
  1 tablespoon tomato paste
  4 medium tomatoes, chopped
  2 bay leaves, crushed
  2 cups white wine
  Salt and cayenne to taste

....

Make little slashes all over the pork. Grind the paste ingredients together in a mortar or blender until the mixture is smooth, and rub the paste into the meat.

If you're using a banana leaf, lightly sear it over a gas flame to make it flexible. Cut it into a rectangle the proper size to wrap the roast. Fold the leaf or foil around the meat, and seal the package with double folds at the edges. Tie the package with string, if you're using a banana leaf. Let the meat marinate in the refrigerator 4 to 8 hours.

Prepare a fire for barbecuing in a covered grill; let the ashes burn down to a light ash color. Cook the meat 3 to 4 hours, until it is tender enough to be shredded from the bones. (Or cook it in a 325° oven for about the same period, until a thermometer placed in the thickest part of the roast registers 180°.)

While the meat cooks, make the salsa. Heat the olive oil in a skillet. Add the onion and garlic, and sauté them until they are limp. Add the peppers, olives, hot peppers, raisins, tomato paste, tomatoes, and crushed bay leaves. Cook the mixture over low heat for 15 minutes. Add the white wine, and cook another 10 minutes. Season the salsa with salt and cayenne. Refrigerate the salsa until you are ready to use it.

When the meat is cooked, shred it, and pour over the meat the juices that have accumulated in the wrapping. Wrap the shredded meat in warm flour tortillas, and serve it with the salsa.

Makes 8 to 10 servings

THE HAITIAN PEASANT DECLARES HIS LOVE

High-yellow of my heart, with breasts like tangerines,

You taste better to me than eggplant stuffed with crab,

You are the tripe in my pepper-pot, the dumpling in my peas, my tea of aromatic herbs.

You are the corned beef whose customhouse is my heart,

My mush with syrup that trickles down my throat.

You are a steaming dish, mushroom cooked with rice, crisp potato fries, and little fish fried brown . . .

My hankering for love follows you wherever you go.

Your bum is a gorgeous basket brimming with fruits and meat.

—EMILE ROUMER (TRANSLATED FROM THE FRENCH BY JOHN PEALE BISHOP)

RUM-GLAZED RIBS CALYPSO

Parboiling the ribs keeps them moist and reduces the time they spend on the grill. You can simmer them ahead of time, then refrigerate them, and finish them on the grill or under the broiler just before serving time.

....

6 pounds pork spareribs, cut
 apart
Salt and pepper to taste
2 cups tomato sauce
1 cup dark rum
1 cup honey
¼ cup red wine vinegar
½ cup minced onion
2 garlic cloves, minced or mashed
1 teaspoon Worcestershire sauce

....

Put the ribs into a large saucepan or a Dutch oven, then cover them with cold water. Bring the water to a boil, and simmer the ribs, uncovered, for 30 minutes. Drain them, discarding the liquid. (This can be done in advance. If you refrigerate the ribs, let them come back to room temperature before you broil or grill them.)

Combine the remaining ingredients in a small pan. Bring the mixture to a boil, and simmer it 5 minutes.

Preheat the broiler, or prepare a fire for grilling.

Broil or grill the parboiled ribs slowly (5 to 6 inches from the heat), turning them and basting them often with the rum sauce. Serve the ribs at once, and provide your guests plenty of napkins for mopping up.

Makes 6 servings

JERKED RIBS

Jerk seasoning is a Jamaican festival in your mouth, at once hot, spicy, pungent, sweet, and irresistible. Some say the name comes from the meat being "jerked" as it's turned over and over on the coals, while others claim the cooks "jerk" the meat from the bones. It really doesn't matter. It's the flavor that counts.

....

*Baby pork ribs (about 1 pound per
 person), cut into serving-size pieces*

....

PARBOILING SEASONINGS:
1 medium onion, quartered
2 cloves
1 bay leaf
Leaves from 1 celery rib
1 teaspoon dried thyme
¼ teaspoon ground black pepper

....

JERK SEASONINGS:
2 tablespoons ground pimento
 (Jamaican allspice)
¼ teaspoon ground nutmeg
1 teaspoon ground cinnamon
2 bunches green onions, chopped
1 Scotch bonnet (or habanero)
 pepper or 6 jalapeño peppers,
 halved but not seeded
⅓ cup red wine vinegar
2 tablespoons vegetable oil
1 tablespoon salt
1 teaspoon ground black pepper
2 tablespoons soy sauce

....

SPICING THINGS UP WITH JERK

One of our favorite dishes is Jamaican jerk, which is becoming almost as popular in the islands as rum and reggae. Created by the Arawaks and perfected by the Maroons, jerk pork is the ultimate island barbecue. Jerked food is hot, there's no denying that, but it is also complex and exciting. The flavors dance like a spicy festival in your mouth. Scallions, onions, thyme, Jamaican pimento (allspice), cinnamon, nutmeg, and fiery Scotch bonnet or bird peppers combine in a pungent medley that is rubbed on the meat before its slow smoke cooking.

These days jerk huts are clustered by the sides of the roads everywhere in Jamaica. The Pork Pit near the Montego Bay Airport and the Ocho Rios Jerk Center have introduced hundreds of visitors to the joy of jerk. In Negril, jerk pits line the two main roads leading in and out of town, and in Port Antonio jerk can be found on West Street near the market.

For our first taste of jerk, we decided to go to the pioneer establishment at Boston Bay, home of the original jerk pits. A haze of smoke from smoldering pimento wood hung over the wooden huts. Jerk stands aren't much for decor, but the cooks were friendly and helpful when it came time to make our selection: pork, chicken, and locally made sausage. Clutching greasy bags, we sneaked through the lobby of our hotel and slunk into our room. No strangers to Caribbean seasoning, we took the precaution of calling room service to provide four cold Red Stripe beers to wash down this feast. When the waiter arrived he had on his tray not four, but six icy beers.

"That's fine," we said, "We ordered only four, but we can put the other two in our little refrigerator."

The waiter smiled wisely and shook his head. "I see you come through the lobby with them bags, and when you call I say to myself, that is no four-beer jerk. That is a six-beer jerk."

Of course, he was right.

Vegetable oil

....

Put the ribs into a pot, cover them, and add the parboiling seasonings. Bring the mixture to a boil, and reduce the heat. Simmer the ribs for 30 minutes or until they are tender. Drain them, discarding the liquid. (The parboiling can be done in advance. If you refrigerate the parboiled ribs, let them come back to room temperature before you grill them.)

Combine the jerk seasonings. Rub the parboiled ribs with oil, and then rub in some of the seasoning mix (about 1½ to 2 teaspoons per pound). Allow the ribs to marinate at room temperature for at least 1 hour.

Prepare a fire for grilling.

Grill the ribs over hot coals, turning them once, until they are brown and cooked through. Serve immediately.

Makes 6 servings

PORK PICADILLO

This spicy hash-like mixture is one of Cuba's most popular dishes. Although it is usually made with beef, we like it with pork. Traditionally, the dish is served with black beans and rice and fried plantains, with a deep-fried egg topping the picadillo. We also like picadillo as a filling for pita bread or Caribbean patties (see page 31), and it's great for breakfast with a poached egg on top.

....

¼ cup annatto oil (see page 7)
1 onion, diced
1 red or green bell pepper, minced
2 garlic cloves, minced
½ teaspoon minced Scotch bonnet (or habanero) pepper, or other minced hot pepper to taste
½ teaspoon cayenne
2 pounds minced or ground pork
3 medium tomatoes, peeled, seeded, and chopped
½ teaspoon ground cumin
2 tablespoons drained capers
¼ cup raisins
¼ cup minced green olives
Salt and pepper to taste

....

Heat the annatto oil in a large skillet over medium-high heat. Add the onion, bell pepper, garlic, minced hot pepper, and cayenne. Sauté them until the onion is softened, about 5 minutes. Add the pork, and cook, stirring of-ten, about 8 to 10 minutes, until the meat is lightly browned and cooked through.

Add the remaining ingredients, and simmer 15 minutes. Season the picadillo with salt and pepper. Serve it hot.

Makes 6 servings

GRILLED LAMB CHOPS WITH CREOLE SAUCE

We both love lamb, and we think this brightly hued sauce with hints of Spanish-island flavors is an ideal accompaniment for baby lamb chops seared on the grill.

....

1 cup walnuts
4 garlic cloves, chopped
½ teaspoon hot red pepper flakes
½ teaspoon salt
3 tablespoons white wine vinegar
2 teaspoons sugar
1 cup tomato paste
1½ cups olive oil
12 small loin lamb chops

....

Toast the walnuts in an ungreased skillet over moderate heat, shaking them occasionally, until they release their aroma. Chop half the nuts coarsely, and reserve them.

Put the remaining nuts into a blender or food processor, and add the garlic, hot pepper flakes, salt, vinegar, sugar, and tomato paste. Blend well. With the machine running, add the olive oil in a thin stream, and continue blending until the mixture is thick and smooth. (This sauce can be made a day in advance; refrigerate it until you're ready to use it.)

Grill the lamb chops on one side for 5 minutes, then turn them, and spread them with the sauce. Continue grilling them until they are done.

Serve the chops sprinkled with the reserved chopped nuts.

Makes 6 servings

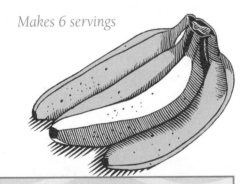

Light-up-the-Grill Dinner

....

CARIBBEAN BLACK BEAN SOUP

◆

GREEN SALAD WITH
CREAMY DILL DRESSING

◆

GRILLED LAMB CHOPS WITH
CREOLE SAUCE

◆

BANANA CHEESECAKE

ROAST LAMB WITH GUAVA AND ROSEMARY

Guavas are native to the Caribbean, where there are dozens of edible varieties. On islands with a Spanish heritage, guava paste is often eaten with cheese for dessert. We purée fresh guavas for this lamb dish when they are available, but canned nectar, available in most supermarkets, works equally well.

....

*1 leg of lamb (6 to 8 pounds with
    bone, or 4 to 6 pounds boned)
Salt and pepper to taste
3 garlic cloves, slivered
2 cups guava nectar
Rosemary sprigs*

....

Preheat the oven to 350°. Rub the lamb with the salt and pepper. With the point of a sharp knife, cut slits in the skin. Put a sliver of garlic and a small sprig of rosemary in each slit.

Place the roast on a rack in a roasting pan. Roast the lamb, basting occasionally with the guava nectar, until its internal temperature reaches 135° to 140° (for rare meat) to 160° (for medium-well-done). Allow about 30 minutes per pound for a boneless roast and 25 to 30 minutes per pound for a bone-in roast.

Remove the roast from the pan, and allow it to rest at room temperature for 10 to 15 minutes. Skim the fat from the pan juices, and reduce the juices on the stove top over high heat until they are slightly thickened. Slice the lamb, and serve it moistened with the pan juices and garnished with rosemary sprigs.

Makes 8 to 10 servings

LEG OF LAMB WITH CALLALOO OR SPINACH AND FETA CHEESE

Goats are more common than lambs on our island, but when we've occasionally tried a goat dish on the menu at the Sugar Mill we've found the guests to be less than enthusiastic. Although we love goat stew, which is a staple at Festival Village during Tortola's carnival, and would travel a long way for a goat roast, we decided to stick with more familiar lamb for this colorful dish.

. . . .

2 tablespoons olive oil
2 tablespoons minced garlic
3 cups fresh callaloo or spinach
  leaves, stemmed
8 ounces feta cheese
2 red bell peppers, roasted, peeled,
  and cut into ½-inch strips
1 boned and butterflied leg of lamb
2 garlic cloves, slivered

A Sophisticated Spring Dinner

. . . .

SMOKED SCALLOPS WITH SALSA

◆

GREEN SALAD WITH CURRY DRESSING

◆

LEG OF LAMB
WITH CALLALOO OR SPINACH
AND FETA CHEESE

◆

CURRIED CITRUS RICE

◆

BANANA BEIGNETS WITH APRICOT SAUCE

Salt and pepper to taste
2 tablespoons fresh rosemary leaves,
  or 2 teaspoons dried rosemary

. . . .

Preheat the oven to 425°. Heat the oil in a skillet. Add the garlic, and sauté it over medium-low heat for 1 minute. Add the callaloo or spinach, increase the heat to medium, and toss the greens until they are just wilted but still green and fresh-looking. Remove the greens and garlic to a bowl, and stir in the crumbled feta.

Spread the cut side of the lamb evenly with the callaloo or spinach mixture. Spread the pepper strips down the center lengthwise. Roll up the roast lengthwise (jelly-roll style), and tie it with kitchen string. Make small slits in the surface of the roast with the tip of a sharp knife, and insert the slivers of garlic into the slits. Sprinkle the roast with salt, pepper, and rosemary.

Place the roast in a shallow roasting pan. Roast it 12 minutes per pound for rare meat (135° to 140°) or 15 minutes per pound for medium (155°). Let the lamb rest for 15 minutes before carving it.

Makes 6 to 8 servings

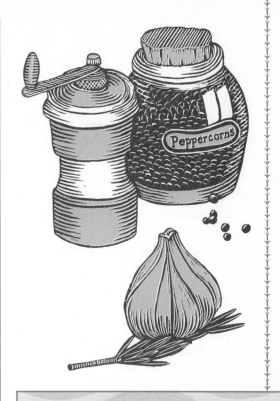

HERB-CRUSTED RACK OF LAMB

There is absolutely no geographical justification for including this recipe here. It isn't even vaguely Caribbean. But our guests love it, we love it, and we'll bet you'll love it, too. Surely these are reasons enough.

. . . .

2 racks of lamb
1 cup toasted bread crumbs
½ teaspoon thyme
1 tablespoon chopped fresh basil, or
    1 teaspoon dried basil
¼ cup toasted pecans
Salt and pepper to taste
Olive oil
About 2 to 3 tablespoons Dijon
    mustard

. . . .

MY THYME IS YOUR THYME

. . . .

Thyme is one of the most popular herbs in the Caribbean. At the open-air market on Saturday morning in Road Town, you can find bouquets of parsley, celery, and thyme, locally known simply as "seasonings."

The tiny oval leaves of thyme release an earthy, pungent aroma that permeates many Caribbean dishes. It is this flavor that bridges the gap between sweet and hot, spicy and delicate, making island spices such as allspice and nutmeg compatible with assertive flavors such as that of Scotch bonnet peppers.

Have the butcher french the bones on the racks. Or, if you're handy with a knife, you can do it yourself by scraping away the thin strip of meat and fat from the ends to the eye, leaving the bare bones. In either case, have the chops cracked at the base for easy carving.

Combine in a food processor the bread crumbs, thyme, basil, toasted pecans, and salt and pepper, and whirl until the nuts are finely chopped and the ingredients are well combined.

Preheat the oven to 400°. Pour a thin film of olive oil into a hot skillet, and brown the racks. Let them cool a bit, then coat the meat with Dijon mustard, and press the bread-crumb mixture into the mustard to make a crust. Arrange the racks on a baking sheet, and cook them for 25 minutes (for medium-rare meat).

Cut the chops apart, and serve them immediately.

Makes 4 servings

SUGAR
ISLAND
SWEETS

SUGAR ISLAND SWEETS

CHOCOLATE DECADENCE

This recipe was given to us by our friend Narsai David, who served Chocolate Decadence in his well-known (though, alas, no longer open) restaurant, Narsai's, in Kensington, California. We think this is the ultimate chocolate dessert.

....

1 pound semisweet chocolate
10 tablespoons unsalted butter
1 tablespoon sugar
1 tablespoon flour
4 eggs

....

TOPPING:
1½ cups heavy cream
1 tablespoon sugar
Shaved chocolate
1 10- to 12-ounce package frozen
    raspberries
¼ cup sugar

....

Preheat the oven to 425°. Butter an 8-inch round cake pan. Line the bottom of the pan with waxed paper or parchment paper, and dust the bottom and side of the pan with flour.

Melt the chocolate with the butter in a double boiler, and remove the mixture to a bowl. Put the eggs and sugar into the double boiler, and beat them over simmering water until the sugar dissolves and the mixture is just luke-warm. Remove the egg mixture from the heat, and beat it until it is thick and pale yellow.

Fold the flour into the eggs. Stir one-fourth of the egg mixture into the chocolate mixture to lighten it, then fold the chocolate mixture into the egg mixture. Bake the cake for no longer than 15 minutes (it should still be almost liquid in the center when you take it out).

Let the cake cool, then freeze it, preferably overnight, before removing it from the pan. To unmold it, carefully dip the bottom of the pan into hot water.

Whip the cream until soft peaks form. Add the sugar, and beat until the mixture is slightly stiff. Cover the top of the cake with the whipped cream, and decorate with the shaved chocolate. Refrigerate the cake until you're almost ready to serve it.

To make the raspberry sauce, purée the frozen raspberries in a blender or food processor. Sieve the purée, and sweeten it to taste with sugar. Spread some sauce on each dessert plate, and place a slice of Decadence on top.

Makes 12 servings

CHOCOLATE CREPES

Chocoholics have been with us ever since the Aztecs, who believed *cac-ahuati*—chocolate—was a gift from

GIVE ME ANY FLAVOR AS LONG AS IT'S CHOCOLATE

When Columbus arrived back in Spain after his voyage to the New World, he presented King Ferdinand with a collection of treasures that included a handful of unpromising brown beans. No one knew what to do with them, and it wasn't until Hernando Cortez drank a delicious brown brew from a golden goblet in the court of Montezuma, emperor of the Aztecs, that any European twigged to the delicious flavor of chocolate. Cortez returned home with more beans and instructions for their preparation.

The Spanish enhanced the flavor by adding sugar, vanilla, and cinnamon to make a delectable chocolate drink. When word leaked out, the chocolate craze swept Europe. By the middle of the seventeenth century, chocolate houses were popular spots for sipping and passing time in intellectual discourse. Chocolate was no longer in the private domain of the aristocracy.

Cacao grows only in tropical areas, on trees up to twenty-five feet tall, with long,

shiny leaves and clusters of pink and white flowers that turn into pods bearing from twenty to fifty beans. After the mature pods are harvested, the beans are removed, then fermented, dried in the sun, and shipped to processing plants.

When cooking with chocolate, remember that it scorches easily. It's best to melt it over simmering water in a double boiler (although some prefer the convenience of the microwave oven). If any water accidentally sloshes into the chocolate it will "seize," that is, become stiff and granular. If this should happen, beat in a tablespoon or so of water that is the same temperature as the chocolate.

Chocolate should be stored at a temperature between 60 and 70 degrees. If it gets too warm, the chocolate will develop a grayish-white film called a "bloom." This doesn't affect the flavor, but it's not very attractive.

For those who love chocolate, there is no mystery about why its botanical name is Theobroma, "food of the gods."

their gods. This chocolate-on-chocolate dessert proves the point.

....

CREPE BATTER:
   1 cup flour
   2 tablespoons unsweetened cocoa
   4 teaspoons sugar
   1 dash salt
   1½ cups milk
   ½ teaspoon almond extract

2 eggs
4 teaspoons melted butter

....

Vegetable oil
Chocolate sauce
Kahlúa
Chocolate or coffee ice cream
Pecans, toasted for 8 to 10 minutes
   in a 350° oven and chopped

....

Put all of the crepe ingredients into a blender or food processor, and whirl until the mixture is smooth. Chill it for an hour, if possible.

Heat a crepe pan over medium-high heat until a drop of water will dance on the surface. Lower the heat to medium. Brush the pan with vegetable oil. Pour in just enough batter to cover the pan's surface. Cook just until the first side is set, about 45 seconds to 1 minute. Turn the crepe, and cook it on the other side for about 5 seconds. Put it on a clean towel to cool. Repeat with the remaining batter, brushing the pan with oil as necessary. Stack the cooled crepes between layers of waxed paper.

When you are ready to serve the crepes, heat the chocolate sauce, and stir in a little Kahlúa. Spoon some ice cream down the center of each crepe, and place the crepes seam side down on dessert plates. Spoon warm chocolate sauce over each serving, and sprinkle with pecans.

Makes 6 servings

CREOLE BANANA CREPES

When choosing bananas at the market, look for plump, well-formed fruit. If you want to use bananas immediately, select uniformly yellow ones. However, since the fruit ripens off the tree, you can pick green ones and allow them a few days to ripen at home.

....

CREPE BATTER:
   1½ cups milk
   4 eggs
   1 cup sifted flour
   2 tablespoons dark rum
   1 tablespoon sugar
   ¼ cup melted butter

....

CREPE FILLING:
   3 tablespoons butter
   2 tablespoons brown sugar
   1 pinch ground nutmeg
   3 bananas, sliced
   1 cup apricot preserves
   1 teaspoon grated lemon zest
   2 teaspoons lemon juice
   2 tablespoons rum

....

Vegetable oil
Sweetened whipped cream
Slivered almonds, toasted 8 to 10
   minutes in a 350° oven

....

Put all of the ingredients for the crepes in a blender or food processor, and whirl until the mixture is smooth. Let it rest 1 hour.

Heat a crepe pan over medium-high heat until a drop of water will dance on the surface. Lower the heat to medium. Brush the pan with vegetable oil. Pour in just enough batter to cover the pan's surface. Cook just until the first side is set, about 45 seconds to 1 minute. Turn the crepe, and cook it on the other side for about 5 seconds. Put it on a clean towel to cool. Repeat with the remaining batter, brushing the pan with oil as necessary. Stack the cooled crepes between layers of waxed paper.

To make the filling, melt the butter in a saucepan. Add the sugar and nutmeg, and cook for 2 to 3 minutes over low heat, until the sugar is dissolved. Add the remaining ingredients, and cook just until they are heated through. If the mixture seems too sweet, add a little more lemon juice.

When you are ready to serve, warm the crepes in the oven, if you like, after wrapping them in foil. Spoon the hot banana mixture into the crepes. Roll the crepes, or fold them in quarters. Top them with whipped cream, sprinkle with toasted almonds, and serve.

Makes 6 servings

Cold Rum Soufflé

Any liqueur can be used in place of rum in this cold soufflé. We also like it with Curaçao, frambois, crème de cassis, and crème de cacao.

....

2 envelopes unflavored gelatin
½ cup water
½ cup rum
6 eggs, separated
¾ cup sugar
1 tablespoon lemon juice
1 cup heavy cream

....

GARNISH:
Slivered almonds
Butter
Sugar

....

Combine the gelatin and water, and stir them in a double boiler over simmering water until the gelatin is dissolved. Add the rum. Remove the top of the double boiler from the heat, let the mixture cool, then chill it until it begins to thicken.

Meanwhile, beat the egg whites until they are foamy. Gradually beat in ½ cup sugar. Add the lemon juice, and beat until the mixture is stiff but not dry.

In another bowl, beat the egg yolks until they are frothy. Gradually beat in ¼ cup sugar, and continue beating until the yolks are thick and lemon-colored. Slowly add the slightly thickened gelatin mixture to the egg yolks, and continue beating until the yolks are light and thick. Fold the beaten egg white into the yolk-gelatin mixture. Whip the cream, and fold it in. Spoon the mixture into champagne glasses, and chill it for at least 2 to 3 hours.

Sauté the slivered almonds in butter, then sprinkle them with sugar. Top each champagne glass with some of the sugared nuts, and serve.

Makes 10 servings

THE LIME LATITUDES

Columbus included limes among the fruits he brought to the West Indies on his second voyage, in 1493, and they quickly established themselves in the warm, moist Caribbean climate. When Spanish settlers made their way to Florida, they took lime seeds with them. The trees flourished in the Florida Keys, and their fruit eventually became known as Key limes.

The Key lime is about the size of a golf ball, and its skin is usually more yellow than green. Its pungent, fresh flavor is found throughout the Caribbean. Limes are, of course, essential to rum punch and other island libations. The juice of this versatile fruit also is used as a meat tenderizer and marinade, as an astringent for the skin, and as a mosquito repellent.

Although Key limes are not readily available in markets outside the areas in which they are grown, other varieties can stand in very well. Just be sure to select fruits that are heavy for their size so they will be nice and juicy.

KEY LIME MOUSSE

Although Key limes have a unique flavor, this tart, cold, and creamy dessert is just fine made with the more common Tahitian or Persian limes.

¾ cup fresh lime juice (preferably from Key limes)
1 envelope unflavored gelatin
4 large eggs, separated
¾ cup sugar
1 cup chilled heavy cream

GARNISH:
Whipped cream
Toasted shredded or flaked coconut (see page 69)

Put ¼ cup of the lime juice into a small bowl. Sprinkle the gelatin over. Set the mixture aside, and let the gelatin soften for 10 minutes.

Whisk the yolks in a heavy saucepan until they are smooth. Whisk in the remaining lime juice, then ½ cup of the sugar. Cook the mixture over low heat, stirring constantly, until it thickens slightly, about 10 minutes.

Remove the pan from the heat. Add the gelatin, and stir until it dissolves. Pour the mixture into a large bowl. Let it cool to lukewarm.

Beat the cream until soft peaks form. Gradually beat in the remaining ¼ cup sugar, and continue beating until the cream is stiff. In another bowl, beat the egg whites until soft peaks form. Fold the whites into the cream. Gently fold the cream mixture into the lime mixture. Divide the mousse among six or more champagne or dessert glasses, and chill the mousse until it is firm.

Garnish each glass with a drift of whipped cream and a sprinkle of toasted coconut, and serve.

Makes 6 servings

LEMON MOUSSE

This tangy mousse is a welcome finale to a rich meal. We like to serve it with a selection of crisp cookies.

....

4 eggs, separated
1½ cups sugar
1 package unflavored gelatin
¼ cup cold water
1 teaspoon cornstarch
Grated zest and strained juice of 3
  lemons
¼ cup Grand Marnier liqueur
1½ cups heavy cream
3 tablespoons confectioners' sugar

....

GARNISH:
Toasted shredded coconut (see page
  69)

....

Beat the egg yolks with the sugar until the mixture is thick and lemon-colored. Sprinkle the gelatin over the water, and let the gelatin soften for 10 minutes.

In another bowl, combine the cornstarch with one-third of the lemon juice, and stir until the mixture is smooth. Stir in the remaining juice, the lemon zest, and the softened gelatin. Mix well, then stir this mixture into the egg-yolk mixture. Pour the ingredients into the top of a double boiler, and cook them over simmering water, stirring constantly, until the mixture is thick. Stir in 2 tablespoons of the Grand Marnier, and cook 1 minute longer. Remove the top of the double boiler from the heat, let the mixture cool, then chill it.

In a large bowl, beat the egg whites until they are stiff but not dry. Whip the cream, and beat in the confectioners' sugar and remaining Grand Marnier. Fold the flavored whipped cream into the egg whites, and then carefully fold the chilled egg-lemon mixture into the whipped cream and egg-white mixture.

Spoon the mousse into glass dishes, and chill it 2 to 3 hours. Top the mousse with sprinkles of toasted shredded coconut, and serve.

Makes 6 servings

ISLAND STYLE: GRENADA

It's called the Isle of Spice because Grenada, with only 130 square miles of land, grows and exports almost half the world's nutmeg and mace, as well as cinnamon, saffron, cloves, and allspice. Grenadians say the very air is perfumed.

It was not always so.

After a lot of feuding with the French, who occupied the island repeatedly, the British finally got permanent possession of Grenada just before the start of the nineteenth century. In 1843, an English sea captain on his way home from Indonesia left behind a few small nutmeg trees, and a thriving industry was born. The spices now appear in dishes on virtually every Caribbean island.

Nutmeg is the pit of a fruit about the size of an apricot. It is described as the pig of Grenada because every part of the fruit is used. The flesh is made into jams and jellies; the crimson webbing around the seed is the spice mace; and the nutmeg—well, there is a joke in Grenada that the military invasion in the fall of 1983 was carried out to make sure there would be enough nutmeg around for eggnogs at Christmas.

KIWI MOUSSE

Now that the kiwifruit is available in produce sections almost everywhere, we can enjoy the refreshing flavor and pretty pale green color of this exotic fruit done up in an elegant mousse.

....

3 eggs
¾ cup sugar
6 tablespoons Curaçao or Grand
    Marnier liqueur
2 cups heavy cream
3 drops vanilla extract
3 kiwifruit, peeled and chopped

....

GARNISH:
1 kiwifruit, peeled and sliced

....

In the top of a double boiler, combine the eggs, ½ cup of the sugar, and 4 tablespoons of the liqueur. Whisk the mixture over simmering water until it is thick. Remove the top of the double boiler from over the water, and continue whisking until the mixture has cooled, 3 to 5 minutes. Chill it in the refrigerator.

In a medium bowl, whip the cream until it is thickened. Beat in the remaining sugar and the vanilla, and continue beating until the cream is stiff. Gently fold in the chopped kiwi and the remaining liqueur, and swirl the egg mixture into the cream. Spoon the mousse into wine glasses or tall parfait glasses. Top each with a slice of kiwi, and refrigerate the glasses until you are ready to serve.

Makes 6 servings

Cappuccino Mousse with Creme de Kahlúa

This simple, foolproof recipe makes light work of almost everyone's favorite dessert.

....

8 ounces semisweet chocolate chips
1 cup heavy cream
1 tablespoon instant espresso or
   instant regular coffee
3 egg yolks
1 tablespoon Kahlúa or Tía
   Maria
1 teaspoon brandy
½ cup heavy cream
1 teaspoon sugar
½ teaspoon vanilla extract

....

Put the chocolate chips into a food processor. Heat the cream and instant coffee until the mixture is very hot, but do not allow it to boil. Pour it into the food processor. Blend for about 1 minute, or until the chocolate is melted.

With the machine running, add the egg yolks one at a time, then the liqueur and brandy. Turn the mixture out into

a bowl, and allow it to cool for about 10 minutes. Whip the cream with the sugar and vanilla until the cream is stiff. Fold the whipped cream into the cooled mousse.

Spoon the mousse into champagne or wine glasses, and refrigerate them until the mousse is firm.

Serve the mousse with a little whipped cream on top.

Makes 6 servings

Coconut Cloud Tart

Its gossamer texture and subtle coconut flavor make this a favorite dessert.

....

CRUST:
   1¼ cups vanilla wafer crumbs
   ¼ cup grated or shredded coconut
   ⅓ cup butter, melted
   3 tablespoons sugar

....

FILLING:
   1 cup grated or shredded coconut
   1 tablespoon unflavored gelatin
   ¼ cup brandy, warmed
   4 eggs
   ½ cup plus 3 tablespoons sugar
   1½ cups heavy cream
   3 tablespoons sugar
   ½ cup apricot jam

....

Preheat the oven to 300°. Spread the coconut in a pie pan, and toast it, stirring it occasionally, for about 6 to 8 minutes. Let it cool.

Heat the oven to 350°. Combine all the crust ingredients, and pat them on the bottom and side of a buttered 9-inch tart pan. Bake the crust for about 8 minutes, or until the top is very lightly browned. Set the baked crust aside to cool.

In a small bowl, soften the gelatin in the brandy. Place the bowl over hot water, and let it sit until the gelatin becomes liquid, about 10 minutes. Beat the eggs with the ½ cup sugar until the mixture is very thick and pale yellow. Beat in the gelatin mixture. In another bowl, beat the cream with the 3 tablespoons sugar until the cream is stiff. Fold the cream and ½ cup of the toasted coconut into the egg mixture.

Spread the apricot jam in the bottom of the prepared crust. Mound the filling in the tart shell, and sprinkle the remaining toasted coconut on top. Chill the tart until it is firm.

Makes 1 9-inch tart

CHOCOLATE TRUFFLE TART

A chocolate filling in a chocolate crust is like catnip for most dessert lovers. This tart is especially nice for picnics, as it holds up well when transported.

....

1¾ cups flour
⅓ cup unsweetened cocoa
⅛ teaspoon salt
¼ cup sugar
¾ cup cold unsalted butter, cut into bits
⅓ to ½ cup cold strong coffee

....

FILLING:

12 ounces semisweet chocolate, melted
⅔ cup sugar
2 tablespoons melted butter
2 tablespoons milk
2 teaspoons Tía Maria
2 eggs, beaten
½ cup finely chopped walnuts, toasted 8 to 10 minutes in a 350° oven

....

Powdered sugar

....

For the crust, put the flour, cocoa, salt, and sugar into a food processor, and blend them by turning the machine on and off three or four times. Distribute the chilled butter pieces over the flour in the processor. Turn the machine on and off several times, until the mixture looks like small crumbs. Add the coffee, and turn the machine on briefly until the contents are well mixed. Using your fingers, press the dough onto the bottom and side of a 9-inch tart pan. Chill the crust for 15 minutes.

Preheat the oven to 350°.

To make the filling, beat the chocolate, sugar, butter, milk, and Tía Maria together with a whisk. Add the beaten eggs and walnuts, and stir. Pour the filling into the chilled tart shell, and bake the tart for 30 to 40 minutes or until the top is dry and firm.

To decorate the tart, place strips of waxed paper in a criss-cross pattern on the top, and sift on powdered sugar. Carefully remove the paper. Serve the tart with vanilla or chocolate ice cream.

Makes 1 9-inch tart

RUM-CHOCOLATE CHEESECAKE

Cheesecake is a much-loved dessert to follow any dinner. Adding rum and chocolate simply embellishes an already superb finale.

....

CHOCOLATE-ALMOND CRUST:
1½ cups chocolate-cookie crumbs
6 tablespoons melted butter
½ cup finely chopped almonds
2 tablespoons sugar

....

FILLING:
8 ounces cream cheese
1½ cups sour cream
6 tablespoons sugar
1 teaspoon vanilla extract
¼ cup rum
1 package unflavored gelatin
8 ounces semisweet chocolate chips, melted

....

GARNISH:
Chocolate leaves or grated chocolate

....

To make the crust, preheat the oven to 350°. Blend together all the crust ingredients. Press the mixture on the bottom and 1 inch up the sides of a 10-inch springform pan. Bake the crust 8 minutes, then let it cool.

Beat together the cream cheese, sour cream, sugar, and vanilla. Put the rum into the top of a double boiler or into a heat-proof bowl, sprinkle on the gelatin, and let it soften 10 minutes.

Stir the gelatin mixture over simmering water until the gelatin dissolves, then beat the solution into the cream-cheese mixture. Beat in the melted chocolate. Pour the mixture into the prepared crust, and refrigerate the cake until the filling is firm.

Before serving, remove the metal ring, and decorate the cake with chocolate leaves or grated chocolate.

Makes 1 10-inch cheesecake

TIPSY TART

With this basic filling, a well-stocked bar at your disposal, and a freewheeling spirit of adventure, you can create an almost infinite number of tarts—each different, all delectable. Choose the most appropriate crust, and proceed.

GRAHAM CRACKER CRUST:
1½ cups graham cracker crumbs (from about 20 crackers)
3 tablespoons sugar
⅓ cup melted butter

COOKIE CRUST:
1½ cups crushed cookies (vanilla or chocolate wafers, or gingersnaps)
¼ cup butter, melted

FILLING:
1 cup sugar
1 envelope unflavored gelatin
4 eggs, separated
½ cup water
Flavorings of your choice (see "Tipsy Tart Flavoring Suggestions")

Preheat the oven to 350°. Mix together all the ingredients for either the graham cracker crust or the cookie crust, and press the mixture onto the bottom and side of a 9-inch tart pan. Bake the crust 10 minutes. Let it cool.

Make the filling: In a small saucepan, stir together ½ cup of the sugar and the gelatin. Blend the egg yolks with the water and flavorings. Cook the sugar-yolk mixture over medium heat, stirring constantly, until the mixture is thickened. Let it cool.

Beat the egg whites until they are foamy. Beat in the remaining ½ cup sugar, 1 tablespoon at a time, and continue beating until the egg whites form stiff, glossy peaks. Fold the gelatin mixture into the meringue, and spoon the mixture into the prebaked 9-inch tart shell. Chill the tart before serving.

Makes 1 9-inch tart

TIPSY TART FLAVORING SUGGESTIONS

Butterscotch Collins Tart

5 tablespoons Scotch whisky
2 tablespoons Scotch liqueur
1 tablespoon lemon juice

Gimlet Tart

6 tablespoons gin
2 tablespoons Rose's lime juice
Juice and grated zest of 1 lime

Daiquiri Tart

5 tablespoons light rum
2 tablespoons lime juice
1 tablespoon lemon juice

Black Russian Tart

7 tablespoons vodka
3 tablespoons coffee-flavored liqueur

BLACK-BOTTOM BANANA CREAM PIE

Almost everyone loves a luscious banana cream pie, but we like to gild the lily by lining the crust with chocolate.

. . . .

1 unbaked 9-inch pie shell
½ cup semisweet chocolate chips
⅓ cup sugar
¼ teaspoon salt
2 cups milk
3 egg yolks
1 cup heavy cream
6 tablespoons cornstarch
1 tablespoon butter
3 bananas
½ cup whipped cream
½ cup toasted shredded coconut (see page 69)

. . . .

Preheat the oven to 400°.

Bake the pie shell for 8 to 10 minutes, until it just begins to brown on the edge. Remove the pan from the oven, and immediately sprinkle the chocolate chips into the shell. Return the pan to the oven just long enough to melt the chips. Spread the chocolate with a spatula to cover the bottom of the pie shell.

Dissolve the sugar and salt in the milk. Whisk the egg yolks with the cream and cornstarch in a heat-proof bowl or the top of a double boiler. Slowly whisk the milk mixture into the egg yolks. Set the bowl or pan over simmering water, and whisk constantly until the mixture thickens to a pudding-like consistency, 7 to 10 minutes. Remove the custard from the heat, whisk in the butter and vanilla, and strain the custard through a fine sieve into a bowl. Put plastic wrap directly on the surface of the custard, and allow it to cool.

Slice two bananas crosswise into the chocolate-coated pie shell. Pour the cooled custard over the bananas at once. Chill the pie for at least 1 hour.

Just before serving, spread the pie with the whipped cream. Peel the remaining banana, score it lengthwise with a fork, cut it into thin crosswise slices, and arrange the slices around the edge of the pie. Sprinkle the toasted coconut in the center, and slice and serve the pie.

Makes 1 9-inch pie

KEY LIME PIE

A tropical classic, this brisk dessert deftly balances sweet and sour on a warm Caribbean night.

....

1 9-inch pie shell, baked at 400° for
    10 minutes and cooled
3 eggs, separated
1 can sweetened condensed milk
½ cup fresh lime juice
2 tablespoons grated lime zest
¼ teaspoon cream of tartar
¼ cup sugar

....

Preheat the oven to 350°. Beat the egg yolks until they are light yellow and thick. Stir in the condensed milk, then the lime juice and zest. Pour the mixture into the prepared crust.

Beat the egg whites with the cream of tartar until they are thick, and very slowly beat in the sugar. Beat until shiny peaks form. Spread the egg whites over the filling, making swirls and peaks.

Bake the pie 15 minutes. Let it cool before serving.

Makes 1
9-inch pie

PAPAYA PIE

When fresh papayas are available, try this island delicacy. Although our local papayas are small and yellow-fleshed, we were lucky enough to get some seeds that produced trees with truly astonishing fruit. Stateside friends tell us their produce departments often sell these large, red-fleshed fruits as "Mexican papayas." Weighing up to ten pounds and full of flavor, these papayas are perfect in this pie.

....

1 9-inch pie shell, baked at 400° for
    10 minutes and cooled
1 tablespoon unflavored gelatin
¼ cup cold water
1 cup puréed papaya
1 cup sugar
3 egg yolks, beaten until light and
    lemon-colored
¼ cup fresh lime juice
4 egg whites
1 pinch salt
1 cup heavy cream
Confectioners' sugar to taste

....

GARNISH:
    Sliced crystallized ginger
    Peeled and sliced papaya or pineapple

....

Sprinkle the gelatin over the water, and allow the gelatin to soften for 10 minutes.

In a saucepan, combine the papaya

purée, ½ cup sugar, and the beaten egg yolks. Cook the mixture over very low heat, stirring constantly, for 20 minutes or until it is thickened. Add the softened gelatin, stir until it is dissolved, and stir in the lime juice. Pour the mixture into a bowl set in a larger bowl of ice, and stir the mixture until it is thickened (but not set). Or place the bowl in the freezer until the mixture is thickened.

Beat the egg whites with the salt until the whites hold soft peaks. Add the remaining ½ cup sugar, 2 to 3 tablespoons at a time, and continue to beat until the meringue is stiff and shiny. Fold the meringue into the custard, and pour the mixture into the pie shell. Chill the pie for 3 hours or until it has set.

Whip the heavy cream, and sweeten it with confectioners' sugar. Put the cream into a pastry tube, and pipe a pretty design onto the top of the pie. Garnish the pie with the crystallized ginger and papaya or pineapple, and slice and serve.

MERINGUE SEASHELLS WITH BANANA CREAM

Meringues are always a good thing to make if you find yourself with leftover egg whites. Piping the meringues into the form of seashells is fairly easy. We try for something resembling a nautilus shell, but be creative—pipe the meringue in any design you like.

....

MERINGUES:
4 egg whites
1 cup sugar
Additional sugar to taste

....

FILLING:
1 cup heavy cream
2 tablespoons banana liqueur
2 bananas, chopped

....

RASPBERRY SAUCE:
10 ounces fresh or frozen raspberries
¼ cup sugar
2 tablespoons dark rum

....

To make the meringues, preheat the oven to 250°. Beat the egg whites until they hold stiff peaks. Gradually beat in 6 tablespoons sugar, and continue beating until the mixture is glossy. Fold in the remaining sugar. Fit a pastry bag with a ½-inch shell tube, and fill the bag with the mixture. Pipe the mixture onto a baking sheet to make twelve shell-shaped meringues. Sprinkle them lightly with sugar, and let them set 5 minutes. Then bake the meringues about 1½ hours, or until they are firm. Transfer them to wire racks to cool.

Whip the cream. Beat in the banana liqueur and sugar to taste. Fold in the chopped bananas, and chill the mixture.

When you're ready to serve, cut the meringues in half horizontally, and spoon some of the banana cream on one half. Sandwich the halves together to form complete shells.

To prepare the raspberry sauce, purée the raspberries, sugar, and rum in a blender or food processor. Strain the mixture to remove the seeds. Spoon some of the sauce onto each dessert plate, and set two meringues on top. Drizzle some of the sauce over the meringues, and serve.

Makes 6 servings

BANANA BEIGNETS WITH APRICOT SAUCE

Crisp and fragile, these delectable fritters are especially alluring with a rum-laced apricot sauce.

....

5 to 6 bananas, cut crosswise into
   1-inch rounds
Lemon juice
Sugar
¼ cup rum
1 cup flour
1 pinch salt
2 teaspoons sugar
⅓ cup warm beer
2 tablespoons melted butter
Vegetable oil, for deep frying

APRICOT SAUCE:
   2 cups apricot jam
   ½ cup water
   2 teaspoons grated lemon zest
   Juice of 1 lemon
   ¼ cup rum

....

Put the bananas into a bowl, and sprinkle them with lemon juice, sugar, and rum. Toss the bananas lightly. Cover the bowl, and let the bananas sit for about ½ hour.

Combine the flour, salt, sugar, beer, and enough water to make the batter the thickness of heavy cream. Add the butter, and allow the batter to stand for about 1 hour.

Heat 2 inches of oil in a large skillet or heavy pot. Beat the egg whites, and fold them into the batter. Drain the banana slices, dip them into the batter, and fry them until they are golden brown. Drain them on paper towels, and sprinkle them with powdered sugar.

To make the apricot sauce, combine all the sauce ingredients but the rum in a saucepan. Bring the mixture to a boil, and then reduce the heat to low. Simmer the sauce for about 5 minutes. Stir in the rum, and serve the warm sauce with the beignets.

Makes 6 servings

BANANA BREAD PUDDING WITH RUM SAUCE

This is a wonderful way to transform stale bread into a delicious dessert. Although bread pudding sounds very homey, this is actually a very sophisticated dish, and one our guests dote on.

Bread pudding can be prepared a day ahead and refrigerated. Rewarm it in a 350° oven, or serve it cold with hot sauce.

....

2 tablespoons unsalted butter
4 bananas, halved lengthwise
4 tablespoons sugar
2 cups heavy cream
4 large eggs
¼ cup dark rum
1 teaspoon vanilla extract
½ pound sliced egg bread, brioche, or
    home-style white bread
⅓ cup raisins

....

RUM SAUCE:
    ¼ cup butter
    ½ cup heavy cream
    ½ cup sugar
    1 pinch salt
    2 tablespoons rum

....

Vanilla ice cream

....

Preheat the oven to 350°. Melt the butter in a large skillet over medium heat. Add the bananas to the skillet, and sprinkle them with 2 tablespoons sugar. Cook them gently until they are golden brown, about 3 minutes per side. Set them aside.

Combine the cream, egg, rum, and remaining 2 tablespoons sugar in a bowl. Lay one-third of the bread slices in a well-buttered 5-by-9-by-3-inch loaf pan. Pour about one-third of the egg mixture over. Top with four banana halves. Sprinkle with half of the raisins. Cover with another third of the bread slices, and pour on another third of the egg mixture. Lay the remaining banana halves in the pan, and sprinkle the remaining raisins over. Cover with the rest of the bread slices and, finally, the remaining egg mixture. Bake the pudding until it is just firm to the touch, 30 to 40 minutes.

To make the rum sauce, melt the butter in a saucepan. Add the cream, sugar, and salt. Bring the mixture to a rolling boil, stirring often. Remove the pan from the heat, and stir in the rum.

To serve the bread pudding, cut it into slices, top it with vanilla ice cream, and spoon on the hot rum sauce.

Makes 6 to 8 servings

GINGERBREAD ROLL WITH CRYSTALLIZED-GINGER CREAM

Gingerbread is a Caribbean favorite. We have taken the idea a step further to create a glamorous roulade filled with cream and crystallized ginger.

....

3 eggs, separated
1 tablespoon butter, melted
½ cup molasses
¼ cup sugar
1 cup flour
¾ teaspoon baking powder
¾ teaspoon baking soda
⅛ teaspoon salt
½ teaspoon ground cinnamon
½ teaspoon ground cloves
½ teaspoon ground ginger
Confectioners' sugar

....

GINGER CREAM FILLING:
1½ cups heavy cream
⅓ cup confectioners' sugar
¼ cup minced crystallized ginger

....

GARNISH:
Sugared grapes (grapes dipped in egg
white and then sugar, and dried)

....

Preheat the oven to 350°. Line the bottom of a 15-by-10-by-1-inch jelly-roll pan with parchment paper, or oil the pan, line it with waxed paper, and oil and flour the waxed paper.

Beat the egg yolks in a large bowl until they are thick and pale yellow. Stir in the butter and molasses.

In another bowl, beat the egg whites until they are foamy. Gradually beat in the ¼ cup sugar, and continue beating until the whites are stiff and shiny but not dry. Fold the egg whites into the yolk mixture. In another bowl, combine the flour, baking powder, baking soda, salt, cinnamon, cloves, and ginger, and gently fold the dry ingredients into the egg mixture. Spread the batter evenly in the prepared pan. Bake the cake 8 to 10 minutes, until it tests done.

Spread a dish towel on your work surface, and sift the confectioners' sugar all over it. When the cake is done, immediately loosen it from the sides of the pan, and turn it onto the sugared towel. Peel off the parchment or waxed paper. Roll up the cake and towel together. Let the cake cook completely on a wire rack, seam side down.

While the cake is cooling, prepare the filling. Beat the cream until it is foamy. Gradually beat in the sugar, and continue beating until soft peaks form. Fold in the ginger.

Unroll the cooled cake, spread it with half the ginger cream, and reroll it. Place the cake on a serving platter, seam side down, and spread the remaining cream on all sides. Decorate the roll by pulling an icing comb or fork down the length of the frosting.

Garnish the roll with the sugared grapes, and slice and serve it.

Makes 12 servings

LEMON SHORTBREAD TART

Limes work equally well in this easier-than-pie dessert.

....

CRUST:
   1 cup flour
   ¼ cup confectioners' sugar
   1 pinch salt
   ½ cup cold butter, cut into bits

....

FILLING:
   1 cup sugar
   2 eggs, lightly beaten
   2 tablespoons flour
   ½ teaspoon baking powder
   3 tablespoons lemon juice
   Grated zest of 1 lemon

....

Preheat the oven to 350°. Combine the flour, sugar, and salt in a mixing bowl, and cut in the butter until the mixture resembles coarse meal. Press the dough into the bottom and part of the way up the side of a 9-inch tart pan with a removable bottom. Bake the crust 20 minutes.

Blend the filling ingredients, and pour the mixture into the partially baked tart shell. Bake the tart another 25 minutes.

Serve the tart warm or cool.

Makes 1 9-inch tart

"LEMON TREE VERY PRETTY . . ."

....

There are so many uses for lemons in the kitchen that it's hard to imagine life without them. Here is a little lemon lore:

♦ A little lemon juice keeps mushrooms and artichokes from darkening.

♦ Lemon butter adds fresh flavor to seafood and vegetables.

♦ To juice half a lemon, stick a fork into it and twist.

♦ If a recipe calls for sour milk or buttermilk and you don't have any, pour 1 tablespoon lemon juice into a measuring cup, add milk to the 1 cup measure, and allow the mixture to stand 5 minutes.

♦ Lemon shells make pretty containers for lemon sorbet, horseradish, mayonnaise, or dip.

♦ To give vodka or gin a nice syrupy consistency and lemony flavor, add lemon slices to the bottle, and put it in the freezer. Let the liquor mellow for about 2 weeks (it will not freeze).

RUM PECAN TORTE WITH BROWN SUGAR-BUTTER CREAM

Ivor Peters, the Sugar Mill kitchen's master of desserts, counts this among his favorites.

....

TORTE:

3¼ cups (about 13 ounces) finely
    ground pecans
¼ cup flour
2 teaspoons baking powder
¼ teaspoon ground nutmeg
½ teaspoon salt
6 eggs, separated
2 cups sugar
¼ cup dark rum

....

BROWN SUGAR–BUTTER CREAM:

3 cups light brown sugar
½ to 1 cup heavy cream
9 tablespoons butter, softened
1 pinch salt
3 ¾ cups confectioners' sugar, sifted

....

GARNISH:

Pecan halves

....

Preheat the oven to 350°. Butter and flour two 10-inch springform pans. In a large bowl, combine the flour, baking powder, nutmeg, and ¼ teaspoon salt. Put the egg yolks and 1 cup sugar in a mixer bowl, and beat until the mixture is doubled in volume and a slowly dissolving ribbon forms when the beaters are lifted, about 5 minutes. Mix in the rum. Fold this mixture into the nut mixture.

In another bowl, beat the egg whites with the remaining ¼ teaspoon salt until soft peaks form. Gradually beat in the remaining 1 cup sugar. Continue beating the whites until stiff peaks form. Gently fold the whites into the pecan mixture, in two additions. Divide the batter between the prepared pans, and bake until a toothpick inserted into the centers comes out clean, about 35 to 40 minutes.

Let the torte cool in the pans for 15 minutes, then release the pan sides. Remove the bottoms, and let the torte cool completely on racks.

To make the frosting, combine the brown sugar, ½ cup of the cream, the butter, and the salt in a small, heavy-bottomed saucepan. Cook the mixture over medium heat, stirring constantly, until it comes to a boil. Let it boil for 5 minutes without stirring it. Remove the pan from the heat, and let the mixture cool. Add the confectioners' sugar, and beat until the frosting is perfectly smooth and well blended. If it is too stiff to spread easily, beat in a little more cream.

Fill and frost the torte layers, using a pastry bag to make a decorative border. Garnish with the pecan halves, and serve.

Makes 12 servings

KIWI AND LIME NAPOLEONS

Our climate makes it almost impossible to prepare our own puff pastry, so we are grateful for the commercially made product, which allows us to create dishes like this luscious dessert. Look for puff pastry in the frozen-foods section of your market.

....

PASTRY CREAM:

1 cup sugar
5 egg yolks
⅔ cup flour, sifted
2 cups hot scalded milk
1 tablespoon unsalted butter
2 tablespoons vanilla extract

....

10 kiwis, peeled
1¼ cups heavy cream, whipped
3 tablespoons grated lime zest
3 limes
8 2½-inch commercial puff-pastry squares, baked according to package instructions

....

To make the pastry cream, gradually beat the sugar into the egg yolks. Continue beating for about 3 minutes, until the mixture is pale yellow and forms a ribbon as it falls from the beater. Beat in the flour. Pour in the milk in a slow stream, beating constantly.

Transfer the mixture to a nonreactive saucepan, and place the pan over high heat. Bring the mixture to a boil, while continuing to beat it until it is smooth. Lower the heat, and continue cooking for about 3 minutes, stirring constantly. Remove the pan from the heat. Beat in the butter and vanilla.

Purée eight of the kiwis in a blender or food processor, and strain out the seeds. Chill the purée.

Fold the whipped cream into the pastry cream. Zest the limes with a zester to make long curls. Peel and section two of the limes. Dice the sections, and squeeze the juice from the third lime. Fold the diced lime and juice into the cream.

To assemble the dessert, pour some of the kiwi sauce onto each dish. Cut the pastry squares in half horizontally, and fill them with the lime-flavored cream. Place them on the beds of sauce. Slice the remaining kiwis, and garnish the plates with the kiwi slices and lime zest.

Makes 8 servings

CHOCOLATE-MANGO OR STRAWBERRY SHORTCAKES

SHORTCAKES:

½ cup unsweetened cocoa
2 cups flour
½ cup sugar
3 teaspoons baking powder
½ teaspoon salt
½ cup cold butter, cut into bits
1 cup heavy cream

....

FILLING:

6 cups cubed mango or hulled strawberries
About ½ cup sugar
¼ cup Curaçao liqueur
1½ cups chilled heavy cream

....

GARNISH:
Confectioners' sugar
Mint sprigs

....

For the shortcakes, preheat the oven to 425°. Sift together the cocoa, flour, sugar, baking powder, baking soda, and salt. Cut in the butter until the mixture resembles coarse meal. Add the cream, and stir the mixture with a fork until it forms a dough. Divide the dough into eight equal pieces, and form each into a rough 3-inch round. Place the rounds on baking sheets, and bake them for 12 minutes or until a tester inserted in the centers comes out clean. Transfer the shortcakes to a rack, and let them cool.

Put 3 cups mango cubes or strawberries into a bowl. If you are using strawberries, mash them. To either fruit, add ¼ cup sugar and the Curaçao, and stir until the sugar is dissolved. Stir in the remaining mango cubes or whole strawberries.

Beat the cream until it holds soft peaks, and then beat in about ¼ cup sugar. Continue beating until the cream holds stiff peaks.

Cut the shortcakes in half horizontally with a serrated knife, and with a metal spatula transfer the bottom halves to dessert plates. (Take care; the shortcakes are delicate and crumble easily.) Top each bottom half with some of the mango or strawberry mixture and some of the cream. Carefully top each serving with a top half of a shortcake, and then the remaining fruit and cream. Sprinkle the shortcakes with confectioners' sugar, and garnish the plates with mint sprigs.

Makes 8 servings

TROPICAL TRIFLE

This most British of all desserts takes an exotic turn when introduced to the flavors of the islands.

....

SAUCE:
8 egg yolks
¼ cup Curaçao liqueur
¾ cup orange juice
½ cup sugar
1 cup heavy cream

....

1½ cups strawberries, puréed and sweetened to taste
1 sponge cake or pound cake, cut into bite-size pieces
¼ cup dark rum
¾ cup pineapple juice
¾ cup sweetened cream of coconut, such as Coco Lopez
1¼ cups guava jelly, heated and slightly thinned with rum
4 cups cubed mixed tropical fruits, such as mangoes, papayas,

pineapple, guavas, and passion fruit

....

GARNISH:

Toasted grated or shredded coconut (see page 69)
Kiwi slices, twisted orange slices, or whole strawberries

....

To make the sauce, combine the egg yolks, Curaçao, juice, and sugar in a bowl or in the top of a double boiler. Whisk the mixture over hot water until it is thick and pale yellow, about 5 minutes. Put the bowl into a larger bowl of ice water, and whisk until the mixture is cold.

Whip the cream to soft peaks, and fold it thoroughly into the sauce. Refrigerate the filling, closely covered with plastic wrap, until you are ready to use it.

Coat the bottoms of 8 to 10 glass goblets or wine glasses with some of the strawberry purée. Place some of the cake pieces in the bottoms of the glasses, using scraps to fill in at the edges.

Mix together the rum, pineapple juice, and coconut cream. Trickle one-quarter of this mixture into the glasses. Add a quarter of the cubed fruit. Spread some of the guava jelly and puréed strawberries onto the remaining cake, and add a layer to each glass. Top with ½ cup of the sauce. Repeat the layering, beginning with the cake and ending with the sauce, until the glasses are full. Cover the glasses, and refrigerate them for several hours or overnight.

Just before serving, garnish the glasses with toasted coconut and kiwi slices, orange twists, or strawberries.

Makes 8 to 10 servings

CHOCOLATE PECAN SOUFFLÉ WITH RUM SAUCE

Rum and chocolate have a special affinity, which is clearly evident in this devilishly delicious dessert. You can make the pudding and sauce ahead and reheat them, although the pudding will sink a bit.

....

4 ounces chopped semisweet chocolate or semisweet chocolate chips
1½ cups (about 5½ ounces) pecan pieces
⅓ cup sugar
¼ cup dry bread crumbs
¼ teaspoon ground cinnamon
½ cup unsalted butter, softened
1 tablespoon dark rum
5 eggs, separated
1 pinch salt

....

RUM SAUCE:

1½ cups milk
⅓ cup sugar
4 egg yolks
2 tablespoons dark rum
1 teaspoon vanilla extract

....

Preheat the oven to 350°. Add 3 tablespoons water to the chocolate, and melt the chocolate in a double boiler or microwave oven. Let the chocolate cool to room temperature.

Coarsely chop the pecan pieces in a food processor. Remove ½ cup chopped pecans. Add 1 tablespoon of the sugar to the remaining nuts, and grind them to a fine powder. Combine the ground pecans, bread crumbs, and cinnamon in a bowl. Mix them well, and set the bowl aside.

In a large bowl, beat the butter with half the remaining sugar until the mixture is soft and light. Beat in the cooled chocolate, and then the rum. Add the egg yolks one at a time, beating until the mixture is smooth. Stir in the ground pecan mixture.

In another bowl, beat the egg whites with the salt until the whites form soft peaks. Beat in the remaining sugar in a slow stream, and continue beating until the egg whites hold firm peaks. Stir one-quarter of the beaten egg whites into the chocolate batter, then gently fold in the remaining egg whites.

Pour the batter into a buttered 1½-quart baking dish. Smooth the top. Scatter the reserved chopped pecans evenly over the surface of the batter. Place the baking dish in a larger pan filled with hot water. Bake the pudding in the middle of the oven for 30 to 35 minutes, just until the pudding puffs and feels slightly firm when pressed with the palm of the hand.

Make the rum sauce while the pudding bakes. Combine the milk and sugar in a pan, and bring the mixture to a boil. Beat the egg yolks in a small bowl. When the milk boils, gradually whisk one-third of it into the yolks. Pour the remaining milk into a bowl set over a pan of simmering water, and whisk in the yolk mixture. Cook the sauce, whisking it constantly, until it thickens, 1 to 1½ minutes. Do not let it boil. Immediately remove it from the heat.

Whisk the sauce for 1 minute as it cools. Strain it through a fine sieve into a bowl, and whisk it for 30 seconds more. Stir in the rum and vanilla.

To serve the pudding, spoon it onto dessert plates. Ladle some of the warm rum sauce over and around the pudding.

Makes 6 to 8 servings

GINGER-POACHED SPICE ISLANDS PEARS

Although pears don't grow in our garden, they are good travelers and arrive on our shores little the worse for wear. Anjou, bosc, and winter nelis pears all hold together well when cooked. We poach them with typical island spices like ginger and cinnamon, but we also like to introduce a note of intrigue with that glamorous stranger, star anise.

....

2 cups water
2 cups orange juice
1 cup sugar
2 tablespoons grated peeled
gingerroot
2 cinnamon sticks
2 star anise or 1 teaspoon aniseed
8 medium pears
2 lemons, halved

....

GARNISH:
Whipped cream
Minced crystallized ginger

....

Combine the first six ingredients in a large, heavy pot. Bring them to a boil. Reduce the heat, and simmer the contents 5 minutes. Remove the pot from the heat.

Cut a thin slice from the bottom of each pear. Core the pear from the bottom, using a vegetable parer. Peel the pears, leaving the stems intact. Rub the exposed flesh with the lemon halves. Add the lemon shells to the pot. Place the pears upright in the pot. Cover the pot, and cook the pears until they are just tender, about 18 minutes.

Discard the lemon shells. Transfer the pears to a bowl, using a slotted spoon. Pour the poaching liquid over them. Cover the pears, and refrigerate them until they are cold, or overnight.

Stand the chilled pears upright on plates. Pour the poaching liquid into a saucepan, and boil it until it is syrupy,

about 5 minutes. Strain the syrup into a bowl, and chill it.

Spoon some of the chilled syrup over each pear. Garnish with a dollop of whipped cream and a sprinkling of minced crystallized ginger, and serve.

Makes 8 servings

AMARETTO ORANGES WITH SORBET

This dessert is made for those occasions when the clock is running faster than you are. Presentation is the key here, so take a little trouble to be sure each plate looks pretty.

....

4 to 5 oranges, peeled and sliced into
thin rounds
¼ cup Amaretto liqueur
1½ pints lemon or grapefruit sorbet
or sherbet

....

GARNISH:
Mint leaves or edible flowers

....

Put the orange slices into a bowl, sprinkle them with the liqueur, and chill them.

Drain the orange slices, and arrange them in a fan pattern on dessert plates. Place a scoop of sorbet at the base of the fan pattern on each plate.

Garnish with the mint leaves or flowers, and serve at once.

Makes 8 servings

BANANA CHEESECAKE

When we have an overload of bananas and the banana daiquiri drinkers can't keep up, we mash some bananas, sprinkle them with lemon or lime juice, and freeze them for later use in this cheesecake.

. . . .

CRUST:
  1½ cups graham cracker crumbs
  ¼ cup sugar
  5 tablespoons butter, melted

. . . .

FILLING:
  1 pound cream cheese, at room
    temperature
  ½ cup sugar
  1½ cups mashed bananas
  ¼ cup banana liqueur
  1 teaspoon vanilla extract
  4 eggs

. . . .

TOPPING:
  1½ cups sour cream
  1 tablespoon sugar

  1 tablespoon banana liqueur
  1 teaspoon vanilla extract

. . . .

Preheat the oven to 350°. Combine the cracker crumbs, sugar, and melted butter in a bowl. Press the mixture into the bottom and part of the way up the side of a 9-inch springform pan.

In a food processor or blender, blend the cream cheese, sugar, banana liqueur, and vanilla until the mixture is smooth. Add the eggs one at a time, blending well after each addition.

Carefully spoon the filling into the shell, taking care not to disturb the crumb crust. Bake the cake in the middle of the oven for 35 minutes.

While the cake bakes, blend the sour cream, sugar, liqueur, and vanilla in a bowl. When the cake is ready, spread the topping evenly over it. Bake the cake 5 minutes more. Transfer it to a rack, and let it cool. Chill it in the refrigerator, covered loosely, overnight.

Remove the side of the pan, and transfer the cake to a serving plate.

Garnish it with fresh banana slices before serving.

Makes 1 9-inch cheesecake

"YELLOW BIRD HIGH UP IN BANANA TREE . . ."

If you think all bananas are the same size and color, you probably haven't been to the Caribbean. Here bananas range from the tiny delicate fruits we call finger bananas, or figis, to large, black-skinned ripe plantains, with all shades of yellow, red, and green in between.

Plentiful and prolific, bananas have been a staple of tropical cuisine for hundreds of years, but it was not until refrigerated boats could transport them that they became well known in North America and Europe. And only in recent years have some of the more exotic varieties become available to adventurous cooks.

Wonderfully nutritious and very digestible, bananas can appear in any course of the Caribbean meal, from banana chips as an appetizer to flamed bananas with rum for dessert. Chutneys, jams, and relishes made with bananas are great favorites, and banana leaves are often used to wrap foods for cooking.

COCONUT RUM FLAN

Flans are very popular in all the Spanish-speaking islands of the Caribbean. Rum, coconut, and coconut cream give this version a tropical twist.

1 cup milk
2 tablespoons heavy cream
⅔ cup sweetened cream of coconut, such as Coco Lopez
1 teaspoon vanilla extract
2 tablespoons dark rum
3 eggs
3 egg yolks
½ cup sugar
¼ cup water
6 pineapple slices
½ cup toasted shredded coconut (see page 69)

Preheat the oven to 350°. Heat the milk and cream in a heavy saucepan until bubbles form around the edge. Do not let the mixture boil. Add the cream of coconut, vanilla, and rum. Heat the mixture until bubbles form, whisking constantly.

Beat the whole eggs and yolks together. Add them to the hot milk mixture, and whisk well over the heat until the custard is smooth and evenly colored. Remove the pan from the heat.

In another saucepan, bring the sugar and water to a boil. Allow the sugar mixture to boil, without stirring, until it is syrupy and brown. When it is caramelized, pour a little of the syrup into each of six custard cups. Swirl each cup so the caramel coats the side and bottom, taking care not to burn yourself. Fill the cups with the custard. Set the cups in a baking pan, and pour water into the pan until it comes halfway up the sides of the cups. Bake the custard for 15 to 20 minutes. It is done when a toothpick inserted in the custard comes out clean.

Let the custard cool to room temperature, and refrigerate it.

When the custard is thoroughly chilled, unmold it by running a knife around the side of each cup. Invert the cups onto a baking sheet. If the custard isn't released within 4 minutes, gently tap the bottoms of the cups with a knife handle.

Serve each mound of custard on a slice of pineapple, and sprinkle the custard with the toasted shredded coconut.

Makes 6 servings

WHERE TO PUT YOUR PARFAIT

Although there are special containers for these layered, gooey delights, a lack of special dishes shouldn't prevent you from serving parfaits. Wine glasses, footed tumblers, or even juice or old-fashioned glasses will work just fine. Clear glass is best, though, because it allows the pretty layers of the parfait to shine through.

COFFEE CARAMEL PARFAITS

Cool and creamy, these parfaits are an ideal make-ahead solution to the dilemma of what to serve for dessert when company's coming.

SAUCE:
1½ cups sugar
½ cup water
½ cup light corn syrup
¾ cup heavy cream
10 tablespoons unsalted butter
⅔ cup sour cream

¼ cup chopped walnuts, toasted for 8 to 10 minutes in a 350° oven

PARFAITS:
⅔ cup sugar
2 cups heavy cream
12 egg yolks
¼ cup instant espresso or regular instant coffee
¼ cup Tía Maria liqueur
1 cup sour cream

GARNISH:
Whipped cream
8 walnut halves

To make the sauce, stir together the sugar, water, and corn syrup in a saucepan over low heat until the sugar

dissolves. Increase the heat, and boil the syrup, swirling the pan occasionally but not stirring, until the syrup is a deep golden brown. Add the heavy cream and butter (the mixture will bubble vigorously when you do so), and whisk until the sauce is smooth. Remove it from the heat, and whisk in the sour cream.

Spoon 1 tablespoon of the sauce into each of eight wine glasses. Sprinkle 1 teaspoon nuts in each glass. Place the glasses in the freezer.

For the parfaits, fill a large saucepan halfway with water, and bring the water to a boil. Whisk together the sugar, ½ cup cream, the yolks, and the instant coffee in the top of a double boiler or in a heat-proof bowl. Set the pan or bowl over boiling water, and whisk the mixture constantly until a candy thermometer inserted in it registers 160°, about 3 minutes. Remove the bowl, and whisk in the white chocolate and Tía Maria.

Combine the remaining 1½ cups cream with the sour cream in a large bowl, and beat the mixture until stiff peaks form. Fold the egg-yolk mixture thoroughly into the cream. Pour ⅓ cup of the parfait mixture into each glass. Chill the remainder. Freeze the parfaits for 1 hour.

If necessary, stir the remaining sauce over low heat just until it is pourable. Spoon 2 tablespoons sauce over each parfait, and sprinkle each parfait with 2 tablespoons chopped walnuts. Place the parfaits in the freez-er until they are set, about twenty minutes.

Divide the remaining parfait mixture among the glasses. Freeze the parfaits 1 hour.

Drizzle 1 tablespoon sauce in zigzag lines over each parfait. Cover the parfaits, and freeze them overnight.

Let the parfaits stand 10 minutes at room temperature before serving. Spoon the whipped cream into a pastry bag fitted with a star tube. Pipe a rosette of whipped cream onto each parfait. Top each with a walnut half, and serve.

Makes 8 servings

SOURSOP ICE CREAM

When our soursop trees are bearing, their slender limbs bend with the weight of the heavy fruit. Removing the seeds is the most taxing part of the preparation. We've found that using the sieve attachment and wooden paddle of our Kitchen Aid mixer separates the fruit from the seeds in record time.

This recipe can also be used to make tamarind ice cream; just substitute tamarind pulp or concentrate for the soursop. Soursop and tamarind concentrates are available in many Latin American markets.

....

5 cups milk
3 cups sugar
4 eggs, beaten
1½ cups soursop pulp or
　　concentrated soursop nectar
½ teaspoon salt
¼ cup lime juice
2 cups heavy cream

....

In a saucepan, scald the milk. Add the sugar, and stir until the sugar is dissolved. Pour the hot milk mixture over the beaten eggs, and beat until the mixture is well blended. Cook it in a double boiler, or in a bowl set over a pan of simmering water, until the custard is thick and smooth. Chill it thoroughly.

Stir the soursop pulp or nectar, salt, lime juice, and heavy cream into the custard, and churn and freeze the mixture according to your ice-cream maker's directions.

Makes 12 servings

SOURSOP

This lumpy green fruit with its creamy flesh and black seeds was introduced into the Caribbean from South America in the sixteenth century. The soursop's sweet, slightly acid flavor is perfect in ice cream. The French missionary Père Labat, who left many descriptions of Caribbean gastronomy in the eighteenth century, tells of a dish of baked soursop with orange-flower water and cinnamon.

PEANUT BUTTER–FUDGE TART

When we first put this on the menu we were a little worried. Peanut butter, we thought—is that really what guests expect when they dine at the Sugar Mill? Since then Peanut Butter–Fudge Tart has become one of our most requested desserts, topping in popularity some of its far more glamorous colleagues.

....

CRUST:
　　1½ cups vanilla wafer crumbs
　　¼ cup sifted confectioners' sugar
　　6 tablespoons melted butter

....

FILLING:
　　8 ounces cream cheese, at room
　　　　temperature
　　1 cup creamy peanut butter
　　1 cup plus 2 tablespoons
　　　　confectioners' sugar
　　2 tablespoons unsalted butter
　　½ cup heavy cream
　　1 tablespoon vanilla extract

....

TOPPING:
　　½ cup heavy cream
　　6 ounces semisweet chocolate,
　　　　chopped, or semisweet chocolate
　　　　chips

....

To make the crust, butter a 9-inch tart pan with a removable bottom. Mix all the crust ingredients in a bowl. Press the mixture evenly on the bottom and side of the tart pan. Refrigerate the tart 1 hour.

To make the filling, beat together the cream cheese and peanut butter in a large bowl until they are thoroughly combined. Add 1 cup confectioners' sugar and the butter, and beat until the mixture is fluffy.

Beat the cream in another bowl until soft peaks form. Add the remaining 2 tablespoons sugar and the vanilla, and continue to beat until stiff peaks form. Stir a third of the cream thoroughly into the peanut-butter mixture. Gently fold in the remaining cream. Spoon the mixture into the crust. Refrigerate the tart until the filling is firm, about 3 hours.

For the topping, bring the cream to a simmer in a small, heavy saucepan over low heat. Add the chocolate, and stir until the mixture is smooth. Let it cool to lukewarm.

Spread the topping over the pie. Refrigerate the pie until it is firm, about 3 hours longer. Serve the pie chilled.

Makes 1 9-inch tart

BANANA BEACH SHORTCAKE

Coconut-laden shortcake layered with bananas and cream and garnished with oranges, kiwis, and strawberries, this dessert is a rainbow of colors and flavors.

....

SHORTCAKE:
⅔ cup plus ½ cup sweetened shredded coconut
2 cups flour
1 tablespoon baking powder
1 teaspoon freshly grated nutmeg
½ teaspoon salt
¼ cup sugar
½ cup unsalted butter, cut into bits
⅔ cup plus 1 tablespoon milk
2½ teaspoons vanilla extract

....

FILLING:
1 cup heavy cream
2 tablespoons sour cream
4 bananas, sliced crosswise

....

GARNISH:
Orange slices
Kiwi slices
Strawberry halves

....

Preheat the oven to 300°.

Spread in a pie pan ⅔ cup coconut, and toast it in the oven, stirring occasionally, for about 6 to 8 minutes.

Sift the flour, the baking powder, the nutmeg, the salt, and 3 tablespoons of the sugar together into a bowl. Cut in the butter until the mixture resembles coarse meal. Add all but 3 tablespoons of the toasted coconut.

Make a well in the middle of the flour mixture, and pour in ⅔ cup milk and 1 teaspoon of the vanilla. Quickly combine the ingredients with about six to seven strokes of a rubber spatula.

Divide the dough into six equal parts, and pat the pieces into 3-inch rounds on a greased baking sheet. Brush them with milk, and sprinkle them with the ½ cup untoasted coconut. Refrigerate the rounds for 15 minutes. Preheat the oven to 375°.

Bake the rounds 20 to 30 minutes, until the rounds are light gold on the edges and their centers are firm and dry.

Whip the cream until soft peaks form. Fold in the sour cream. When you are ready to serve, split the shortcakes, and spoon some banana slices on the bottom half of each. Top with a dollop of cream. Replace the top of the cake, and top it with a few banana slices and more cream. Garnish with orange slices, kiwi slices, and strawberries, and serve.

Makes 6 servings

A Dinner of Caribbean Flavors

VEGETABLE FRITTERS WITH
FIRE CORAL HOT SAUCE

◆

GREEN SALAD WITH AVOCADO AND
PARSLEY DRESSING

◆

TRADE WINDS CHICKEN WITH
PINEAPPLE SALSA

◆

BLACK BEANS AND RICE WITH RUM

◆

BANANA BEACH SHORTCAKE

BRANDY ALEXANDER TART

Combining dessert and an after-dinner drink is not only efficient, it's delicious.

....

CRUST:
 1½ cups crushed Oreo cookies
 ¼ cup unsalted butter

....

FILLING:
 1½ teaspoons unflavored gelatin
 ⅓ cup water
 ¼ cup sugar
 ¼ teaspoon salt
 4 egg yolks
 ¼ cup cognac or brandy
 ¼ cup crème de cacao
 1 cup heavy cream

....

To make the crust, combine the crushed cookies and butter. Reserve 1 tablespoon of the mixture for garnish. Press the remainder firmly and evenly onto the bottom and side of a 9-inch tart pan. Chill the crust.

To make the filling, sprinkle the gelatin over the water in a medium saucepan. After about 5 minutes, when the gelatin is softened, stir in the sugar, salt, and egg yolks. Set the pan over low heat, and cook the mixture, stirring, until the gelatin dissolves and the mixture thickens slightly. Do not allow it to

come to a boil. Remove the pan from the heat, and let the mixture cool for several minutes. Slowly stir in the brandy and liqueur (if you add them rapidly, the sauce may curdle). Pour the mixture into a shallow bowl, and refrigerate the mixture until it is cool but not jelled.

Whip the cream until it holds firm peaks. Fold the cream into the thickened gelatin mixture (the filling will be thinner than other gelatin fillings). Turn the filling into the chilled crust. Sprinkle the reserved cookie crumbs over the top of the tart. Refrigerate the tart for several hours.

Allow the tart to stand at room temperature for about 20 minutes before serving.

Makes 1 9-inch tart

CORDIAL COFFEES

Give your dinner party a special finale with one of these memorable coffee drinks.

MOCHA DELUXE: For four servings, heat 1 ounce chocolate with 1 cup whole milk in the top of a double boiler over simmering water. When the chocolate is melted, beat the mixture with a rotary beater until it is smooth and well blended. Add 3 cups strong coffee, and stir in about 3 to 4 tablespoons sugar.

CAFÉ ROYALE: Place a teaspoon over a demitasse cup of coffee. Put a sugar cube on the teaspoon, and fill the teaspoon with rum. Light the rum. When the flame dies, pour the contents of the spoon into the coffee, and stir.

KAHLÚA COFFEE: Add 2 tablespoons Kahlúa to a cup of rich coffee. Top with whipped cream, and sprinkle with grated orange zest.

ALMOND COFFEE: Add 2 tablespoons Amaretto liqueur to a cup of hot coffee, and top with a dollop of whipped cream and toasted almonds or crumbled almond pralines.

PIÑA COLADA CAKE

Even those who don't know much about the Caribbean have heard of that smooth grown-up milkshake, the piña colada. Here the same flavors appear in a cake that is sure to make your guests ask for seconds.

....

6 egg whites
1½ cups sugar
4 egg yolks
½ cup vegetable oil
½ cup water
1 teaspoon vanilla extract
1½ cups flour
3 teaspoons baking powder
1 dash salt
¼ cup pineapple juice
2 tablespoons white rum
¼ cup sweetened cream of coconut, such as Coco Lopez

....

FROSTING:
6 tablespoons butter
1 pound confectioners' sugar, sifted
1 egg
¼ cup heavy cream
1 teaspoon vanilla extract
¼ cup drained crushed pineapple
1 tablespoon dark rum

....

8 ounces toasted sweetened shredded coconut (see page 69)

....

Preheat the oven to 350°. Beat the egg whites until soft peaks form. Gradually beat in ½ cup sugar, and continue to beat until the whites are very stiff.

Whisk together the egg yolks, oil, water, and vanilla in a bowl. Sift together the remaining 1 cup sugar, the flour, the baking powder, and the salt.

Fold the flour mixture into the beaten yolks, and mix well. Fold in the beaten egg whites. Pour the batter into two 8-inch cake pans. Bake the cake for about 25 minutes, until it shrinks from the sides of the pans and the tops spring back when touched. Turn the cake out onto racks, and let it cool.

In a small bowl, mix together the pineapple juice, rum, and cream of coconut. Brush both cake layers with this mixture.

To make the frosting, beat together the butter, confectioners' sugar, egg, cream, vanilla, and coconut or almond extract until the mixture is smooth and creamy. Combine half the frosting with ¼ cup crushed pineapple, and spread the mixture on the bottom cake layer. Put the top layer in place. Stir the dark rum into the remaining frosting. Frost the cake, and sprinkle the top with toasted coconut.

Makes 1 8-inch layer cake

WHITE CHOCOLATE AND TOASTED ALMOND CHEESECAKE

This is another creation of Sugar Mill chef Ivor Peters. White chocolate is traditionally made from cocoa butter, milk solids, sugar, and flavorings, but

other vegetable oils are often used now in place of the cocoa butter. Look for white chocolate made wholly with cocoa butter rather than substitute fats.

....

CRUST:

    2 cups graham cracker crumbs
    6 tablespoons butter, melted

....

FILLING:

    2 pounds cream cheese, at room
        temperature
    2 cups sugar
    1 tablespoon cornstarch
    5 whole eggs
    2 egg yolks
    1 cup melted white chocolate
    ¼ cup Amaretto liqueur
    1 cup almonds, toasted 8 to 10
        minutes in a 350° oven and minced
    ¾ cup heavy cream

....

GARNISH:

    1 cup heated and strained apricot
        jam
    1 cup almonds, toasted 8 to 10
        minutes in a 350° oven and minced

....

Grease a 10-inch springform pan. To make the crust, mix the crumbs and butter together. Press the mixture evenly onto the bottom of the pan. Chill the crust while you make the filling.

Preheat the oven to 400°. Cream the cheese in a mixer or food processor. Stir together the sugar and cornstarch,

and beat them into the cheese mixture. With the machine still running, add the whole eggs, yolks, melted chocolate, Amaretto, and almonds, and beat until the mixture is smooth. Beat in the cream. Pour the filling into the crumb-lined pan, and level the surface.

Bake the cake for about 1¾ hours, or until the filling is just set. Allow the cake to cool in the pan.

When the cake is cool, remove the side of the pan. Heat the apricot glaze, and brush it on the side of the cake. With your hands, press the minced toasted almonds onto the side. Chill the cake before serving it.

Makes 1 10-inch cheesecake

ICY ISLAND TORTE

    1 cup graham cracker crumbs
    3 tablespoons sugar
    ½ teaspoon grated nutmeg
    6 tablespoons melted butter
    2 cups vanilla ice cream
    2 cups pineapple sherbet
    1 cup sweetened cream of coconut,
        such as Coco Lopez
    1 cup crushed pineapple, thoroughly
        drained
    1 cup toasted coconut (see page 69)

....

Preheat the oven to 350°. In a bowl, combine the graham cracker crumbs, sugar, nutmeg, and melted butter, and stir until all the crumbs are moistened with the butter. Press the crumbs into the bottom of a 9-inch springform pan. Bake the crust for 8 to 10 minutes, then let it cool, and chill it.

In a large bowl, beat together the ice cream, sherbet, coconut cream, and pineapple. Turn the mixture into the cracker crumb–lined pan, and freeze the torte overnight.

When you are ready to serve, sprinkle the torte with the toasted coconut, remove the side of the pan, and cut the torte into wedges.

Makes 1 9-inch torte

CHILLED IRISH COFFEE TORTE

Cold desserts are understandably popular in the islands, where we prefer our Irish coffee in frozen form.

. . . .

CRUST:
1½ cups crushed Oreo cookies
⅓ cup butter, melted
2 tablespoons Kahlúa
3 tablespoons sugar

. . . .

FILLING:
1 quart coffee ice cream, softened

. . . .

TOPPING:
½ cup heavy cream
1 tablespoon sugar
1 teaspoon instant coffee
1 tablespoon Irish whisky

. . . .

Preheat the oven to 350°. Mix together the crust ingredients, and press them into the bottom of a 9-inch springform pan. Bake the crust for 8 to 10 minutes. Let it cool.

Fill the springform pan with the ice cream, and freeze the torte. When you are ready to serve, beat together the cream, sugar, instant coffee, and Irish whisky, and pipe the mixture onto the top of the ice cream filling.

Makes 1 9-inch torte

COLD AMARETTO SOUFFLÉ

Cold soufflés like this, actually egg custards stiffened with gelatin and enriched with whipped cream, are also known as Bavarian creams. Opulent yet light and airy desserts, they are easy to prepare but make a very grand entrance indeed.

. . . .

2 envelopes unflavored gelatin
½ cup water
½ cup Amaretto liqueur

6 eggs, separated
¾ cup sugar
1 tablespoon lemon juice
1 cup heavy cream, whipped
1 dozen amaretti cookies or other
   crisp macaroons, crushed

....

GARNISH:
   Slivered almonds
   Butter
   Sugar

....

In a small bowl, soften the gelatin in the water for 5 minutes. Place the bowl over simmering water, and stir

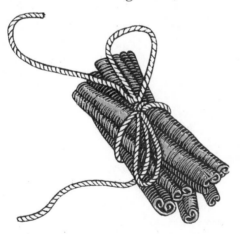

until the gelatin is dissolved, about 10 minutes. Remove the pan from the heat, and add the Amaretto. Let the mixture cool, then chill it until it begins to thicken.

Meanwhile, beat the egg whites until they are foamy. Add ½ cup sugar gradually, beating constantly. Add the lemon juice, and beat until the mixture is stiff but not dry.

In a separate bowl, beat the egg yolks until they are frothy. Gradually add ¼ cup sugar, beating until the yolks are thick and lemon-colored.

Add the slightly thickened gelatin slowly to the egg yolks, and continue beating until the mixture is light and thick. Fold the beaten egg whites into the gelatin mixture. Fold in the whipped cream. Fold in the crushed cookies. Spoon the soufflé into champagne glasses, and chill them.

Sauté the almonds in butter, and sprinkle them with sugar. Sprinkle the almonds over the soufflé in the glasses, and serve.

Makes 10 servings

TRADE WIND COCKTAILS

TRADE WIND COCKTAILS

Rum is, of course, the favorite libation in the islands. Old island hands usually take theirs simply with soda and lime, but everyone loves the extravagant tropical drinks that have come to be identified with the Caribbean. Here are a few recipes we've collected during our years in the islands.

SUGAR SYRUP

Keep this in a jar in the refrigerator, and you'll be ready to make any island drink.

....

½ cup sugar
½ cup water

....

Combine the sugar and water in a saucepan. Bring them to a rapid boil. Simmer the syrup for a minute or two. Let the syrup cool, and use it as directed for the drink of your choice.

PIÑA COLADA

Piña coladas are to the Caribbean what white wine is to a Manhattan singles' bar. The whining of blenders concocting this drink is the back beat of almost every bar in the islands.

To make a blushing colada, a lovely drink that glows with a sunset-pink hue, simply add a splash of grenadine.

....

¾ cup crushed ice
1½ ounces dark rum
½ ounce brandy
4 ounces pineapple juice
2 ounces sweetened cream of
    coconut, such as Coco Lopez
Grated nutmeg
1 pineapple spear
1 maraschino cherry

....

Put the ice into a blender. Add the remaining ingredients, and whirl until the mixture is frothy. Serve it in a tall 12-ounce glass, garnished with the pineapple and maraschino cherry.

Makes 1 serving

PAINKILLER

Most people agree that the first sighting of this drink was at the Soggy Dollar Bar in Jost Van Dyke. No matter its origins, it's become one of the most popular libations in the BVI.

....

1 cup crushed ice
1½ ounces dark rum
3 ounces pineapple juice
3 ounces orange juice

2 ounces sweetened cream of
coconut, such as Coco Lopez
Orange slices

....

Put the ice into a blender. Add the remaining ingredients, and blend until the mixture is frothy. Serve it in a 12-ounce glass garnished with orange slices.

Makes 1 serving

THE VOLCANO

Although most of the mountain peaks in the Caribbean are docile, occasionally one begins spitting and steaming. When that happens, it's time to reach for this drink.

....

4 ounces light rum
2 ounces pineapple juice
1 ounce papaya juice
1 teaspoon sugar syrup (see page
238)
Juice of 1 lime

....

Put all the ingredients into a cocktail shaker with ice cubes. Shake until the ingredients are well combined. Strain the liquid into a tall glass filled with ice cubes, and serve.

Makes 1 serving

COCO TEQUILA

The Caribbean sea laps a portion of the east coast of Mexico, where tequila replaces rum as the tipple of choice.

....

½ cup crushed ice
1½ ounces tequila
½ ounce sweetened cream of coconut,
such as Coco Lopez
½ ounce lemon juice
1 teaspoon maraschino liqueur

....

Put the ice into a blender, and add the remaining ingredients. Blend until the mixture is thick and smooth. Pour the mixture into a chilled champagne glass, and serve.

Makes 1 serving

COFFEE RUMBA

Iced coffee is a popular afternoon refresher in the islands, but when it's time for sundowners, this drink supplies a Caribbean kicker.

....

1 ounce dark rum
1½ ounces sugar syrup (see page 238)
1 ounce heavy cream
Cool strong coffee
Vanilla-flavored sweetened whipped cream

....

Put the rum, sugar syrup, and cream into a 12-ounce glass, and stir. Add two or three ice cubes, and fill the glass with coffee. Garnish with a dollop of whipped cream, and serve.

Makes 1 serving

I DON'T WANT A WHITE CHRISTMAS WITH PLENTY OF SNOW

I WANT A BRIGHT CHRISTMAS WITH RUM AND CALYPSO!

—THE GREAT JOHN L, CALYPSONIAN

MANGO MOON

When the full moon takes on that gorgeous peachy glow, we call it a "mango moon." This is the ideal moon-watcher's libation.

....

2 ounces dark rum
½ teaspoon Triple Sec
1 ounce mango nectar
1 tablespoon lime juice
1 lime slice

....

Put the rum, Triple Sec, mango nectar, and lime juice into a bar shaker filled with ice cubes. Shake until the ingredients are well combined. Strain the liquid into a wine glass. Garnish with a lime slice, and serve.

Makes 1 serving

BANANA DAIQUIRI

The daiquiri took its name from a little mining town near Santiago, the old capital of Cuba; the drink is said to have been invented by one of the foremen of the mine. Ernest Hemingway liked the daiquiris at the Floridita Bar in Havana, where he ordered doubles without sugar. As time went by, the simple daiquiri went through a sea change, first when it met shaved ice and the blender, and later when the sugar was replaced by various tropical fruits, such as pineapples, mangoes, passion fruit, and, of course, bananas.

....

½ cup crushed ice
1½ ounces light rum
Juice of 1 lime
½ ounce Cointreau
1 small banana
1 lime slice

....

Put the ice into a blender. Add the rum, lime juice, Cointreau, and banana, and whirl until the mixture is thick and smooth. Serve it in a large stemmed glass, garnished with the lime.

Makes 1 serving

YELLOW BIRD

One of the islands' favorite rum drinks is named for the bird that also inspired one of the Caribbean's best known songs. Yellow birds are not much bigger than hummingbirds, and if you put a saucer of sugar outside they'll gather from miles around to enjoy a sweet treat.

....

½ cup ice cubes
1 ounce light rum
½ ounce Triple Sec

½ ounce banana liqueur
½ ounce Galliano
1 orange slice

....

Put all the ingredients except the lime into a bar shaker, and shake vigorously until the contents are thoroughly chilled and frothy. Pour them, including the ice, into a tall 12-ounce glass. Garnish with the orange slice, and serve.

Makes 1 serving

GULF STREAM COOLER

The term *rum running* refers to the Prohibition-era smuggling of rum from Caribbean islands into the United States. Many rum-running ships depended on the favorable currents of the gulf stream to facilitate their illicit journeys.

....

1 ounce light rum
1 ounce dark rum
1 dash grenadine
1 dash Curaçao
Juice of 1 lime
1½ ounces unsweetened pineapple
   juice
1 pineapple spear
1 mint sprig

....

Put the ice into a blender. Add the rums, grenadine, Curaçao, and juice, and whirl until the mixture is frothy. Pour it into a tall glass, garnish with the pineapple and mint, and serve.

Makes 1 serving

Rum Punch

Every island—in fact, every bartender on every island—has a unique recipe for rum punch. This is the one we use at the Sugar Mill.

. . . .

½ cup ice cubes
1½ ounces dark or light rum
½ ounce Triple Sec
2 dashes Angostura bitters
Juice of ½ lime
2 ounces orange juice
2 ounces pineapple juice
2 ounces guava nectar
2 dashes grenadine
1 lime slice
1 maraschino cherry
1 grating of nutmeg

. . . .

Put the first nine ingredients into a bar shaker, and shake vigorously until the contents are thoroughly chilled. Pour them, including the ice, into a large glass. Garnish with the lime, maraschino cherry, and nutmeg, and serve.

Makes 1 serving

Rum Cooking in the Caribbean

. . . .

There is much disagreement among islanders about the ins and outs of cooking with rum. Some state flatly that cooking with rum is a waste of a good drink, while others consider a bottle of rum a kitchen staple. In St. Thomas, a cook might put a jigger of rum into bread pudding for her family, whereas on St. Barts a French-trained chef sets aside the brandy to flame a fresh lobster in rum. Cooks vary in their opinions about rum's best uses. Some say you should never pair rum and fish, explaining that the strong liquor would overpower the delicate fish. Others wouldn't dream of cooking the catch of the day without a splash of rum. Some fastidious cooks say you should use a different rum for every culinary undertaking: a light gold for flavoring delicate dessert, a dark Jamaican for a moist, dark chocolate mousse. Others have a favorite potion they depend on for all occasions.

The one thing all experienced Caribbean cooks agree on is that rum should be used with a light hand, so its flavor doesn't overwhelm those of good fresh foods.

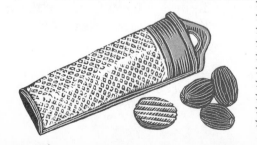

HIBISCUS COCKTAIL

A pretty pink drink that mirrors the color of some of our beautiful island flowers.

....

1½ cups shaved ice
9 ounces dark rum
6 ounces white Dubonnet wine
1½ ounces grenadine
2 tablespoons lime juice

....

Put the ice into a blender. Add the remaining ingredients, and blend until the mixture is frothy. Pour it into chilled champagne glasses, and serve.

Makes about 6 servings

CARIBBEAN CHAMPAGNE

Although it's hard to improve on champagne in its unadorned state, we love the gilding of the bubbly.

....

½ teaspoon light rum
½ teaspoon banana liqueur
1 dash orange bitters
4 ounces chilled brut champagne
1 kiwi or ½ orange slice

....

Pour the rum, banana liqueur, and bitters into a chilled champagne glass. Stir gently, garnish with kiwi or orange, and serve.

Makes 1 serving

GINGER LIMEADE

The pungent bite and aroma of fresh ginger make this a refreshing choice to have by your side when lounging on the beach or by the pool on a warm afternoon.

....

5 ounces gingerroot, minced
4½ cups boiling water
1¼ cups lime juice
1 to 1¼ cups sugar
¾ cup rum
Lime slices

....

Combine the ginger and hot water. Allow the ginger to steep for about 1 hour. Pour the liquid through a strainer; discard the ginger. Add the lime juice and sugar to the ginger water, and stir until the sugar dissolves. Cover the mixture, and chill it from 1 hour to 1 week. When you are ready to serve, add the rum, and pour the limeade over ice in tall glasses. Garnish with lime slices, and serve.

Makes about 6 servings

ISLAND STYLE: BARBADOS

*T*here are those who say that Barbados is more English than England. Not long ago, for instance, employers requested that a series of cricket matches not be televised on weekdays until after the afternoon tea break, to discourage absenteeism. But even the somewhat stodgy British culinary influence couldn't quell the Caribbean desire for fiery food. The Bajans—short for Barbadians—are hearty eaters, with a taste for spicy dishes, such as their version of souse, a combination of various odd parts of the pig steeped in lime juice, herbs, and blazing hot peppers. It is often served with a highly seasoned pudding made from yams.

The wealth of the sea surrounds Barbados, but the creature most associated with the country is the flying fish. It is simply prepared, lightly breaded and pan-fried, and "Flying Fish Bajan Style" appears on menus throughout the West Indies.

The hills of the northern half of the island are covered with sugarcane, still an important crop on an island that produces several well-known brands of rum, notably Mount Gay and Cockspur. It is said that the first commercial rum was produced in Barbados in 1647, shortly after the island was settled. The late Victor Bergeron, creator of the worldwide chain of restaurants known as Trader Vic's, where rum drinks evolved into flamboyant fruit-laden fantasies of gargantuan proportions, once wrote that rum was first known as "killdevil" and later as "rum bouillon," but by 1667 the most popular drink in the islands was known simply as rum.

Barbados rums are amber-colored and have a full but light aroma that some people compare to the finesse of a fine brandy. Their clean flavor makes them very good mixers for all kinds of punches and mixed drinks.

REGGAE REVENGE

*T*his is a terrific Caribbean punch, perfect for a party.

....

1½ cups sugar
Grated zest of 2 limes
4 ounces lime juice
8 ounces orange juice
2½ cups medium-strength hot tea

2 bottles dark rum
2 bottles dry sherry
1 cup brandy
1 to 2 bottles chilled dry champagne
Fruit slices

....

With the back of a spoon, mash together the sugar and lime zest in a large mixing bowl. Add the lime juice, orange juice, and tea, and stir thoroughly. Refrigerate the mixture until it is cool. Add the rum, sherry, and

brandy. Stir until the contents are well mixed, cover the bowl, and let the punch mature in the refrigerator for at least 6 hours. Just before serving, pour the punch over a block of ice in a punch bowl, and add champagne to taste. Garnish with fruit of the season.

Makes about 20 servings

THE REEF BASHER

Another delicious libation for a gang of guests.

. . . .

10 cups papaya nectar
2 cups dark rum
5 cups carbonated ginger beer

. . . .

Combine the papaya nectar and rum in a large punch bowl over a block of ice. Just before serving, add the ginger beer. Garnish the bowl with tiny orchids or gardenias.

Makes about 20 servings

INDEX

<![CDATA["\x00"]]>

R